CERTAIN ASPECTS OF MORAL COURAGE

BY COMPTON MACKENZIE

Novels and Romances

SINISTER STREET
SYLVIA SCARLETT
GUY AND PAULINE
CARNIVAL
FIGURE OF EIGHT
CORAL
THE VANITY GIRL
ROGUES AND VAGABONDS
THE ALTAR STEPS
THE PARSON'S PROGRESS
THE HEAVENLY LADDER
HUNTING THE FAIRIES
WHISKY GALORE
KEEP THE HOME GUARD TURNING
THE MONARCH OF THE GLEN
BEN NEVIS GOES EAST
THE RIVAL MONSTER
THE RED TAPEWORM
POOR RELATIONS
APRIL FOOLS
RICH RELATIVES
BUTTERCUPS AND DAISIES
WATER ON THE BRAIN
VESTAL FIRE
EXTRAORDINARY WOMEN
EXTREMES MEET
THE THREE COURIERS
OUR STREET
THE DARKENING GREEN
THE PASSIONATE ELOPEMENT
FAIRY GOLD
THE SEVEN AGES OF WOMAN
THE OLD MEN OF THE SEA
THE FOUR WINDS OF LOVE:
THE EAST WIND THE SOUTH WIND
THE WEST WIND THE NORTH WIND
MEZZOTINT
THIN ICE
THE LUNATIC REPUBLIC

Verse

POEMS 1907
KENSINGTON RHYMES

Play

THE LOST CAUSE

History and Biography

EASTER EPIC, VOL. I
ALL OVER THE PLACE
GALLIPOLI MEMORIES
ATHENIAN MEMORIES
GREEK MEMORIES
ÆGEAN MEMORIES
WIND OF FREEDOM
MR. ROOSEVELT
DR. BENES
PRINCE CHARLIE
PRINCE CHARLIE AND HIS LADIES
CATHOLICISM AND SCOTLAND
MARATHON AND SALAMIS
PERICLES
THE WINDSOR TAPESTRY
THE VITAL FLAME
I TOOK A JOURNEY
COALPORT
REALMS OF SILVER
THE QUEEN'S HOUSE
THE SAVOY: LONDON
MY RECORD OF MUSIC
GREECE IN MY LIFE
CATS' COMPANY
CATMINT

Children's Stories

SANTA CLAUS IN SUMMER
TOLD
MABEL IN QUEER STREET
THE UNPLEASANT VISITORS
THE CONCEITED DOLL
THE ENCHANTED BLANKET
THE DINING-ROOM BATTLE
THE ADVENTURES OF TWO CHAIRS
THE ENCHANTED ISLAND
THE NAUGHTYMOBILE
THE FAIRY IN THE WINDOW BOX
THE STAIRS THAT KEPT ON GOING DOWN

Essays and Criticism

ECHOES
A MUSICAL CHAIR
UNCONSIDERED TRIFLES
REAPED AND BOUND
LITERATURE IN MY TIME

Certain Aspects of Moral Courage

SIR COMPTON MACKENZIE

DOUBLEDAY & COMPANY, INC.
Garden City, New York
1962

Library of Congress Catalog Card Number 62-7660

Printed in the United States of America
First Edition in the United States of America

To Wendy Wood

Whose friendship I have enjoyed for thirty-five years and who throughout those years has never failed to show the moral courage of a Scottish patriot

Contents

Acknowledgments

I am very grateful to the authors, literary executors and publishers concerned for permission to quote extracts from the following books: H.R.H. the Duke of Windsor's *A King's Story*, Cassell Ltd.; Sir J. M. Barrie's *Courage*, Hodder & Stoughton Ltd.; John Dickson Carr's *The Life of Sir Arthur Conan Doyle*, John Murray Ltd.; Norman Douglas's *Looking Back*, Chatto and Windus Ltd.; William Douglas Home's *Half-Term Report*, Longmans Green Ltd.; Ludovic Kennedy's *Ten Rillington Place*, Victor Gollancz Ltd.; D. H. Lawrence's *Apropos of Lady Chatterley*, William Heinemann Ltd.; William Park's *The Truth about Oscar Slater*, The Psychic Press; Hesketh Pearson's *Life of Oscar Wilde*, Methuen Ltd.; *The Trial of Lady Chatterley*, ed. by C. H. Rolph, Penguin Books Ltd.

For permission to quote from correspondence, I would like to thank the following: The Society of Authors, as the literary representative of the Estate of the late James Joyce, for an extract from James Joyce's letter to Miss Harriet Shaw Weaver, dated December 17th, 1931, quoted in Richard Ellmann's *James Joyce*, Oxford University Press; to Mr. Adrian Conan Doyle for extracts from Sir Arthur Conan Doyle's letter to his mother, dated 29th January, 1907, and from the dossier sent to the Home Office; to Laurence Pollinger Ltd. and the estate of the late Mrs. Frieda Lawrence for an extract from D. H. Lawrence's letter to M. and A. Huxley, dated 15th August, 1928, quoted in *The Letters of D. H. Lawrence*, William Heinemann Ltd.; to Countess von Moltke for an extract from Helmuth James Graf von Moltke's letter to his sons, published in *A German of the Resistance*, Oxford University Press.

I would also like to express my appreciation to the following, who have helped me with material for this book: Mr. Leslie Jackson and Mr. Eamonn Andrews (Chapter XI); Helmuth

Graf von Moltke, Dr. Eugen Gerstenmaier, Raban Graf Adelmann and Herr Hans von Herwarth, until recently German Ambassador in London (Chapter XIII).

I have made my own translations of the Greek passages in this book. Some of the material in Chapter XII appeared in a book called *Calvary*, published during the war by the Bodley Head, profits from the sale of which went to the Lord Mayor of London's Air Raid Distress Fund.

I

In search of a definition

THE EXPRESSION "moral courage" is a late arrival in English. The first instance of it cited in the *Oxford English Dictionary* comes from the second volume of *Lacon* or *Many Things in a Few Words*, a well-expressed series of aphorisms by Charles Caleb Colton published in 1822. "Oliver Cromwell's hypocrisy neutralised his moral courage never his physical."

If, as we may presume, Colton was the first person to put moral courage on the printed page, a brief outline of his own life is worth giving. He was born in 1780, educated at Eton, elected to King's College, Cambridge in 1796, and in 1801 after graduating he was presented by his college to the rectory of Prior's Portion, Tiverton, tenable with a fellowship. Here in 1812 he published one of his sermons and the first book of *Hypocrisy: a Satire in Three Books*. Colton was more renowned as a sportsman, particularly as a good fisherman, than as a divine. In 1818 his college gave him the living of Kew and Petersham where his eccentricities for a parson were excessive. He wore military dress. He said it was cheaper to live in London than at his living. So he took squalid lodgings over a marine-store with a few books including Defoe's *History of the Devil* and a number of fishing-rods. Presently, he carried on a business as a wine-merchant, entertained visitors with the best wine and talked brilliantly. He got into difficulties through gambling and was associated with Thurtell about the time the latter murdered Mr. Weare in 1823. Colton disappeared and it was believed for a while, that he too had been murdered by Thurtell. In fact he had gone to America, whence after a period in Paris he returned to claim his living. This was too much for his college who had appointed a successor. Colton now visited America again and finally settled in Paris where he was a familiar figure at the gaming-tables in the Palais Royal. He gained at one time £25,000 but lost it all later and in the words of a friend was supported by his " aged mother, and was above distress." One of Colton's observations in *Lacon* was that no one ever committed suicide from bodily anguish, thousands had done so from mental anguish. This remark he would himself prove false. In 1832 a painful disease demanded a surgical operation, rather than undergo which Colton killed himself in the house of his friend Major Sherwell at Fontainebleau.

Charles Caleb Colton himself must have had a considerable amount of moral (or immoral) courage to carry off a career not very suitable for a clergyman, and it is ironical that in his own death he should exemplify the distinction between moral and physical courage, to which it would seem he was the first to direct attention.

The first attempt to define precisely moral courage was not made until 1862, when Sir James Fitzjames Stephen, seventeen years before he became a judge, laid down in an essay: " Moral courage is readiness to expose oneself to suffering or inconvenience which does not affect the body. It arises from firmness of moral principle and is independent of the physical constitution." Inconvenience is hardly a felicitous alternative to suffering. Moral courage would be too assertive a claim for an expression of opinion or a course of action which merely led to interference with one's personal comfort or ease. Mental suffering, opprobium or unpopularity are surely more appropriate to moral courage than inconvenience. " Unpopularity " may sound as flimsy as " inconvenience " but we may reflect that the moral cowardice of so many politicians is due to their fear of unpopularity and its adverse effect upon the voters on whom their careers rely. Furthermore, if we restrict moral courage too straitly and deny any physical constitution, we may be driven to deny to physical courage any moral constitution, and certainly such a denial could not be sustained.

Sir Fitzjames Stephen himself was severely bullied when he went to Eton because he expressed independent opinions in a society which frowned as severely on independence of mind as the most doctrinaire communism or fascism in our days or as once upon a time Rome and Geneva frowned. The fact that he persisted in his opinions argued physical courage as well as moral courage because in the forties of the last century bullying at public schools was a ferocious business. It was so bad in the case of Stephen that his parents removed him from Eton and sent him to King's College, London, where as a day boy he was no longer a prisoner in school. Stephen's career later was never marked by any conspicuous display of moral courage, although he was always known for his forthright opinions. He was the judge who presided over the Maybrick case by which time he was already beginning to show signs of the mental deterioration which led to his retirement from the Bench a year or two later.

In 1889 Mrs. Maybrick, an American woman married to a Liverpool cotton broker, was found guilty of poisoning him with arsenic. She was reprieved at the last moment by the Home Secretary, Henry Matthews, but suffered imprisonment for fifteen years. Her case was an abortion of justice for which Mr. Justice Stephen must be held chiefly responsible, although his mental failure does not acquit three successive Home Secretaries—Henry Matthews, H. H. Asquith and Matthew White Ridley of surrendering to what may be called expedient opinion in a decision to cover up legal and official blundering at the expense of a luckless woman.

Repeated efforts were made to obtain Mrs. Maybrick's release, with which her own counsel, Sir Charles Russell, associated himself, although he was not able to affirm his belief in her innocence without breaking the tradition of his profession. In a careful brief submitted to Mr. Asquith, when a change of government sent him to the Home Office, it was urged among other reasons for releasing Mrs. Maybrick, "that the Judge in summing up placed himself in a position where his mind was open to the influence of public discussion and prejudice, to which was probably attributable the evident change in his summing up between the first and second days; and he also assumed facts against the prisoner which were not proved."

We can believe that if Mr. Justice Stephen's mind had been in the condition it was when he laid down that definition of moral courage on which the *Oxford English Dictionary* depends, he would have admitted his inability to administer justice and have retired from the Bench before he did, in which event the irony of quoting a definition of moral courage by a man whose moral courage apparently failed him at the end would have been avoided.

As too often happens the Home Secretary's decision at the last moment to reprieve the unfortunate Mrs. Maybrick was regarded as a way of avoiding responsibility for the death of what might be an innocent person without having the courage to admit that the trial was a miscarriage of justice. The decision of Mr. Henry Matthews was thus announced:

"... the Home Secretary, after the fullest consideration and after taking the best legal and medical advice had advised Her Majesty ... to commute the punishment to penal servitude for life, inasmuch as, although the evidence leads clearly to the conclusion that the prisoner administered and attempted to administer arsenic to her husband with intent to murder, yet it does not wholly exclude a reasonable doubt whether his death was in fact caused by the administration of arsenic.... We understand the course adopted has the concurrence of the learned judge."

In the words of *The Times* when commenting on the reprieve —"It makes things comfortable all round." Sir Charles Russell, Mrs. Maybrick's advocate, commenting upon the reasons given by the Home Secretary for the reprieve, declared that Mrs. Maybrick "was to suffer imprisonment on the assumption of Mr. Matthews that she had committed an offence, for which she was never tried by the constitutional authority and of which she has never been adjudged guilty."

Lord Russell after he became Lord Chief Justice, continued at intervals to plead for Mrs. Maybrick. He failed to persuade

Mr. Asquith and he failed to persuade Mr. Asquith's successor as Home Secretary, Sir Matthew White Ridley, to whom he wrote:

> "The foundation on which the whole case for the Crown rested was rotten, for there was in fact no murder; on the contrary the deceased had died from natural causes. . . . If I were called upon to advise, as head of the Criminal Judicature of this country, I should advise you that Florence Maybrick ought to be allowed to go free."

Her freedom was not granted until four years after the death of her advocate when in 1904 she emerged from fifteen years in Woking and Aylesbury gaols and returned to the United States where in 1941 she died in her eightieth year. It may be significant that Lord Russell was an Irishman, and therefore less liable than English politicians to succumb to one of those attacks of moral cowardice by which from time to time they are infected. Let it be added quickly that such a remark is not intended to suggest that English politicians make a habit of paying more attention to the claims of their career than to their conscience. As elected representatives of the English people, they know that the English believe with more fervour than any other nation that things should be made comfortable all round, and it would not be difficult to sustain the paradox that what looks like moral cowardice was in fact moral courage to allow injustice to an individual in the interest of what was believed to be the public good.

We may discern a repetition of the Government's attitude over the case of Mrs. Maybrick in their attitude towards a fresh inquiry into the case of Timothy John Evans who was hanged in 1949 for the murder of his baby daughter with the further charge of having murdered his wife. The chief witness for the Crown was John Christie who at that date had already strangled two women and buried them in the garden of 10 Rillington Place, and who, after leaving the court garlanded with compliments from the Bench and the prosecution went out to strangle within the next two or three years his own wife and three prostitutes. It was an unsatisfactory trial because Mr. Justice Lewis, himself a sick man on the edge of death, was clearly incapable of grasping anything except that Evans had confessed to the murders. However, it was asking too much of a British Court of Justice to divine the true character of John Christie; on the evidence as presented and without the advantage of hindsight probably any of us serving on that jury would have given the verdict they did. Mr. Chuter Ede, who was Home Secretary at the time, could not be blamed for refusing a reprieve, but since then he has had the courage to admit that a mistake was made and that almost certainly an innocent man was hanged.

After the Christie trial, there was naturally a demand for an Inquiry and in 1953 Sir David Maxwell Fyfe, who was then the Home Secretary, appointed Mr. Scott Henderson, Q.C., to hold a preposterously hurried inquiry which was severely criticised in the House of Commons at the time. Yet Mr. Scott Henderson had done what he was expected to do. In the words of *The Times* about the Maybrick case, he had made things comfortable all round.

Mr. Ludovic Kennedy has now written a book, *Ten Rillington Place* which ought to make things uncomfortable all round until a fresh inquiry is held in public and not in private.

A sad lapse into moral cowardice on the Bench was shown by Mr. Justice Darling in June 1918 when Miss Maud Allan brought a libel action against Pemberton Billing, M.P., whom in 1916 the temporarily besotted electors of East Herts had voted for as an Independent to represent them in Parliament. Pemberton Billing was publishing a toilet-paper edition of Horatio Bottomley's *John Bull* in which he professed to expose all sorts of scandals for the titillation of readers as credulous as the electors of East Herts. He affected a blatant patriotism that was afraid of nobody and, on the strength of service with the R.N.A.S. earlier in the war, claimed to advise the public about air defences; the public disturbed by the Zeppelin raids paid attention to him, and this mountebank rascal for whom the most charitable excuse is the approach of delusional insanity enjoyed for a year or two a pinchbeck popularity.

Maud Allan was a dancer of the Isadora Duncan type—all

wriggling arms and pseudo-Attic attitudes. In the present period of brassières and bikinis Maud Allan would seem fully dressed; to the Edwardians she appeared half-naked. Pemberton Billing published in his paper a lewd paragraph accusing Maud Allan of being a sapphist active in the corruption of other women. He bragged that by forcing a libel action he would expose the dangerous spread of lesbianism, and chose to attack particularly Maud Allan's Dance of the Seven Veils in Oscar Wilde's play *Salome*. Whether the performance of the plaintiff was or was not indecent was soon lost sight of in the case because Pemberton Billing who was conducting his own defence, proceeded with the witnesses he called to mix pro-Germanism with unnatural vice in an attack upon a number of well-known people, in the course of which Mr. Justice Darling completely lost control of the case and the court. The first mistake he made was to allow the defendant to call witnesses to testify that Maud Allan's brother had been executed in California for the rape and murder of a young girl. What this had to do with Maud Allan's performance in *Salome* the judge did not venture to explain to the plaintiff, and indeed it remains inexplicable. Pemberton Billing encouraged by such an exhibition of judicial feebleness now called witnesses to testify to the existence of a German " Black Book " which was said to contain the names of various prominent people in Great Britain who would be useful to the Germans owing to their indulgence in unnatural vice and therefore vulnerable to blackmail if they refused to be useful. After admitting this false and in any case irrelevant testimony Mr. Justice Darling in an attempt to retrieve his reputation for promoting laughter in court asked if *his* name was in the Black Book. " Yes, it is." Pemberton Billing shouted, whereupon Mr. Justice Darling turned pale and rose hurriedly to adjourn the court amid a babel such as never before had disgraced a British court of justice. As the judge left the bench Lord Alfred Douglas threw his top hat at him. Alfred Douglas had had a grievance against Darling since he lost his libel action against Arthur Ransome five years before, when he believed that the judge had summed up against him.

What *The Times* called a "Scandalous Trial" came to an end on 4th June, 1918, with a verdict for Pemberton Billing from a jury as besotted as the electors of East Herts. Mr. Justice Darling cannot be exonerated from bearing the main responsibility for allowing this trial to degenerate into a bear-garden and it is difficult to explain the failure to preserve his own dignity and the dignity of the bench merely by his occasional displays of cheap levity to which the account of his life in the *Dictionary of National Biography* attributes that failure. "The Pemberton Billing case was a shocking example and went far to lower the status of the Bench. In this instance he insisted on trying the case against the wish of the defendant, who alleged without contradiction, that a few weeks before in a civil case Darling had said of him that he did not believe him on his oath. Darling often allowed himself as judge to be grossly insulted by witnesses and laughed with them and at them." That may be so, but what turned that court into a bedlam was the sudden pallor of the Judge and his abrupt rising from the Bench when in answer to what he supposed to be a flippant question Pemberton Billing shouted "Yes." Why did not the Judge immediately commit the plaintiff for contempt of court? Was it a temporary collapse of moral courage in fear of what the rapscallion might say next? Was he himself to be a victim of the hysteria he had allowed to prevail by his handling of the case? Anyway, Darling never recovered his control and the jury found for the defendant so that to the loss of status suffered by the Bench was added in the minds of many a feeling of contempt for a British jury. It was said at the time that the "Black Book" was in fact a list of names made by a German traveller for the firm of Mercedes as possible purchasers of their cars.

It is fortunately rare in these days for a judge, at any rate in our country, to be called upon to display moral courage in defence of justice; but they were not always so carefully protected against criticism of their judicial competence.

In the churchyard of Sutton Coldfield in Warwickshire may be read this epitaph:

As a warning to Female Virtue
and a humble monument to Female Chastity
this stone marks the grave
of
Mary Ashford
who in the 20th year of her age
having incautiously repaired
to a scene of amusement
without proper protection
was brutally violated and murdered
on the 27th of May, 1817

Lovely and chaste as is the primrose pale
Rifled of virgin sweetness by the gale,
Mary! the wretch who thee remorseless slew
Avenging wrath, which sleeps not, will pursue,
For though the deed of blood be veiled in night
Will not the Judge of all the earth do right!
Fair blighted Flower! The Muse that weeps thy doom
Rears o'er thy sleeping Form this warning tomb.

This tombstone was put up by public subscription after Abraham Thornton had been found not guilty of the murder and rape of Mary Ashford thanks to his good luck in having as the judge at the Warwickshire Summer Assizes of 1817 Sir George Sowley Holroyd who had been raised to the King's Bench in the previous year and whose summing up at the trial caused the jury to return a verdict of "not guilty" in six minutes without leaving the box.

The verdict was received with indignation all over England. Almost every newspaper in the country reviled Mr. Justice Holroyd with accusations that would not be tolerated to-day. Wild statements were made about the witness for the defence being bribed to commit perjury. An unfortunate constable who had testified that the prisoner had spontaneously admitted to having had connection with the girl before she was found drowned in a gravel pit full of water was sacked from the police office with great disgrace as having been "guilty of gross misconduct." Parsons preached from their pulpit about Abraham

Thornton's guilt and Mary Ashford's sad fate. *The Mysterious Murder or What's the clock, a melodrama in three acts founded on a tale too true* was performed in Birmingham and was a popular offering by strolling players until it was displaced from their repertoire by *The Mysterious Murder of Maria Marten in the Red Barn.*

Presently various Warwickshire busybodies who were convinced of Abraham Thornton's guilt decided to finance an "appeal of murder" which as the law stood in 1817 could be lodged against a man acquitted of murder by the heir-at-law of the alleged victim. So Mary Ashford's elder brother, a small, illiterate and nervous young labourer was persuaded to play his part. Various eminent lawyers in London were consulted about the prospect of success for such an appeal and presently the writ of appeal was issued, Abraham Thornton was arrested and kept in gaol until the appeal was heard in November. The appellants felt confident of winning their case and getting Thornton hanged provided the appellee did not challenge the appeller to mortal combat to decide whether he was guilty or not. This right had not been invoked since the reign of Charles I, but it was still on the statute book. Such a juridical contest had to be fought in lists sixty feet square and if the appellee was defeated he was to be hanged on the spot. If the appellee killed the appeller or maintained the fight from sunrise to sunset he was to be acquitted. The worthy busybodies who believed in Thornton's guilt did their best to prevent poor little William Ashford's being challenged to fight by digging up what they thought was fresh evidence against Thornton.

The first hearing took place in November in Westminster Hall round which a mob collected to hoot the appellee when he arrived from the Marshalsea. The belief in Thornton's guilt had not been confined to the lower classes. Crabb Robinson wrote in his diary that "no one seemed to have any doubt of the prisoner's guilt, but he escaped owing to the unfitness of a profound real property lawyer to manage a criminal trial." This reflected public opinion in general about Mr. Justice Holroyd, but the probity of his mind was not affected by adverse public opinion after plea and counter-plea had dragged on until the 20th of April, 1818. Abraham Thornton was finally acquitted but he had to leave the court by a private door behind the Bench to avoid a furious mob still persuaded that he was guilty. It was lucky for him that Mr. Justice Holroyd sat with the Lord Chief Justice and two other judges. Later Mr. Justice Holroyd's son wrote *Observations upon the case of Abraham Thornton* in which he suggested as an explanation for Mary Ashford's death that she turned faint and fell into the pit. This was presumably his father's opinion, but it seemed more likely that she tried to wash out stains of blood upon her white dancing shoes and in doing so slipped from the steep bank into the deep water.

It may have been a recognition of Holroyd's moral courage which had led Sir Francis Burdett to engage him as counsel in his suit against Mr. Speaker Abbot and the Sergeant-at-Arms for wrongful arrest in 1811. Certainly Sir Francis Burdett displayed outstanding moral courage himself as an English politician. He never hesitated to incur the unpopularity of his own class by supporting causes and persons of which and of whom they disapproved. It is surprising that nobody has written a life of this fox-hunting squire of ancient lineage who was prepared to be fined £2000 and be sent to prison for three months at the Leicester Assizes of 1820 because he would not sacrifice freedom of speech and dared to denounce the behaviour of the authorities in the Peterloo affair. We talk to-day as if freedom of speech has been an age-long British privilege. We should not enjoy it to-day without the moral courage of men like Sir Francis Burdett who believed that truth and justice demanded the respect of men and who were determined to give fearless voice to that respect.

If respect for truth be accepted as a powerful inspiration of moral courage, Pilate's question may be asked, What is truth? In the Greek: τί ἐστιν ἀλήθεια; the absence of the definite article distinguishes "truth" from "the truth" which Jesus Christ emphasised. In the vulgate "*quid est veritas?*" Pilate's question is exactly translated but the lack of a definite article in Latin destroys the emphasis on "*the* truth." Bacon in his essay on truth seemed to suppose that Pilate was jesting when he asked the question. " What is truth ? said jesting Pilate and would not stay for an answer." About the same time Bishop Andrewes was rebuking Pilate in a sermon because he went on his way before he had the answer. " He deserved never to find what truth was." We can feel that Pilate displayed moral cowardice when he handed over to his enemies One in whom he could find no fault at all, but Bacon showed a failure to grasp the motives of human conduct when he accused the Roman procurator of flippancy. Shakespeare would never have made such a mistake, and here is one more piece of internal evidence to show the impossibility of Bacon's having written the plays of Shakespeare.

Pilate's question about truth was in answer to Jesus Christ's claim that He came into the world to bear witness unto the truth. " Every one that is of the truth heareth my voice." The Gospel narrative makes it clear that Pilate surrendered Jesus to the Jews only when they threatened to denounce him as disloyal to Cæsar and certainly suggests that in surrendering Jesus, Pilate was being false to what in his heart he already knew was *the* truth. Pontius Pilate was not the stuff of which martyrs are made but when he is condemned for his moral cowardice let it be remembered that St. Peter out of physical cowardice did not seem at that moment the stuff of which martyrs are made.

At this point let it be said that examples of moral courage will not be sought among those illumined by a lively faith in what they believe to be the revealed truth of whatever religious body they are members. If it be granted that one of the main inspirations of moral courage is truth it is not intended to seek it in revealed truth. The present writer does not feel capable of adding any observations of value to the rich chronicles of hagiography. Truth in his view of moral courage will be a humbler kind of truth based upon the individual's own sense of justice. Truth and justice can be so closely interwoven, that it may be impossible to claim for either the direct inspiration of moral courage. There may be some significance in the fact that the first definition of moral courage was not made until the security of faith was being assailed by the development of human knowledge.

Although truth and justice may be the most powerful impulses to show moral courage, there are others. Compassion is one of these. Tentatively it can be suggested that this is the main influence upon those who urge the abolition of capital punishment. It is recognition of compassion's part that leads the upholders of capital punishment to accuse the abolitionists of sentimentality in being more sorry for the murderer than for his victim. This is nonsense but with it some organs of the popular Press played upon the emotions of their readers so successfully that many candidates for Parliament were afraid to support abolition for fear of losing votes and the result was the muddle-headed Homicide Act of 1957 which made murder with robbery a capital crime and allowed the poisoner to escape the gallows. That illogical qualification shows how flimsy is the argument that capital punishment is a deterrent to murder. The poisoner always works on a calculated plan of action and therefore is able to consider whether or not his taking another's life is worth the risk of his own; the violent thief is usually at the mercy of an instant emotion. The only arguable plea for capital punishment is the right of society to retribution in this world with the prospect of life in another, but since what used to seem to the great majority of civilised humanity the assurance of another life beyond the grave has come to seem to more and more people less certain, a feeling for the value of human life has become deeper and more widespread. This may seem a paradoxical claim to make at a time when mankind is so much preoccupied with weapons of destruction. Nevertheless, it is a claim that can be sustained and if compassion animates those who urge the abolition of the death penalty it is not a sentimental compassion for the mental agony inflicted upon a condemned man but a dread of destroying the miracle of life.

When in the eighteenth century offences against the law that to-day would not earn a month in prison were punished with the death penalty, the severity of the penal code had no serious effect on the prevalence of crime. When it made no difference to the fate of a highwayman or footpad whether he had killed his victim or merely robbed him of a few pieces of silver, there were no more murders then than there were when men like Sir Francis Burdett succeeded in lightening the excessive severity of the penal laws. In those days the sacredness of life on earth was not greatly regarded because a life in the world to come was taken for granted except by a comparatively small minority of philosophers.

Nor was the long-drawn ordeal of the condemned cell inflicted either upon the condemned man or his gaolers once upon a time. Those who believe in capital punishment may have arguments for its retention, but surely no reasonable argument can be found for retention of the sickening mumbo-jumbo that accompanies it from the moment that the judge dons the black cap with what looks like a pen-wiper balanced on the top of his wig, to the reading of the burial service over the condemned man before he is dead. Moreover, it was more merciful to launch the condemned man into eternity twenty-four hours after he was sentenced than to keep him shivering on the brink of that dread gulf for nearly three weeks. Hanging is an atrociously archaic way of killing a human being and the self-satisfied modernity of the electric chair is just as atrocious. The administration of a strong sleeping draught to the condemned man every night from which one night he does not awake, seems a more civilised alternative to our present barbarous procedure, if capital punishment through the influence of backward minds be retained.

Then arises the question of reprieve. No man should be compelled to bear the burden carried by a Home Secretary. His moral courage must be often strained to breaking point when he is asked to decide whether a human being is to live or die and, distasteful though it be to have to say this, there must have been times when a Home Secretary's moral courage has failed him under the temptation of expediency masquerading as justice. In the present climate of opinion, besides the abolition of capital punishment, there is an outstanding demand upon the moral courage required to secure another reform. I refer to the recommendation of the Wolfenden Report that homosexual behaviour between two adults of over twenty-one should no longer be treated as a criminal offence. With various organs of the popular Press booming away in a diapason of morality, Members of Parliament are frightened to let common sense guide them for fear of losing votes. Their moral courage does not rise to it in case they may themselves be suspected of sympathy with homosexuality.

The apparent increase of homosexuality is due to the fact that men and women talk about it much more freely. It was always widely spread in our country, even when it was a capital offence. To make it an offence against the criminal law is to encourage homosexuality because stolen fruit tastes sweeter and because the greatest encouragement of all is the penalty of prison for the homosexual offender. Blackmail, all too often leading to the suicide of the victim, is encouraged by that preposterous clause in the Criminal Law Amendment Act of 1886, and here we are in the second half of the twentieth century without the moral courage to delete it from the statute book. So long as the energy of the police is exhausted by the control of traffic and their attention preoccupied with trapping homosexuals outside public lavatories or young people making love in motor cars, the streets of our great cities will be as inadequately patrolled as they are to-day, and the crimes of violence will increase. Even down-to-earth common sense often demands moral courage for a display of it.

Besides truth, justice, compassion and common sense there is another spring for moral courage and that is self-respect. This may include a man's duty to the other four, but it can all too easily become self-esteem, egotism, pride, vainglory and self-will. Pride is included with some hesitation because the layman may feel nervous about defining the qualities of a deadly sin that has puzzled eminent moral theologians to define with exactitude in complete agreement with one another. That pride can be a virtue is shown by the qualification proper pride and if we accused such an ignoble creature as Hitler of pride we might justifiably feel that we were committing *lèse-majesté* against Satan.

II

Abdication from an Empire

IT HAS BEEN NOTED that the earliest instance of an example of moral courage quoted by the *Oxford English Dictionary* was taken from Charles Caleb Colton who wrote of Cromwell that his " hypocrisy sometimes neutralised his moral courage never his physical." Foreigners for a long time now have imputed to the English a predilection for hypocrisy and it may be that it is this very hypocrisy which seems to deprive them at times of moral courage. A hypocrite in classical Greek was an actor, and it is not used in the pejorative sense of outward show until the Gospels where the Pharisees pretended to a piety they inwardly lacked by the ostentation of their phylacteries and ritualism.

The English do not lay claim to virtues they do not possess nor are they conscious of pretence in their attitude about sex, liquor, gambling, religion and class; but they are essentially a romantic nation who have produced the greatest poetry since the ancient Greeks and who have had a clearer notion of justice than any nation since the Romans. They have not produced any actors or actresses of outstanding genius on the stage unless their blood has been mixed with Jewish or Celtic blood. On the other hand, few nations have produced equally accomplished actors off the stage. One may offer as an example Stanley Baldwin, and the beauty of his performance was his complete unawareness that he *was* acting. Like his first cousin Rudyard Kipling, another fine actor off the stage, he believed in the romantic effigy he had made of himself, and therefore they both believed equally in the reality of their work. Both suffered disillusionment. For Kipling it came with the South African War; for Baldwin it did not come until the Second World War. What seemed to so many the hypocrisy of Baldwin's handling of the Abdication was true but that hypocrisy was not of belief or behaviour; it was a romantic vision of himself saving the Crown and in the process of salvation displaying moral courage under fearful odds. There were some who said that Baldwin took advantage of the Abdication to protect himself against the disastrous result of lulling the British public with the soothing syrup of safety first. This may be doubted. Baldwin's vision of himself did not allow him to perceive the least evidence of self-aggrandisement from the time he helped to overthrow Lloyd George until he retired from the political scene, bewildered after the outbreak of war by the ingratitude of the people by whom he felt he was owed so much. It could be argued that nobody who creates an image of himself can ever display moral courage because he will always be at the mercy of the imagined self. This may well have been true of Cromwell, and the occasional lack of moral courage to which Colton refers may have been due to an unwillingness to subvert the character of himself he had built up.

It may be remarked of the Prime Ministers during the last seventy years that none of those who achieved high political office with an ancestral background of privilege like Salisbury, Rosebery, Balfour and Sir Winston Churchill felt called upon to present an idea of themselves up to which they had to live. That was equally true, however, of Lloyd George who was always almost recklessly himself; he never gave up to party what was meant for mankind.

Mr. Attlee, as Prime Minister, never seemed handicapped by having to present to the world an idea of himself up to which he had to live. Therefore, when he decided that the time had come to stop dodging the issue with one excuse or another and to abdicate from the Empire of India in the name of Britannia ten months before that abdication was due, he could afford to obey his common sense and perform an act of moral courage. The intention of the British Government to hand over India by

June 1948 was widely disbelieved and most Indians were convinced that an excuse would be found to postpone independence. The pessimism of Lord Wavell about the future was intense, and the speeches of the Opposition at home did nothing to convince India that Great Britain did seriously intend to abdicate in June 1948. It was then that Mr. Attlee had the notion of asking the King to create Lord Louis Mountbatten a viscount and obtain his appointment as Viceroy to replace Lord Wavell. It was an inspired choice because Lord Mountbatten would achieve what no British Viceroy had achieved in ninety years. He realised that the only way to avoid civil war was to persuade Pandit Nehru to accept the partition of the sub-continent into India and Pakistan, and he offered India freedom in August 1947 if Pandit Nehru would accept partition. That Mr. Attlee would authorise him to make such an offer required from the Prime Minister a very great deal of moral courage. And that moral courage was sustained not by any devotion to truth and justice but by Mr. Attlee's simple common sense, armed with which he refused to be deflected from his purpose by the sonorous rhetoric of the Right. To imagine where we should have been to-day without that common sense of his is an unpleasant nightmare.

On 15th August, 1947, independence became a reality instead of a dream for the fulfilment of which India had hoped so long, except for a few bold spirits, with that Oriental quietism which is always prepared for disappointment. On that August morning Britons all over India and Pakistan appeared like persons transfigured and suffused by a radiance of goodwill shed by the people they had ceased to rule.

It was tragic that the partition could not be accomplished without such loss of life in the Punjab, which, it may be added, was grossly exaggerated by those at home opposed to the decisive speed with which the future of India and Pakistan was settled. I heard a member of the previous Cabinet declare on a public platform that nearly ten million people had been killed. In fact the sum total of the lives lost was not half a million, and of these the great majority were lost through disease, hunger, exposure and floods. It is to be remembered that in Bengal, where communal rioting the year before had caused so many deaths there was no disorder. This was due to the influence of Mahatma Ghandi who must be revered as an outstanding example of moral courage in this century.

And let due praise be given to the moral courage of the officers of the old Indian Army. In circumstances that might have demoralised any army composed of men who suddenly found themselves with a split allegiance, these officers crowned with glory the end of the old Indian Army. It was not just a matter of discipline; it was discipline fortified by moral courage. The behaviour of the Indian Army in 1947, which Rudyard Kipling esteemed so much less highly than the British Army in India, might have restored that faith of his which was sapped by the South African War. Alas, there was no Kipling left to write in his own incomparable way about the India of fifty years after he had known it.

The example set by the British officers was loyally sustained by the Indian and Pakistani officers during those critical days when partition was being effected. What is more officers were able to see the example they set sustained with equal fidelity by the troops under their command and above all by those wonderful subahdars and jemadars and risaldars with the Viceroy's commission. The gratitude that Great Britain owes to those men ought to be expressed in the shape of a stone memorial somewhere in Whitehall.

The men of the old Indian Army inevitably were often called upon to oppose popular opinion and for many years they had been held up as mercenaries to be scorned by those who were working for Indian freedom. To-day both in India and Pakistan the Army is regarded as a bulwark. Indeed, in Pakistan the worsening political situation was saved by the intervention of the Army.

We are gratified when we hear that both in India and in Pakistan the armies look back with pride to the tradition of military service under British leadership and are determined to preserve that grand example. Let us remember in our gratification that for years the Indian Army officer was regarded with condescension by the British Army officer. Let us remember that for years the Poona colonel was a butt for facetious playwrights and novelists for whom it was easier to produce a stock character stuffed by convention than to create a genuine character inspired by experience.

Lord Mountbatten himself was called upon to show a good deal of moral courage, and he was fortunate in having a man like Pandit Nehru as the leader of Indian opinion. Lord Mountbatten's heart was set on India's joining the Commonwealth when independence was achieved and at one time he was almost alone in his belief that this would happen. He and Lady Mountbatten won what no previous Viceroy or Vicereine had ever won, and that was the love of the Indian people. Edwina Mountbatten, demonstrating the power of love by her single-hearted devotion, did much to erase from the memory of the Indian people the slights of those who believed that it was necessary to maintain their position by a display of superiority. Day after day she and that remarkable woman Rajkumari Amrit Kaur, who had been appointed Minister of Health, used to rise in the small hours and fly to cholera and typhus camps and spend the day comforting the stricken, but Lady Mountbatten was never too tired to be the perfect hostess when she returned. There was a photograph published in one of the glossy weeklies in which she was standing with old Mr. Rajagopalachari's arm round her waist. I used to be enraged by hearing her criticised for a lack of dignity in allowing such a photograph to be taken. Those who criticised her would none of them have had the moral courage to defy by such an action the comments of what once upon a time used to be known as "Society." She was completely fearless and to no woman in this century that owes so much to women, does our country owe more.

Her courage as Vicereine was outstanding because British Society in India was ridden by the self-protective femininity of the memsahib kind which has always sapped our colonial position from the point of view of the colonised. It can be called self-protection because it is fed by the instinctive urge of womanhood to promote the survival of the fittest.

In considering the evolutionary urge of woman to promote the survival of the fittest it may not be extravagant to attribute to that urge the imperious demand for female rights which marked the beginning of this century. This is not to suggest that women conscious of the mess that men looked like making of the world demanded political rights for themselves to avert complete disaster. Yet that passion for equality with men which fired the suffragists could hardly have been sustained without an instinctive conviction of its necessity for the future of humanity.

Do not let us forget that it was the women of Britain who fought a desperate battle and won a victory for women all over the world. Some of us who can remember the fight of the militant suffragists find it incredible now that the stupidity and brutality of those who resisted the demand of votes for women could have been tolerated for so long and that in the end women were given political rights because they had played their part in a great war.

The war was an excuse for politicians to grant with apparent grace and goodwill what they had so obstinately refused to grant before the war. No votes would have been granted to women unless the militant suffragists had come into action. Was that action an example of moral courage or of physical courage? Extreme physical courage was needed for many of the deeds they performed during the ten years of the continually more bitter struggle to which they had dedicated themselves. Physical courage alone would not have sustained that struggle for so long a time. Moreover, the feats of daring themselves required a great deal of moral courage because many of them inevitably aroused hostility and were accused by lukewarm believers in women's suffrage of damaging the cause by their violence. It required a great deal of moral courage to face the humiliating ordeal of being forcibly fed during a hunger strike. Year in year out from the brief twilight of the Unionists in 1905 to the gloaming of the Liberals that began with the declaration of war in 1914 the militant suffragists defied what seemed a growing weight of popular opinion against their methods. It was amusing (except for the victim) when a young suffragist attacked with a dog-whip a Baptist minister in Aberdeen railway station under the misapprehension that the unfortunate pastor was Mr. Lloyd George trying to escape in disguise from the Mænads. It was not amusing when pictures were destroyed and churches burnt. There were stalwarts like the late Lord Pethick-Lawrence, whose wife Mrs. Pethick-Lawrence was such a redoubtable leader, and that old paladin Henry Nevinson who defended the violence of the suffragists, and that required much moral courage in the worsening climate of public opinion. But when we have paid tribute to the physical courage of the women it is their moral courage which has most to be admired, and it was that which won them their victory.

What will always puzzle an observer of the political scene in Britain is the repeated failure to grant what must inevitably be granted in the end until the strength of the demand has been demonstrated by violence. So it was with the women suffragists; so it was with Ireland; so it was with Palestine; so it was with Cyprus. The result is that when what appears to be a surrender to violence is finally made it seems to savour unhappily of moral cowardice. Yet when Mr. Attlee and his Government acted with moral courage over our Indian Empire and so averted what must have been a struggle even more bloody than any of the others there was a large body of opinion that believed they were displaying moral cowardice.

It is equally easy to accuse Neville Chamberlain of moral cowardice at Munich, whereas in fact his hope of peace was sustained by great moral courage. Deplorable as it seemed to many of us at the time and even more deplorable as it seems to all of us to-day with the hindsight granted by the revelation of Germany's unreadiness for war in 1938, Chamberlain himself did show real moral courage in defying precedent as a Prime Minister by getting into a plane for the first time in his life and flying off to see Hitler personally. We are apt to forget now the length of time during which so many people in our country were infected by an admiration for Hitler. In 1933 just after he became Chancellor I was gibing at this admiration in the *Referee* for which I was writing every week a column of comment. At that time there was a silly season agitation in the Press about the threat to our rivers from the behaviour of musquashes who were being bred for their fur and had escaped.

I wrote these lines:

"We *must* squash the musquash
The musquash, the musquash,
For if *we* don't squash the musquash,
The musquash must squash us.
And we really ought to squash Hitler too."

I received a letter from the editor to say that so many readers had written to protest against my gibe at Hitler that he must ask me to abstain from such gibes in future. I replied that I could not abstain because I considered Hitler was a menace to Europe; then I offered my resignation from the weekly column which was at once accepted.

The wild cheers which greeted Chamberlain when he stood with King George VI on the balcony of Buckingham Palace to receive the acclamations of London for what had happened at Munich were all too soon to be forgotten. It may be true that Chamberlain looked at life through the wrong end of a municipal drain-pipe, as Sir Winston Churchill is reputed to have said. It may be true that Chamberlain set out from Munich in much the same mood as he had often set out from Edgbaston to settle a dispute in the Birmingham City Council. Nevertheless, within the limitations of a small mind he performed an act of moral courage, even although paradoxically that act of moral courage was inspired by the moral cowardice of his advisers.

A grand example of moral courage after the wretched Munich business was the resignation of Duff Cooper, the First Lord of the Admiralty, because "he profoundly distrusted the foreign policy the Government were pursuing and seemed likely to continue to pursue." The great mass of popular opinion in Britain had welcomed Chamberlain's postponement of war as peace in our time. After the debate on the Government's foreign policy Chamberlain was encouraged to consider himself a statesman of vision by 366 votes to 144, and Duff Cooper joined Mr. Winston Churchill in the wilderness.

In his speech to the House after his resignation, Duff Cooper spoke words which to-day are still vibrant:

"During the last four weeks we have been drifting daily nearer to war with Germany. We never said until the last moment, and then in the most uncertain tone, that we were prepared to fight. We know that information to the opposite effect was being poured into the ears of the head of the German State, and that he had been reassured and fortified in the opinion that in no event would Britain fight.... Throughout these days, the Prime Minister has talked to Hitler in the language of sweet reasonableness, but he would have been more open to the language of the mailed fist. Mr. Chamberlain returned from Berchtesgaden with proposals wrapped up in a cloak and called self-determination. They meant partition of a country, cession of territory. Sweet reasonableness has won nothing except terms which a cruel and revengeful enemy would have dictated to a beaten foe after a long war.... Crueller terms could hardly be devised than those of the Berchtesgaden ultimatum. I said to myself that if these terms were accepted it would be the end of all decency of conduct of public affairs in the world.... Having accepted partition, Czechoslovakia should have been saved the humiliation of having to submit to the ignominy and horror of invasion. After Naboth had agreed to give up his vineyard he should have been allowed to pack up his goods. The German Government, having got their man down, were not to be deprived of the pleasure of kicking him, or the German Army of its loot. Britain was left with a tremendous commitment—to guarantee and defend a frontier that she had at the same time destroyed. It was as though we had dealt a man a mortal blow and at the same time insured his life."

Those words and the action of him who spoke them evoked hardly even the most tepid commendation at the time because the country was still under the spellbound relief of having escaped war. The criticism of those who deplored Munich was drowned in the noise of the ovations that greeted Neville Chamberlain on his return to England. Earlier that year Mr. Anthony Eden had resigned from the Foreign Office because he disapproved of the way in which the Prime Minister was playing the part of the Secretary of State for Foreign Affairs by dealing directly with Mussolini over his head. Mr. Eden's resignation won popular approval. That was not difficult to win. The country was not afraid of going to war with Italy.

III

The influence of Public Schools

EVER SINCE THE FIRST WORLD WAR there has been an inclination to denigrate the heroic aspect of man. We seem to welcome more and more cordially any evidence of weakness in heroes. It is difficult not to suspect that this delight in iconoclasm is the sign of a moral weakness in ourselves, or perhaps it might be nearer the mark to call it a moral jealousy. That jealousy of the past is recurrent in human nature. Two and a half millenniums ago the younger generation in Athens was inclined to resent the unfavourable comparisons being drawn between their youthful behaviour and that of the preceding generation which had produced the tough veterans of Marathon. Those of us who were boys in the last decade of the nineteenth century can recall the burden of the Victorian past lying heavily upon our shoulders, we who seemed to have nothing but the dull fag end of it to contemplate. No wonder the South African War excited us, and equally no wonder that many of us who had been too young to take an active part in that war became nauseated by jingoism and welcomed Mr. Somerset Maugham's cynical view of military heroism in his novel *The Hero*, which perhaps significantly has so far not been republished. Nevertheless, the disillusionment of the South African War did not affect the willingness of youth to sacrifice itself in immensely greater numbers when the call came in 1914. Yet within a decade after the Great War came to an end the egg-head critics of the moment were calling Rupert Brooke's poetry romantic rhetoric. The business of exploiting the weaknesses of revered figures was started by Lytton Strachey with his book *Eminent Victorians* and was continued by a number of second-rate writers whose work often hardly rose above the level of a gossip-writer's paragraph. Lytton Strachey may have written in the spirit of a mischievous (sometimes malicious) old maid but the result was a brilliant entertainment, a sort of mental strip-tease at the end of which truth never revealed herself completely naked. Florence Nightingale, Dr. Arnold, Cardinal Manning and General Gordon had all been revered as people of high moral courage and Strachey's apparent ability to explain it away could be impeached as a deleterious influence upon morals by those who believe in the potentially evil influence of books. In fact Lytton Strachey's work was the effect of the contemporary mood not the cause of it. That mood is apparent in the early novels of Aldous Huxley which were so stimulating to the young people of the nineteen-twenties, but whose characters would seem as unreal to the young people thirty years later as to the young people of the twenties seemed the characters of the nineties of which decade in fact they were a long delayed afterbirth. Now, just as the nineties and the Edwardian decade were romanticised, the decade of the twittering twenties is being romanticised by the revengeful whirligig of time, and that decade which believed itself to have debunked the past with such success is being presented in a mist seen through rose-tinted spectacles.

How far was the attitude of the twenties in our country responsible for the moral cowardice which displayed itself at Munich? Moral cowardice there certainly was, even if the man who voiced it was himself morally courageous. Surely the path to the ignominy of Munich was laid out in the previous decade when Great Britain, France and Italy surrendered to Turkey and sacrificed Greece, when the League of Nations surrendered to Mussolini and condoned the outrage of the Corfu bombardment, when Austen Chamberlain made a secret agreement with Italy about Abyssinia and had to stammer excuses at Geneva after the little Negus prompted by France asked awkward questions, and when later the Japanese were allowed to have their way in Manchuria.

But even as these words are written the memory of the

Spanish Civil War returns in which many young men who had not so long ago been voting in University debates that nothing would persuade them to fight for King and country played a gallant enough part. Nevertheless, I believe that some words I wrote twenty years ago are alarmingly applicable to-day:

> "After the Great War of 1914–18, people sat back and declared that another great war would mean the end of civilisation. Pamphlets were published to warn the world what appalling weapons and poisons would obliterate humanity. Pacificism was feverishly preached on the text that war was too horrible, but its missionaries forgot that only experience teaches and that a younger generation would be excited but not warned by books like *All Quiet on the Western Front.* Meanwhile, for two fatal decades audiences sought a deliberate thrill from gangster films and plays, and readers woke up to the fact that the thrills and kicks they had been administering to themselves, thrills and kicks more pernicious to moral stamina than any hashish or cocaine could supply, were expressions of such a *zeitgeist* as not even the far-sighted Goethe might have discerned upon the way."

The poison-gas and bacilli with which the ardent and admirable missionaries of peace hoped to frighten humanity into behaving itself proved to be as ineffective as the bogies with which nursemaids used to threaten obstreperous children. Will the H-bomb be any more successful because it is called "the deterrent"? This dangerous belief in the power of a name is prevalent in Britain. Call gaolers or warders prison-officers and to the bureaucratic mind a measure of prison-reform has been carried through. Talk of the free world and by some credulous alchemy we begin to believe that the part of the world in which we live really is free.

Let it be admitted at once that the H-bomb is a much more certain threat to civilisation than poison-gas, so much more certain that if war comes the reality will undoubtedly be much worse than anything we imagine beforehand. Let it also be admitted that the existence of this dreadful weapon does make the nations who possess it able to swallow and digest much tougher *casus belli* than once upon a time. If the H-bomb were called the "dissuasive" such an epithet could be accepted. To use so positive a word as "deterrent" is to encourage an unjustifiable confidence and an imaginary security. Half the country took the phrase "collective security" as a tranquilliser before the last war. It was hush-a-bye baby to a cradle in the tree-top, and the bough broke.

So long as only the United States and the U.S.S.R. possessed the H-bomb, it was possible to feel that war could come only by the accident of human error. Then Britannia decided that her dignity must be preserved by making the H-bomb herself with the natural result of suggesting to France that her dignity required an H-bomb. We may expect that in due course any nation large or small will need its H-bombs as a *nouveau riche* needs a grouse-moor and his wife a mink coat to establish status. Should these H-bombs be allowed to multiply, a third war is inevitable. Should such a war come it assuredly will mean the end of civilisation. At this moment in the destiny of mankind a tremendous gesture of moral courage by a great nation might save the world, and perhaps only Britain is capable of making such a gesture.

Britain can display a maddening stupidity, all the more maddening because one knows that when the stupid fit has passed she will atone for it by an abundant, indeed sometimes an excessive generosity. As this book is being written news keeps coming in of the glorious reception that the Queen is being given by the peoples of India and Pakistan. That reception is the tribute paid by a sub-continent to express its appreciation of and gratitude for the act of moral courage performed on 15th August, 1947. In the long tale of empires gained and lost there is no comparable abdication of power.

It was said above that Lord Attlee had been inspired by common sense to display his moral courage and listening to him on television recently when he was being asked about events and personalities in his life we heard Lord Attlee in that appropriately dry, slightly pedagogic voice of his dismiss that tremendous decision to withdraw from India as a piece of obvious common sense. Let it be just that: it still remains a superlative manifestation of moral courage which, whatever embarrassment the epithet may cause him, makes Lord Attlee a great man. What statesman still active is capable of an even greater and much harder display of moral courage by leading Britain to set an example to the world and dropping all the H-bombs she has, unexploded, into the deepest part of what would then be the well-named Pacific Ocean?

It may be argued that for this country to face the certainty of being destroyed on the chance of being able to remain long enough available as a base for American bombers is itself an act of moral courage. That may be true, but it would be a barren act because it would die with the island that made it.

But argument does not come into it. There is no argument about faith, and it would demand from the country that disarmed herself to set an example to the rest of the world of an incandescent act of faith.

The reaction to Mr. Khrushchev's offer to disarm was discouraging. That offer may have been bluff, but if bluff, why was the bluff not called? Instead the critics all started to point out the difficulties of disarmament, and the amount of preliminary discussion that would be needed before agreement was reached about the way in which it was to be put into effect. At the end one was left with the impression that Mr. Khrushchev's critics regarded his proposal as a piece of unfair propaganda intended to embarrass them. Nobody seems to wonder whether beneath all the showmanship there may not be an anxious desire to find an excuse to prevent the Chinese from arming themselves with atomic weapons and in the course of time turning Moscow into a satellite of Peking.

The American obsession with a sudden attack on the United States by the Soviet Union is an intelligible obsession after Pearl Harbour; but so long as that obsession endures it will be a threat to the peace of the world. And let it be remembered that so long as the Americans remain obsessed by the fear of this sudden attack the Russians will suppose the Americans capable of launching such a sudden attack upon themselves, and thus is nurtured another threat to the peace of the world. Neither side is secure against the mistaken panic of an individual, and all too easily the great deterrent might become the great detergent, wiping humanity from the earth.

Yet even as one pleads for the moral courage to set an example to the world by disarming one has to respect the attitude of those who prefer the possibility of being obliterated to what they believe would be surrender to an ideology fatal to the future of mankind. One may suspect a lack of imagination in such stalwarts which leads them to believe that this Armageddon on the edge of space will end in victory for them, but we have no right to dismiss courage as mere stupidity. It was a shock to many of us when Aneurin Bevan gave his support to the advocates of the H-bomb for Britain, but in giving that support Aneurin Bevan was displaying the moral courage with which he was so bountifully endowed. It is sometimes a much more difficult decision for a man of character to follow a majority than a minority, and although the decision he took may have been the wrong decision he was never more admirable than when he took it.

In 1945 just before the General Election I said to him that I hoped the Tories would win because I thought that the difficulties of any Government faced with the task of steering the country through the years of recovery after the war would be so formidable that those difficulties would be associated with whatever party was in power and that as a result that party would not return to power for a long time.

"We *must* win the election," he said. "And we *must* face the responsibility of governing the country. We have run away from that responsibility for too long."

Silenced by the measured gravity of the tone in which he made that reply, so abruptly different from his usual bubbling speech, I asked myself how I could have supposed for a moment that Nye Bevan would let his faith be played upon by expediency. Yet he could consult expediency when it seemed necessary. About the time of the notorious comparison of the Tories to vermin, which convinced his opponents that he was a potential

Robespierre, he said to me, "But I must be strident. If I am not strident in Ebbw Vale they will be saying, 'Ah, there's Nye Bevan going the way of Ramsay MacDonald and running after the duchesses and the marchionesses and forgetting he is one of ourselves.'"

The inspiration of Aneurin Bevan's moral courage, which was persistent, may have been mainly a longing for truth and justice but there was in him a solid stratum of common sense which had he lived would have combined with his other qualities to make him a great Prime Minister. In the middle of the last war when Bevan was showing the greatest moral courage in criticising the conduct of the war I could always make good solid, unimaginative conservative opinion splutter by observing that a few months after a third world war came Nye Bevan would be called upon like Lloyd George and Winston Churchill to lead the country. He was looked upon as a destructive force by those for whom the wind of change only meant a damned uncomfortable draught. In fact he was a creative force. His object was not to bring down the privileged to a lower level but to raise the underprivileged to partake of the fullness of life.

I never heard Nye Bevan advocate the abolition of what in England are paradoxically called public schools. He found himself easily at home with those who had had a different kind of education from his own, and he was never inclined to call the grapes sour. He wanted the working classes to enjoy the privilege of a public school education and the only thing he criticised in the public schools was their failure to follow the intentions of their founders by allowing class to count in the award of their scholarships. He welcomed the more progressive spirit of Oxford and Cambridge in this regard. Yet I in old age feel more and more doubtful of the value of a public school education and increasingly apprehensive of the present tendency to covet a grammer school education as something superior to the education of a secondary school. The obstinate survival of class consciousness in England, particularly south of the Trent, is more responsible than anything else for the curious fits of moral cowardice to which the English are prone, and that class consciousness is based fundamentally on the public schools. In Scotland on the other hand fits of moral cowardice on a national level have nothing to do with class consciousness but seem to be a survival of the religious anxiety that tormented the Scots for a century and a half after the Reformation. The moral superiority of the English over so many other nations establishes itself by their ability to recognise, without ever admitting it of course, their own mistakes and bear no ill will in consequence of them. Moral superiority is not being used in the sense of claiming better morals but superiority of morale. One of the handicaps of this moral superiority is so strong a conviction of being in the right that in the struggle the other side almost always has to resort to physical force before the English are able to grasp the possibility of their being in the wrong. When they have been hard enough hit they yield with grace like good sportsmen and respect the other side for nearly beating what they, the English, consider the best side in the world. To an embittered exile like Lord Elcho the willingness of the English to treat with a stubborn foe seemed contemptible. " In the month of March 1778," he wrote in his *Journal*, " seeing that the English ministers were endeavouring to arrange terms of peace with the American rebels, I wrote a letter to Lord North in which I remarked to him that since the Government had come to treat with the rebels in America, they ought to extend a little of their clemency to me, a rebel Scot, and permit me to return to my native land after an exile of thirty-two years. The English are the most inconsistent and the most stern nation in the world when they have their enemies in their power.... To-day they see that they cannot conquer the American rebels, who defeat them on every occasion. Thereupon they humble themselves before them and offer all sorts of terms of accommodation while they treat their Scottish rebels with the utmost haughtiness, hardship and cruelty after having vanquished them. What difference is there between the Americans who wish to form themselves into a republic and renounce the sovereignty of George III, and the Scots who renounced the sovereignty of George II and wished to recognise a Prince of the Scottish House of Stuart in place of the House of

Hanover, which is German and foreign. . . . But ferocious in prosperity and abject in adversity—that is the national character of the English. . . . Their hatred towards all nations in Europe is well known. They cannot even tolerate their subjects the Irish. Their conduct towards their subjects in America brought upon them a civil war. Their animosity against their own compatriots in Scotland is such that a turmoil arises when the King appoints a Scotsman to be his Minister; yet without Scotland what could they do? The Scots are their mainstay in all their wars. . . ."

Elcho would have found confirmation of his opinion of the English toward enemies who had nearly beaten them by their generosity to the Boers, to the Germans, to the Jews, to the Irish and to the Cypriots. Elcho failed to divine the reason for this in the sporting Englishman's admiration for an opponent who had shown himself almost as good as an Englishman. Yet what must sometimes be set beside the readiness of the English to forgive their enemies is an equal readiness to forget their friends.

We have spoken of the English when it would have been more accurate to speak of the English governing class, and until not so long ago that governing class was almost exclusively the product of the English public school.

It may surprise many people to learn that when in 1861 the Public Schools Commission went into the question of their endowments there were only nine schools in the country recognised as public schools. These were Eton, Winchester, Harrow, Rugby, Shrewsbury, Westminster, Charterhouse, St. Paul's and Merchant Taylors. To-day the public schools accepted as such must be at least fifty.

The definition of a public school in the *Concise Oxford Dictionary* is an " endowed grammar (usually boarding-) school preparing pupils chiefly for universities or public services, often maintaining discipline with help of pupils."

That maintenance of discipline with the help of the pupils may be the source of what sometimes appears to be moral cowardice among English people because it begets fear of the result of nonconformity and impresses on the growing boy the sacred duty of not being different from other boys.

In May 1864 Charles Dickens made a speech in the presence of the Provost of Eton in the course of which he declared:

> "I believe there is not in England any institution so socially liberal as a public school. It has been called a little cosmos of life outside, and I think it is so . . . as far as I know, nowhere in the country is there so complete an absence of servility to mere rank, to mere position, to mere riches as in a public school. A boy there is always what his abilities or his personal qualities make him . . . of the frank, free, manly, independent spirit preserved in our public schools, I apprehend there can be no kind of question. . . ."

Dickens had sent his eldest son to Eton and may therefore have felt that he had to justify such a step with that vast public of his who thought *David Copperfield* a much more vital picture of youth than *Tom Brown's Schooldays* of Thomas Hughes or *Eric or Little by Little* of Dean Farrar or as a later generation would regard H. A. Vachell's *The Hill.* The shock given to established public-school opinion of nearly fifty years ago by novels like *Sinister Street* or *The Loom of Youth* of Alec Waugh is difficult to realise to-day. Nevertheless, that demand for conformity still exists in the public schools of less antiquity, just as one finds among parvenus an occasionally excessive anxiety to do the right thing, often with the result of overdoing it.

This rigid doctrine setting forth the importance of not letting down the side sets a problem to somebody who may think that the side is wrong, but in nine cases out of ten the man educated at a public school will surrender his private convictions for what he believes to be the value of unity. Ten years ago the Establishment would have signified to anybody who used the word the Established Church of England. To-day the Establishment means the combination of the higher Civil Service with the Law supported by the opinion of what used to be called the governing classes. That Establishment is permeated with the public-school spirit and one has had an example of its strength in the refusal so far to institute a public inquiry into the Evans case. Evans was supposed to have strangled his wife and the Establishment hopes to avoid the accusation of having strangled Evans. It is more important in the view of the Establishment that the remains of an innocent man should stay in a felon's grave than that the Establishment should have to admit a miscarriage of justice. Such an admission might encourage the pernicious superstition that there is one law for the rich and another for the poor. The sacred impartiality of British justice must not be impugned. Disciplined opinion must be maintained.

The strength of the Conservative Party has been the power of the whips to enforce discipline and there is an amusing resemblance between their methods and the methods of prefects with small boys. Neither the Liberal Party nor the Labour Party has been able to use the whip as effectively as the Tories, and therefore the Conservative Party has not been able to produce as many examples of political moral courage as the other two parties.

The outstanding example of Duff Cooper has been mentioned, and to that might be added the example of Sir Winston Churchill when as a young man he crossed the floor of the House to join the Liberal Party. One must be old enough to remember the mood of the country nearly sixty years ago to appreciate the political moral courage of Winston Churchill's decision at that date.

Mussolini's fascism when it started looked like an attempt to apply the public-school ethos of England to Italian politics, and the original marchers to Rome whom the Duce himself followed by train looked and behaved like boy scouts on the way to a jamboree. The very methods of dealing with their opponents recalled bullying scenes in the school stories of once upon a time. It is useful to remember that Mussolini's early fascism was cordially welcomed by the majority of the British governing classes, educated in public schools. However, as always when man prefers physical force to moral force he degenerates into an earlier form of himself and his behaviour moves away from man towards mandrill. The possible play on words, so useful to the setters of crossword puzzles, reminds us that when man allows himself to be drilled into a uniform pattern for the purpose of inflicting that pattern upon others he can all too easily acquire some of the characteristics of a ferocious baboon. The Fascists failed to compete with the barbarism of the Nazis perhaps because the much more ancient civilisation of Italy was unable to revert so easily as the comparatively recent civilisation of Germany. Nevertheless, the Fascists could be barbarous enough, and one of their victims was a man I knew and admired, a man whose moral courage was infrangible.

Giovanni Amendola was a journalist born in 1882 who in 1919 was elected Deputy for Sarno, standing as a Democratic Liberal, and became Minister for the Colonies in the Bonomi and Facta governments which preceded the fascist revolution. He was a strong and outspoken opponent of fascism, and with others tried hard to persuade King Vittorio Emmanuele to proclaim martial law. However, the little King let himself be persuaded into supporting fascism and in October 1922 he called on Mussolini to form a Cabinet.

The voice of Amendola was almost the only one in the existing Cabinet to denounce the objectives of the fascist *coup d'état* and the way in which it had been achieved, and he never compromised with his belief that the triumph of fascism would be a fatal misfortune for the country. He was marked down for silencing. In March 1924 the police forbade the meeting at which he was to make an election address in Naples after he had been roughly handled by Blackshirts whose expenses were paid by order of the General Secretary of the Fascist Trades Unions. A month later Amendola was again assaulted by hired ruffians after attending a prohibited meeting in Rome.

A week before the murder of Matteotti, the Socialist Deputy, a crowd of Blackshirts gathered outside the Chamber of Deputies, shouting for Mussolini and demanding the liquidation of the Opposition. As the Deputies left the Chamber, Amendola and another ex-Minister, Di Cesaro, were set upon by the Blackshirts, and at the same time other Blackshirts beat up members of the staff of *Il Mondo*, the journal which Amendola had founded in 1921.

Then on 10th June came the foul murder of Matteotti in which Mussolini himself was involved. Sixteen years later on another 10th June he would be involved in the murder of his country. Amendola played a leading role in the investigations of the Matteotti murder, and as the evidence of Mussolini's part in it piled up the Opposition hoped that the little King would dismiss the fascist Cabinet and appoint a constitutional Cabinet drawn from the Opposition. The little King, however, assured Mussolini of his support, and the campaign of Blackshirt violence was encouraged.

In July Amendola obtained possession of two memorandums which established conclusively the complicity of Mussolini and the fascist leaders in the murder. Those documents were presented to the King by Bonomi, an ex-premier. The King refused to take any action. Mussolini published a denial that he had ever been involved in an attack on any of his opponents and mentioned particularly Amendola. At this very moment he was encouraging his thugs to finish Amendola off more skilfully than the murder of Matteotti had been managed.

On 20th July a thousand Blackshirts and mobsters assembled outside Amendola's hotel in Montecatini and threatened him with their violence. The police on being appealed to for protection against the mob when he left in his car for Pistoia sent a lorry filled with *carabinieri*, but soon after Amendola's car left the hotel the lorry disappeared, and Amendola himself was dragged out of his car and brutally beaten up. From the injuries he received Amendola died on 6th April, 1926, aged forty-four. Ten days after the bludgeoning of Amendola the King decreed an amnesty for all those involved in the Matteotti affair. If Giovanni Amendola may be held up as a splendid example of an Italian's moral courage King Vittorio Emmanuele II will serve to illustrate an Italian's moral cowardice, and yet that moral cowardice was accompanied by physical courage of a high order.

Giovanni Amendola must have had as much physical courage as he had moral courage to endure what he did, but however much we admire that physical courage we must admire even more that moral courage which sustained his spirit to resist the popularity of fascism and the exhilaration of the flowing tide. I am proud to have met a man who even in the nineteen-twenties could not have been called anything less than a hero.

When one cites the treatment given to Amendola as a possible outcome of the public-school attitude carried to extremes we must not forget the comparable violation of the individual's right to choose his own behaviour in an industrial dispute. Conformity is demanded from the members of trades unions as obstinately as from public school boys. Compulsory membership of a trade union is insisted upon as rigorously as compulsory games at a public school. This demand is sometimes carried so far as to dictate to which union a worker shall belong. If we admire the moral courage of a Duff Cooper we must admire equally the moral courage of men who are prepared to suffer not loss of office but, what to them may be even more precious, loss of comradeship, because they are not prepared to accept the verdict of the majority in what may seem to them coming out on an unnecessary and ill-advised strike. It is a heavy test of man's devotion to a principle when he is sent to Coventry. It was a heavy test for prep-school boys when they were sent to Coventry by their fellows, but it was a penalty no longer in use at public schools by the beginning of this century, possibly because it had become a recognised penalty at girls' schools. The origin of the phrase was the treatment of difficult royalist prisoners sent to the Roundhead-ridden town of Coventry.

Clarendon in his history of the Great Rebellion writes: "At Bromigham (Birmingham), a town so generally wicked that it had risen upon small parties of the King's, and killed or taken them prisoner and sent them to Coventry, declaring a more peremptory malice to his majesty than any other place."

Whatever Coventry's reputation in the seventeenth century we must not forget the exemplary behaviour of its citizens when Lady Godiva provided people with such a magnificent example of moral courage.

It does not seem extravagant to speculate whether five hundred years hence moral courage will be a comprehensible demonstration of human virtue. The evolutionary trend of humanity seems to be in the direction of the bees, the ants and the termites in the evolution of insects. The only counter-revolutionary process seems to depend upon the ability of woman to develop her independence of man sufficiently to preserve the individual. Yet, although the domination of the female was strong enough to maintain the spider, the earwig and the praying mantis it must be remembered that the female is equally dominant among the community insects by evolving the sterile worker among the bees and the ants, and that monstrous termite matriarch. In any kind of comparable human society in the far future moral courage would not be a virtue but an offence.

We cannot believe that a man like Aneurin Bevan would have been afraid to defy his fellows if he had been convinced that they were taking a wrong course of action, but some of us should feel happier about the political maturity of the working classes if we saw more leaders on the horizon with the qualities of a Bevan. Although one wise man may be worth a hundred dullards, nobody has succeeded in devising a political system of minority rule that was tolerable. Whether we believe in a God or do not believe in a God this tiny green world of ours rolling around our small sun in the midst of the unimaginable infinity of the universe turns to nonsense unless we believe that this creature called man can increase his moral strength to keep pace with the achievements of his brain. To quote some words of my own:

> "Democracy puts a strain upon the faith of humanity which can become unendurable in hours of disillusionment. Yet democracy, which provides the only rational view of a Divine political purpose, has survived so many assaults from without, so much undermining from within, that to deny the possibility of ever attaining the goal towards which it moves so slowly, so painfully and sometimes so disgracefully, is to declare all the years of recorded history more useless than a heap of dead leaves and to offer them as a bonfire to the destructive and evil spirit of misdirected evolution."[1]

[1] *Mr. Roosevelt.*

Yes, there can be no doubt that the majority must have the last word, but that must not deprive the minority, even a minority of one, of having any word at all, and there is something peculiarly mean, and childishly mean at that, in sending a worker to Coventry because he refuses to belong to a trade union. There is little to choose morally between beating up a man physically and beating him up mentally.

IV

Those who stood by Oscar Wilde

IN THE COURSE OF the moving and generous tribute Mr. Macmillan paid to Aneurin Bevan in the House of Commons he wondered why "a man who had, all through his life, been a somewhat controversial figure should have ended by commanding such general admiration and affection." The answer is that in the end the British people respect the man who has spoken his own mind, regardless whether that speech coincided with the popular prejudice of the moment. Irritated although they may often have been at the time by Bevan's fearless honesty of word or action, they had gradually come to realise that the armour of consistent honesty had blunted the arrows of criticism and left the man against whom they were aimed a figure to be respected and loved. The British people will always concede their admiration of moral courage at last, even if many of them have been maddened when it seemed to challenge at the time their own ability to display it and therefore stung.

On the other hand, the British people in spite of their own reputation for hypocrisy with other nations will ultimately turn against a former idol whom they have grown to suspect of it.

An example of this was the almost savage way in which they turned against Lord Baldwin after the last war began. Yet all that Baldwin had done was to flatter and cosset the mood of the country at the time and perceive in himself the incarnate expression of it.

The danger of hypocrisy, by which is meant the presentation of an idea of oneself to the world that lays upon the person who presents it a continuous responsibility of living up to the figure of himself he has created for others to accept as the reality, is that the maintenance of it too often puts an unbearable strain upon his moral courage. Even when the Delphic admonition (γνῶθι σεαυτόν) Know Thyself has been heeded the knowledge may be so depressing that the trappings of the projected self are retained to hide and warm the nakedness that reality seems likely to reveal. In its lowest form hypocrisy is a deliberate pretence. The outwardly pious Catholic or Protestant who profanes the sanctity of his religion by honouring the letter and dishonouring the spirit is not worth discussion. The hypocrisy with which we are concerned is an idealistic attempt for the failure of which we must have compassion, and be it added, compassion animated by humility but never tinged with that contempt which humility forbids. "But for the grace of God there goes John Bradford."

Sir J. M. Barrie was an example of the projected personality that concealed the real self, and he is chosen here for an example of such a projection among authors rather than Rudyard Kipling, Bernard Shaw, George Meredith or any other of the notable authors of a previous generation who had to live up to what seems now a projected personality because in his Rectorial Address delivered to the students of St. Andrews University on 3rd May, 1922, Barrie chose "Courage" for his theme. In contrast to the projected personalities Thomas Hardy and H. G. Wells may be cited as examples of authors who were not playing a part and were always their real selves.

At the time Barrie's address made a profound impression; re-reading it to-day one seeks for an explanation of an enthusiasm that seems out of tune with the mood of the moment when young people were beginning to wear ready-made reach-me-down cynicism as their mental attitude.

The address starts off with a typical expression of luscious Barrie sentiment inspired by a typical declaration of Barrie modesty.

"You have had many rectors here in St. Andrews who will continue to bloom long after the lowly ones such as I am are dead and rotten and forgotten. They are the roses in December; you remember someone said that God gave us memory so that we might have roses in December. But I do not envy the great ones. In my experience—and you may find in the end it is yours also—the people I have cared for most and who have seemed most worth caring for—my December roses—have been very simple folk. Yet I wish that for this hour I could swell into someone of importance, so as to do you credit."

In fact Barrie cared a great deal more for people of rank inherited or earned; the simplicity of Thrums was for him a piece of picturesque sentimentality.

"You must excuse me if I talk a good deal about courage to you to-day. . . . It is the lovely virtue—the rib of Himself that God sent down to His children.

"My special difficulty is that though you have had literary rectors here before, they were the big guns, the historians, the philosophers; you have had none, I think, who followed my more humble branch, which may be described as playing hide-and-seek with angels."

Imagine any of Barrie's predecessors talking like that—Smollett or Scott or Galt or even R. L. Stevenson who could occasionally trip along by the edge of sentimental humbug and nearly fall right in. It is not surprising to hear Barrie admit that his puppets seem more real to him than himself, and then go on to explain that McConnachie is the unruly half of himself who does the writing:

> "I am the half that is dour and practical and canny, he is the fanciful half."

There was never a more practical and canny writer than Barrie, and his work was wrought with immense skill never to suggest unruliness. McConnachie's fancy was preoccupied with amazement at the height that the young Scots journalist from Thrums had attained in the great world of London.

Barrie went on in his address to flatter his youthful listeners with the notion that the future welfare of the nation rested upon their courage in sharing responsibility for national affairs with those elders who, although not directly responsible, had allowed the country to drift into the war that had finished just over three years earlier. Then in case he might be suspected of pacificism he went on to say:

"The end will indeed have come to our courage and to us when we are afraid in dire mischance to refer the final appeal to the arbitrament of arms." He advised his listeners to avoid the current youthful cant of the moment about the old men and the war, although of course he avoided anything like a clear denunciation of it by using a word like cant but preferred to sentimentalise youth's attitude, " Avoid calling us ugly names; we may be stubborn and we may be blunderers, but we love you more than anything else in the world, and once you have won your partnership we shall be welcoming you. . . . Do not stand aloof, despising, disbelieving, but insist on coming in and helping. After all we have shown a good deal of courage; and your part is to add a greater courage to it."

Phrase after phrase of abstract advice followed without a single practical suggestion for the youth of St. Andrews except that they should work more at modern languages. He went on, after a few pages of truisms like the value of hard work or people being what they make themselves, to cite Henley, Stevenson and Meredith as examples of courage but always in phrases clouded by sentiment. At last he did give a concrete example of courage by reading the letter he had received from Captain Scott, written in that frozen Antarctic tent when the end was very near. Yet even then Barrie had to spoil the poignant beauty of that last letter by sentimentalising about it.

Barrie seemed unable to disentangle moral courage from physical courage. The courage shown by Henley, Stevenson and Meredith was in the face of illness. He gave no example of purely moral courage and one cannot help asking if Barrie himself, knowing what moral courage was, lacked the moral courage to praise as a virtue the courage of a man who will maintain and proclaim his own beliefs even at the cost of unpopularity. His friends covered up what might have looked like affectation by presenting him to the outer world as a whimsical genius incapable of behaving in any way other than that in which he did behave. When his wife left him for Gilbert Cannan his friends praised his generosity in allowing her £300 a year. Nobody spoke of the lack of understanding and exclusion of her from his own social life which drove her into seeking solace from a younger man. Addison Bright, his agent, a little man hardly as big as Barrie himself, used to talk of him in terms of idolatry, and without doubt his skilful management of Barrie's affairs contributed greatly to his material prosperity. Yet when Addison Bright was discovered to have been running a company playing Barrie's plays in Canada without paying Barrie his rightful percentage, Barrie did not forgive him and Addison Bright went off to Switzerland and shot himself. Barrie was generous to prodigality when he was indulging his own heart but he had less generosity for anybody who was in danger of piercing to the reality masquerading under the appearance of McConnachie. It was a stock joke that Barrie used to wait until the Press correspondents and camera men had all seen him at some public function before he scuttled away to avoid publicity. One great quality Barrie did possess and that was a complete lack of jealousy. He did genuinely enjoy the success of younger men and wish them well.

Soon after Barrie's Rectorial Address, F. E. Smith delivered his Rectorial Address at Glasgow. In this he spoke of the glittering prizes at which his listeners should aim in life and the critics of the Press were voluble in contrasting the cynicism of such advice to students with the nobility of Barrie's advice to the young people at St. Andrews. Only recently Lord Boothby's Rectorial advice at St. Andrews to get the most out of life and enjoy it to the full was considered a sad falling away from the lofty moral standard hoisted by his precedessor. Although Lord Birkenhead possessed and Lord Boothby possesses more moral courage than Sir James Barrie, neither of them may have felt he was justified in preaching it to an audience. Barrie protested in his Rectorial Address that this was his first and would be his last public appearance, and that he never could or would have made it except to a gathering of Scottish students. This may have been true but what he failed to tell his hearers was that nobody was more eager for publicity for his work than himself and took more trouble to secure it, always provided that it was managed whimsically, like the statue of Peter Pan in Kensington Gardens, and that it would always be publicity of the right kind achieved in spite of his own efforts to prevent it.

George Bernard Shaw was mentioned earlier as an author who created a projection of himself. To this he adhered consistently throughout his very long life, and it is fair to point out that there were times when he had to display a good deal of moral courage in not letting down that projection of himself. He incurred much odium after the outbreak of the First World War by suggesting that the Germans were hardly more culpable than the other Great Powers for what happened in 1914. He was immediately accused of being a pro-German, a mental attitude which in the state of public opinion at the time seemed hardly less atrocious than the atrocities the Germans were believed to be committing in Belgium, a few of which were true but most of which were either false or greatly exaggerated. Shaw certainly did have a benevolent feeling for the Germans because they had recognised his stature as a playwright before it was recognised in Britain, but pro-Germanism at that date connoted a desire for the Germans to win the war and even a willingness to help them to win it, and I recall the outcry against Shaw with astonishment at the depths of stupidity into which intelligent men can sink when their intelligence is distorted by the emotion of the moment. I have long been puzzled by the ability of the English to believe in their possession of *sang-froid*, using as they so often will a French term for a quality of which they are proud but about which they do not want to show off. *Morale* (spelt wrongly), *élan*, and *esprit de corps* at once occur as examples. They are also prone to use French terms for something of which they are ashamed and of which, although it is a common failing of their own, they wish to suggest its rarity in England. *Laissez-faire*, *mauvaise honte* and *faux bonhomme* are examples.

That the English are unusually capable of showing sang-froid in the face of danger nobody will deny but it is in danger that demands physical courage. When moral or mental courage or even simple common sense is called for the English are less reliable.

There was a disagreeable instance of the emotional excitability of which the English are capable at the beginning of the last war when another author was accused of pro-Germanism. This was when P. G. Wodehouse after being released from the internment camp and accommodated at the Adlon Hotel in Berlin was asked to give some broadcasts to reassure his readers, particularly in the United States, that he had not been and was not being ill-treated. I listened to every one of those broadcasts and, although as broadcasts they were very far from being vintage Wodehouse and although Wodehouse himself had failed to grasp that the Germans were using him for their own ends, there was not a word to suggest that he sympathised with Nazis or approved of Nazis. He merely talked about being caught at Le Touquet and how odd it was suddenly to see a German soldier climbing over the wall into one's garden and how uncomfortable the journey had been into Germany and how glad he was to find himself in a decent hotel again.

Yet the news of those broadcasts roused such a storm of indignation in Britain that Wodehouse has not felt inclined to return home since. (For a time few booksellers would allow his books to be shown.) Questions were asked in Parliament by fatuous back-benchers and answered with deprecating timidity by obedient Under-Secretaries. The *Daily Telegraph* started a correspondence to which various authors contributed. I hope those correspondents are as much ashamed of themselves to-day for their display of self-righteousness as a few of us were ashamed of them at the time.

It was mortifying for an author to find so many of his fellow-authors yapping along with this "common cry of curs." One letter came from A. A. Milne, the father of Christopher Robin, and was couched in terms that reminded one of *Eric or Little by Little*. More in sorrow than in anger Milne wrote to say that Wodehouse had never had any real sense of responsibility and to illustrate this deficiency which any decent prefect would frown on, Milne went on to recall an occasion when Wodehouse had said to him that he would like to have a son but that he would not like to have him until he was old enough to get his house colours. This was too much for my sang-froid, and I wrote to the editor of the *Daily Telegraph* to say that I had listened to all the broadcasts and that there was nothing in them to which even the stupidest intelligence officer in the country could take exception, adding that in any case the last person to sneer at the putative paternity of Mr. P. G. Wodehouse was Mr. A. A. Milne who himself had enjoyed such a profitable paternity. This letter the editor refused to print; I was out of step with the rest of the cadet corps. Altogether that correspondence was a deplorable display of kicking a man when he was down. This the British are so sure is something of which they are incapable that it is surprising they have not found a French phrase for such un-British behaviour.[1]

Nothing like this attack on P. G. Wodehouse had happened to Shaw a quarter of a century earlier. Nevertheless, it was felt seriously that this time the clowning of G. B. S. had gone just a little too far, and that he was in danger of turning into a pantaloon.

The Oscar Wilde case was a considerable challenge to moral courage, and a sad exposure of the lack of it, of which we may still perceive indications in the reaction of the popular Press and vulgar opinion to the Wolfenden Report.

Wilde himself lacked moral courage. Indeed, it could be said that it was this very lack which led to his downfall. A long career of exhibitionism, or as it was called in the nineties of the last century "posing," had blinded him to the realities of life. He could not believe that he would not emerge with all the honours from any court of law. A fortnight after the great success of the first night of *The Importance of Being Earnest* at the St. James's Theatre the porter of the Albemarle Club presented Wilde with Lord Queensberry's card on which, his spelling unable to keep pace with his temper, the Marquess had written

[1] Since these remarks about P. G. Wodehouse were written Evelyn Waugh has put the whole foolish business into perspective by an admirable article in the *Sunday Times*.

"*To Oscar Wilde posing as a somdomite.*" When Wilde allowed himself to be persuaded by Lord Alfred Douglas to apply for a warrant for criminal libel against his hated father, he was challenging the gods by his own hubris or reckless pride. I recall that grey Saturday afternoon in the front of March 1895 and walking down Regent Street from a matinée of Hengler's Circus (which was where the Palladium stands to-day) to catch a red Hammersmith bus at Piccadilly Circus. In those leisurely days the newspaper sellers could lean their placards along the pavement, and I can see now with the mind's eye a black and buff placard of the old *Pall Mall Gazette:* WELL KNOWN DRAMATIST AND SPORTING PEER. RESULT.

The result was to be the trial and acquittal of Lord Queensberry at the Old Bailey on 5th April. There is little doubt that if Wilde had left England immediately after the collapse of his action he would not have been stopped, but he could not bring himself to take the decisive step and that evening he was arrested at the Cadogan Hotel.

Charles Hawtrey and Charles Brookfield, who had both been acting since January at the Haymarket in Wilde's play *An Ideal Husband*, gave a dinner to Queensberry to get the thanks of a Marquess for the amount of mud they had stirred up on his behalf. It was a pity that the actors who attached as much significance as they both did to being gentlemen should have given a performance so far removed from gentlemanly behaviour. It is refreshing to turn from these two gentlemen to Alfred Taylor who, in spite of being a pimp, had the moral courage when offered the choice of being prosecuted with Wilde or giving evidence against him to choose prosecution.

It will be difficult for people to-day to realise the shock the Wilde case gave to London, or to comprehend the ability of civilised people to behave like yahoos. The refusal of bail by the Bow Street magistrate before the first trial on 26th April and the difficulty Wilde had in getting a judge to grant him bail for the fortnight before the second trial is fantastic. It is sad to reflect that Asquith was the Home Secretary and that the Liberals were in power, but there is no doubt that public opinion, fed with such garbage by the Press as makes our contemporary Press at its worst appear comparatively clean and decent journalism, was merciless; the Unionist victory at the General Election that year was undoubtedly helped by a vulgar belief that morals had degenerated under a Liberal Government. So at this date an obviously moribund Government sensing public criticism was anxious to present itself to the British electorate as a stern guardian of morality.

George Alexander kept *The Importance of being Earnest* running until the first trial at the Old Bailey but obliterated Wilde's name from the programmes. Bill posters were employed to stick paper over Wilde's name on the placards; I can recall watching them at work on the way to school.

On 7th May Wilde was released on bail fixed at the exorbitant sum of £5000; the second trial was to be held a fortnight later. Half of this sum was guaranteed by Lord Douglas of Hawick, Queensberry's eldest surviving son, and the Reverend Stewart Headlam.

Headlam was a Christian Socialist who hardly knew Wilde but who had been outraged by the manner in which he thought Wilde was being found guilty by officialdom, the Press and the public before the jury had given a verdict. Headlam who had already had trouble with the ecclesiastical authorities about his Socialist Guild of St. Matthew was worried about his proposed action because he feared he would be accused of having done it to get some cheap publicity. In an autobiography he did not live to finish Headlam wrote. "I knew quite well that this action of mine would with many people damage my already damaged reputation and that it would sadly try some of my best friends whom I had already tried a good deal." Headlam was not wrong. It is depressing to find that intelligent Liberal journalists like Sir Henry Norman and H. W. Massingham could be willing to break up their friendship with Headlam because he had come to the help of Oscar Wilde. One of the High Church Christian Socialist parsons who worked with Stewart Headlam on the Guild of St. Matthew resigned. I knew Father "Jimmy" Adderley, as he was always called. He was a son of old Lord

Norton and did fine work in the East End. How he could ever behave as he did in the Wilde business is difficult to comprehend: it must have been the prevailing hysteria at the time. The Rev. C. L. Marson, whom I knew well later as a humorous High Church parish priest and collector of folk-songs with Cecil Sharp, was another cleric who behaved without charity. He tried to raise feeling against Headlam, who was a friend of his, before a London School Board election meeting. How a man of culture, wit and charm could behave with such mobster vulgarity is a mystery. Headlam was a member of the London School Board from 1888 until 1904 and when it was abolished went on to serve on the London County Council until he died in 1924. He was one of the non-conforming products of Eton and Trinity College, Cambridge.

When Wilde was let out on bail for that ghastly fortnight before the second trial he went to the Midland Hotel at St. Pancras Station where Lord Douglas of Hawick had booked two rooms. They were sitting down to dinner when the manager came in and ordered Wilde out of the hotel. Wilde tried hotel after hotel all over London but was refused hospitality at every one. At last long after midnight he reached his mother's house in Oakley Street, Chelsea. From here Ada Leverson, the wife of a well-to-do Jewish business man and the wittiest woman in London, took him to stay with herself and her husband in Courtfield Gardens. In the words of Hesketh Pearson who has written such an excellent life of Oscar Wilde:

> "But first they summoned their servants together, and Ernest Leverson spoke to them: 'You most of you know Mr. Wilde and have waited upon him. You know now the dreadful thing that has happened to him; you know of what he is accused; you know that he is out on bail. Now your mistress and I would like him to come and stay with us here until he is a free man again, but before inviting him I feel it right to ask you to tell me with frankness whether you think you will be able to make him comfortable. . . .' There was a pause, during which the butler and the cook exchanged glances. The butler cleared his throat and pronounced the

verdict: 'Well, sir—sir and madam—speaking for myself and I think for the rest of us—well, sir, we've most of us read the case, but we know Mr. Wilde, and we have always been proud to wait on him, and proud we shall still be, sir, if I make so bold—we'll all of us do all we can to make the poor gentleman comfortable.'"

The indomitable Stewart Headlam called for Wilde every morning of the trial and drove him to the Old Bailey. This Christian behaviour raised a mob round his house in Bloomsbury, threatening to break all his windows. For rousing this sort of behaviour the Press must bear the blame. With the exception of the *Daily Chronicle* and *Reynolds News*, it was a disgrace to journalism. The *Daily Mail* was still just a year away from being born, and the licence to print filth that the Press allowed itself, before the success of the *Daily Mail* taught Fleet Street that filth did not pay in a cheap family newspaper, is hardly realised to-day.

The Government pressure in the case of Oscar Wilde almost turned from prosecution into persecution. Sir Frank Lockwood, Q.C., the Solicitor-General, took every unfair advantage he could, but then his nephew by marriage had been mentioned as a practising pederast and the Solicitor-General felt a little extra moral indignation was required, in spite of his nephew's name being suppressed early on in the case by agreement behind the scenes.

Wilde was further unfortunate in having Mr. Justice Wills on the Bench at his second trial. Wills professed to have been more shocked by the enormity of Wilde's crimes than by any case he had ever had before him.

"It is no use for me to address you. People who can do these things must be dead to all sense of shame, and one cannot hope to produce any effect upon them. It is the worst case I have ever heard.... I shall under such circumstances be expected to pass the severest sentence that the law allows. In my judgment it is totally inadequate for such a case as this. The sentence of the Court is that each of you be imprisoned and kept at hard labour for two years."

Had Mr. Justice Wills ever looked at the Old Bailey Session

Papers of the previous two centuries? He would have found in them case after case to shock him far more than the case of Oscar Wilde and Alfred Taylor. He would certainly have been shocked by the behaviour of the Bishop of Clogher who was caught *in flagrante delicto* with a guardsman in a tavern off the Haymarket, and he would surely have been appalled by Mother Clap, who kept two male brothels in Holborn frequented in feminine attire by some of the veterans of Oudenarde and Malplaquet. But after all Mr. Justice Wills was easily shocked. Nine years earlier when presiding over the Claverton Street Mystery in which Adelaide Bartlett was accused of murdering her husband with chloroform Mr. Justice Wills had been terribly shocked to learn that contraceptives had been found in the trouser-pockets of the late Mr. Bartlett after his death and on top of this that he had a book called *Esoteric Anthropology* which the monthly nurse admitted she had looked at.

> " Apparently there are people who can read these books and see no shame in them. Annie Walker (the nurse) seems a respectable woman, and she says there is not a word immoral or improper in the book from the beginning to the end. Gentlemen, it has been my unpleasant duty to look at this book . . . I cannot sitting here have such garbage passed under my eyes and then allow it to go forth that an English judge concurs in the view that it is a specimen of pure and healthy literature. It is one of those books, in my judgment, which under the garb of sanctimonious purity, obtains entrance, probably, into many a household . . . it scatters its poison and does its mischief. The women of the present day are used to strange things—things which would have startled us in the time of my boyhood; and it is such reading as this that helps to unsex them, and to bring them to a place like this day after day to listen willingly to details which, even to men of mature life, like yourselves and myself are distasteful and disgusting.
>
> " If you care to verify what I say, I have put down upon a piece of paper references and passages met with in my inspection of this book which not only justify me in expressing

myself with regard to it in language such as this, but compel me to do so. To my thinking, it should excite a feeling of pity for the unhappy woman made in early life the companion of a man who could throw such literature in her way, and encourage her to read it."

We may surmise that if Mr. Justice Wills had been told that Mr. Bartlett had lent his wife *Lady Chatterley's Lover* he might have directed the jury to find that in poisoning her husband with chloroform she had been fully justified; indeed, he might have suggested that the jury should add a rider to applaud her for doing so.

Oscar Wilde was not given an hour's remission from the savage sentence passed upon him, and his life was ruined. A few feeble attempts were made to petition the authorities for clemency. Bernard Shaw signed one; he was the only author of any note who did. Efforts were made to get George Meredith to head a petition but that encased egotist flatly refused.

It is hard to believe that decent people could display the pusillanimity that was displayed by them in that May of 1895, but so it was—actors, authors, politicians and the rest of them, yes, so it was.

Disgust is relieved by the following statement published after Oscar Wilde was broken by Society and the Law, and that it is relieved by a Christian parson practising what he preaches adds something to that sense of relief.

"I became bail for Mr. Oscar Wilde on public grounds: I felt that the action of a large section of the Press, of the theatrical managers at whose houses his plays were running, and of his publisher, was calculated to prejudice his case before his trial had even begun.

"I was a surety, not for his character, but for his appearance in Court to stand his trial. I had very little personal knowledge of him at the time. I think I had only met him twice; but my confidence in his honour and manliness has been fully justified by the fact that (if rumour be correct), notwithstanding strong inducements to the contrary, he stayed in England and faced his trial.

"Now that the trial is over, and Mr. Wilde has been convicted, I still feel that I was absolutely right in the course I took, and I hope that, after he has gone through his sentence, Mr. Wilde may be able with the help of his friends, to do good work in his fresh life. June 1st 1895."

When Wilde was released on 19th May, 1897, Stewart Headlam and Robert Ross were waiting for him in a brougham outside Pentonville. Many members had resigned from Headlam's Christian Socialist Guild since he went bail for Wilde but that did not prevent him from keeping a promise he had made to meet Wilde on his release. They drove immediately to Stewart Headlam's house, 16 Upper Bedford Place. It was six o'clock in the morning. Over the first cup of coffee he had tasted in two years Headlam and he talked about Dante.

In recalling the moral courage of Stewart Headlam and Robert Ross, that of Reginald Turner and More Adey must not be forgotten. The story of the three years left to Wilde, and indeed of the circumstances surrounding the whole miserable business from the moment that fatal action against the Marquess was taken, has been so bedevilled by the prodigal inventions of Frank Harris that the part played by Robert Ross is now irreparably distorted, for which Bernard Shaw's credulity is partly responsible. I met Harris once at the old Savile Club in Piccadilly nearly fifty years ago and still retain the impression made on me then that it was a liar who was entertaining the company. I recall being told of his sniffing dubiously at the claret his host had ordered for dinner. "What's the matter, Harris? Isn't your wine all right?"

"Oh, yes, I suppose the wine's quite all right for this club of seedy prigs," was the reply of a guest who had to maintain a reputation for saying what he thought and to hell with good manners.

In the spring of 1905 I was at Ross's house in Hornton Street, Kensington, on the evening of the day that the first edition of *De Profundis* was published. There were present also Lord Alfred Douglas, Reginald Turner and More Adey. More Adey was the vaguest man I ever met and he must have performed what for him would have been a miracle of concentration by arriving at the right time on the right day to accompany Oscar Wilde and Stewart Headlam to the Old Bailey for the second trial. Reginald Turner, the most consistently and effortlessly witty man I ever knew, was a natural son of the first Lord Burnham, and for some time wrote and edited 'London Day by Day' in the *Daily Telegraph*, the precursor of William Hickey *et hoc genus omne*. For these two columns his salary was £500 a year. All the best cracks in *The Green Carnation* were noted down by Robert Hichens from Reggie Turner's conversation, when he, Reginald Turner and E. F. Benson were on holiday in Egypt. Turner wrote several novels, but in them spontaneity of wit deserted him and he never had a success. As he said to me once when we were talking about first editions. "It's my second editions which are the rarities. Indeed, they're unprocurable." He left England to live in Italy where he remained the delight of many friends. There is a feeble attempt at a portrait of him in *Aaron's Rod* by D. H. Lawrence, the local preacher in whom disapproved of wit was a flippant affectation. Reginald Turner was with Robert Ross by Wilde's death-bed.

That evening in Hornton Street Ross was reading some of the letters he had been receiving about the book. I recall only two of these. There was one from Bernard Shaw commenting on the ability of Wilde to pose even in prison and there was another from George Alexander in which he said that the book had made him shed tears. George Alexander had shown a feeble lack of moral courage throughout the Wilde affair, and when Wilde went bankrupt Alexander bought for a song the acting rights of *The Importance of Being Earnest* and *Lady Windermere's Fan*. Perhaps the tears he shed after reading *De Profundis* fretted his conscience, for when the plays were revived he paid royalties to Wilde's estate and in his will left the copyright to Vyvyan Holland, Wilde's surviving son. Alexander himself must have realised something of what Wilde had gone through when he was charged with misbehaving himself with an elderly street walker on a dustbin in the area of his own house in Pont Street. Several distinguished writers including Pinero, Barrie and (I think) A. E. W. Mason rallied round to give evidence of character at the police court, all testifying to the impossibility of such misbehaviour by a man whom none of them had ever heard tell a *risqué* story—another of those humbugging Gallicisms to describe something so rare in England as not to have a word for it. The Magistrate gave Alexander the benefit of the doubt, but the dark lantern of the rubber-soled policeman which shone down into that Pont Street area was not censured. Although Alexander was given the benefit of the doubt, and although the audience gave him a most cordial reception that night, he must have passed through a *mauvais quart d'heure*.

While Ross was reading the letters that evening Alfred Douglas was fidgeting and scratching himself with his back to the fire, standing on the fender from time to time and sliding off it with an irritating clang. Reginald Turner and More Adey probably already knew that Ross had not published the part of *De Profundis* which blamed Alfred Douglas for so much of what had happened, but of course I was unaware of this at the time and when Douglas began to criticise Wilde's manner of life in Paris after he was released from prison I remember feeling embarrassed by the sudden change in the atmosphere of that room in Hornton Street. Then Ross said something which particularly annoyed Douglas who slid from the fender, kicked it with a crash, and strode out of the room. Presently he came back in his astrakhan-collared great-coat and standing in the doorway said, "You don't know what you're talking about, Robbie." With this he slammed the door behind him and left the house.

In 1912 Martin Secker published a book about Oscar Wilde by Arthur Ransome, and Alfred Douglas sued for libel. Ross provided the defence with the suppressed portion of *De Profundis*; Douglas lost his case. Thence onward Douglas carried on a vendetta in print against Ross of such viciousness that he was driven into bringing a libel action against his enemy. On that occasion the jury disagreed but the malevolent hounding of him by Alfred Douglas severely affected his health and probably shortened his life. His devotion to Wilde was not only courageous but also practical, and nobody deserved less than he the sneers at him in Mr. St. John Ervine's *A Present Time Appraisal of Oscar Wilde* published in 1951. I have never understood why St. John Ervine concerned himself with Oscar Wilde as a pederast when as a Belfast man he might have concerned himself so much more valuably with that high-born pederast, William of Orange.

To commemorate the centenary of Oscar Wilde's birth the London County Council placed a plaque on the house in Tite Street, Chelsea, where he had lived. It was my privilege to unveil this plaque in 1955, the Mayor of Chelsea being present. We are given to reflecting with due amazement on the material changes that have taken place during the last sixty years; we ought to reflect with equal amazement at the moral transformation. It may be doubted if anybody alive in London in 1895 could have imagined such a gathering as attended the unveiling of that plaque; it would have seemed an utterly incredible event.

Nevertheless, we should beware of being too complacent about that moral transformation. One of the popular newspapers of the moment has uncovered what it calls the " lavender establishment." The members of it are anxious to abolish capital punishment, are opposed to the restoration of flogging for criminals, desire to see the recommendations of the Wolfenden Report carried out, and in fact are generally guilty of offending against good honest healthy barbarism. It is difficult for us to-day to understand how a civilised society could have conducted itself as it conducted itself in that April and May of 1895. Let us remind ourselves that in A.D. 2061 people will find it just as difficult to understand how the ghastly mumbo-jumbo of hanging a man could still have survived in a civilised society a hundred years ago. Yet in spite of the relics of old unhappy far-off things that remain we surely can believe that we are nearer to appreciating that heart-searching rebuke of Jesus Christ to the scribes and Pharisees when they brought to him a woman saying: " Master, this woman was taken in adultery in the very act. Now Moses in the law commanded us that such should be stoned; but what sayest thou? This they said, tempting him, that they might have to accuse him." And then after a silence while He stooped and wrote with His finger on the ground He rose and gave an immortal example of moral courage with that reply, "He that is without sin among you, let him first cast a stone at her." And they which heard it, being convicted by their own conscience, went out one by one, beginning with the eldest even unto the last."

That rebuke may be read by us as a Divine admonition which shamed those who heard it long ago in Judæa; alas, it was not an admonition which has been greatly honoured since by humanity. Is it moral presumption to ask with hope whether we are not more aware of its force to-day than in any preceding generation? We are reproached for our greater tolerance as evidence of a lower standard of morals and the criticism implies that we mistake tolerance for what is really a lazy inability to care. Nevertheless, it must be argued that the impossibility of society behaving to-day as it behaved towards Oscar Wilde is due to our wider knowledge of human difficulties than once upon a time. "Judge not that ye be not judged." Surely that evangelical precept may be seen at work upon the human mind which desires to see prison reformed, slums eradicated, wealth shared within reason, opportunity enlarged, and all the many other handicaps that ruin the lives of those less fortunate alleviated. One must be an old man to appreciate what a weight has been lifted from the social conscience of the British people by the Welfare State. One must be able to remember what London was like seventy years ago before one should venture to complain about the manners and morals of contemporary London. I am not trying to claim for Christians the responsibility for the clearing of the social conscience; I am merely pointing out that what a number of wise and compassionate non-believers are doing to-day was advocated and enjoined by the first Christian of all.

For me one of the outstanding instances of the moral courage of Jesus Christ was His treatment of the Sabbath. A very faint idea of the hostility He had to encounter may be gauged from the reaction of present-day Sabbatarians to any mild proposals for the lightening or brightening of Sunday. These Sabbatarians are not prepared to accept Jesus Christ's statement that the Sabbath was made for man not man for the Sabbath. Sabbath-worship to-day, or rather Sunday worship (the old Jewish Sabbath is being worshipped among Christians only by the Seventh Day Adventists), is most fervid in the Highlands and Islands of Scotland. Some years ago I pointed out to an old lady in Skye that an excessive devotion to the Sabbath was contrary to the words of Our Lord. "The Sabbath was made for man not man for the Sabbath, Mrs. Mac——" I reminded her. She shook her head with a sigh, and replied that no doubt he was after saying a lot of things for which he was sorry when he returned to his Heavenly Father. I bowed, realising that argument with passionate Sabbatarians is not a feasible proposition.

We may wonder how many M.P.s will have the moral courage to support the proposals to remove from the statute book some of the anachronisms of the Sunday Observance Act. Sabbatarians and Prohibitionists between them can swing many votes.

V

Some examples from the past

REFLECTIONS UPON MORAL COURAGE in Christian precepts leads to reflections upon examples of moral courage in the Old Testament. There are many instances among the prophets, but this moral courage is inspired by religious belief and like the moral courage of the martyrs and confessors is outside the field of what some may consider the narrow range of the definition.

As we turn from story to story in the Old Testament we often find a background of morality so utterly different from any Christian concept of morality that the unwillingness of the medieval Church to have the Old Testament translated into the vulgar tongue becomes more and more intelligible.

It is easier to gather from Greece and Rome examples of moral courage within our modern comprehension. Immediately there leaps to the mind the figure of Socrates, the example of whose life and teaching is as valuable for us to-day as it was nearly two and a half millenniums since. He was indicted when he was about seventy years old for impiety and corruption of youth. The impiety attributed to him was his rejection of the gods acknowledged by the State and his introducing strange deities. This was based on the claim of Socrates to be guided by a *daimonion* which we can either regard as the equivalent of what we call genius or merely as the first recognition of what we call the voice of conscience. Xenophon pointed out that Socrates disapproved of speculation about the nature of the universe or the laws that governed the phenomena of the heavens. He used to wonder whether scientists who worried themselves over the the solution of such problems believed that their knowledge of human affairs was so complete that they needed fresh fields in which to exercise their brains. He thought it unprofitable to argue and disagree about scientific theories before one had decided what was beautiful, what was ugly, what was just, what was unjust, what was courage, what was cowardice, what was a state and what was a statesman.

There are moments in the times we live in when some of us wish that less attention could be given to the problem of life on Venus or Mars and greater attention to the much more urgent problem of life on Earth.

The corruption of youth alleged against Socrates had nothing to do with homosexuality as one of the leader writers in the newspaper edited by Jack Horner recently supposed in an impassioned defence of morality against the corruption of the Wolfenden Report. The corruption of which Socrates was accused was a matter of politics. The reign of terror which the Thirty Tyrants had imposed on Athens in 404 B.C. had only just been replaced by the reconstituted democracy when Socrates was put on trial, and Critias, one of the most ruthless of the Thirty Tyrants, as a young man had been an associate of Socrates. So too had Alcibiades whom Athens still regarded as the man most responsible for her defeat and humiliation by Sparta. It was remembered against Socrates that when he was on the council it had fallen to his lot to preside in the assembly when the people had wanted to condemn to death the Arginusæ generals by a single vote. They were being impeached because, although they had won the last sea-fight that Athens was to win, they had failed to rescue the survivors clinging to disabled triremes. To condemn all the generals to death by a single vote was illegal and Socrates in spite of the popular outcry and the threats of many powerful persons refused to put the motion to the vote. "It was more to him," Xenophon said, "that he should keep his oath and obey the law than to humour the people and submit to threats." In the turmoil of conflicting politics this display of moral courage in defending the law against a democratic violation of it was held against him as a sign of his anti-democratic feelings. His courageous defiance of the Thirty Tyrants when ordered to accompany four others to arrest a proscribed victim on Salamis by going back to his own house was forgotten. It should be realised that Athens in that bloodstained year 404 B.C. was an early manifestation of fascism except that there were thirty tyrants instead of one.

Socrates was not merely pre-eminent for moral courage at a time when the Greeks had not yet found a word for it; he was also endowed with great physical courage and saved the life of Alcibiades at Delium.

Socrates was put on trial in the spring of 399 B.C. before 501 judges. He was found guilty by 280 votes to 220 so that no casting vote was required. The accuser demanded the penalty of death, and the rule was that after his conviction the accused should propose an alternative penalty. Socrates after expressing surprise at the unexpected smallness in favour of conviction went on to propose as an alternative to death that he should be fed in the Prytaneum at the expense of the State. This annoyed his judges and so yielding to the anxious entreaties of his friends Socrates proposed a fine. At first he suggested a mina of silver, and then went on to say that his friends proposed a fine of thirty minas for the payment of which they offered themselves as sureties.

However, by that time Socrates had so much annoyed his judges by what they considered his flippant attitude that they voted for death with an increased majority. The speech Socrates made after his condemnation as recorded by Plato in the *Apologia* is one of the noblest utterances of a human being our world has known. A piece of the peroration may be quoted:

> " Let us consider how much hope there is that death is a good thing, for death is one of two states: it is either nothingness where the dead are conscious of nothing or, as some say, it is a migration of the soul to another place. If it be unconsciousness like a dreamless sleep, what a wonderful boon death would be! I think that if anybody, even the great King of Persia, chose some night on which he had slept without dreaming and compared it with the other nights and days of his life he would not think that any of them had passed more pleasantly. So if such be the nature of death,

I count it a boon, for then the whole sum of time would be no longer than a single night.

" On the other hand if death be a migration from here to some other place and if what we are told be true, that all the dead are there, what greater good could there be, my judges? What would any of you give to meet with Orpheus and Hesiod and Homer? I should like to die often if what we are told is true. I should find the life there wonderful, and when I met men of old who had lost their lives through an unjust judgment I should enjoy comparing my experience with theirs. But my greatest pleasure would be to spend my time in examining the people there to find out who among them is truly wise and who thinks he is wise when he is not. What would you not give, my judges, to examine him who led the mighty army against Troy, or Odysseus himself, or innumerable others, men and women? Surely the conversation and company of such would be a boundless happiness.

" So you too, my judges, must face death with hope and always remember that no evil can come to a good man either in life or after death, and that the gods will not abandon him. What has happened to me has not happened by chance, and I see clearly that it was better for me to die now and be set free from trouble. I bear no ill will to those who accused me or to those who condemned me.

" And now the time has come for me to depart. I go to die, and you to live; but which of us goes to the better lot is plain only to the god."

Usually the condemned man was given the fatal hemlock within twenty-four hours, but no executions were allowed when the sacred galley was voyaging to Delos, and therefore Socrates had to await its return. He was a month in prison where he was visited continuously by friends. There is no doubt that he could have escaped with their help and that his judges would have been relieved by such an escape.

In that moving dialogue of Plato, the *Crito*, we are told why Socrates refused this offer to help. Crito urges his friend to escape and declares that most people will think his friends were too mean to spend the money on bribing his gaolers and will never believe that he refused to escape. To this Socrates replies by asking his friend why we should care so much what most people think. For him the only opinion worth heeding is the opinion of the most reasonable men, and they would understand why he had not chosen to escape.

Crito insists that one has to pay attention to public opinion because the public is all powerful. Socrates shakes his head and so the long argument about the necessity of what we to-day call moral courage goes on; and in the end Crito surrenders and argues no more.

It was to Crito that Socrates uttered his last words before the paralysing hemlock reached his heart.

"Crito, we owe a cock to Asclepius. Pay it and do not neglect to do so."

Crito gave his word and asked if Socrates had anything else to say. There was no reply.

"Such was the end," said Phædo, "of our friend who was of those we had known in our time the best, the wisest, the fairest of them all."

Socrates was the outstanding example of moral courage in the ancient world and when we contemplate that figure outwardly of such ugliness but inwardly of such rare beauty we must think of him only as a philosopher. He began his career as a sculptor, being apprenticed to his father Sophroniscus. When Pausanias was gathering material for his great work of topography in the second century A.D., there was still to be seen near the Propylæa on the Acropolis a group or relief of the Three Graces which tradition attributed to the hand of Socrates. He was also a frequent visitor at the house of Aspasia which meant to say that he was moving in the best Athenian society, for the milieu of Aspasia was a combination of Grosvenor Square before the First World War with Bloomsbury, or in other words rank and fashion with brains. On top of that he had a considerable experience of active service as a hoplite.

In the *Symposium* of Plato there is a vivid description of the Potidæa campaign. At that date Alcibiades would have been about twenty-three and Socrates about forty. Alcibiades says that Socrates surpassed not only himself but everybody else in his ability to stand the hardships of that exacting campaign. If they were cut off and had to go short of food, Socrates minded it least of all. If food was plentiful, Socrates tucked into it with more pleasure than anybody else and, though he did not like drinking, if he was persuaded by his mess-mates to drink he could beat all of them at it and do so without ever getting drunk himself.

> "But it was in his ability to stand the weather—and the winters in that part of the world are terrible—that he was most wonderful. I remember one particularly hard frost when those of us who had to go out used to wrap ourselves up with tremendous care and even bind felt and sheepskin round our shoes. Yet Socrates used to go out in that weather in the same coat as he always wore and could walk barefoot on the ice more easily than we could in our shoes. . . . On another occasion he became absorbed in some problem at dawn and stood in the same spot, working on it for hours. . . . In the evening several of the Ionians—it was summer-time now—brought out their pallets and rugs after supper to sleep in the cool, for they were anxious to see if Socrates would continue to stand in the same place all night. Well, he stood there till sunrise and then he walked away after offering a prayer to the sun . . . and on the day of the battle (of Delium) in which I won the prize for valour it was Socrates who saved my life, for I was wounded, and he would not leave me but helped me to save both my armour and myself. I did my best, Socrates, to persuade the generals to award the prize for valour to you, but when the generals, with an eye on my social pull, were still anxious to award the prize to me, you were much more insistent than they were that I should have it."

The brains beneath the bronze helmets of ancient Greece and the brass hats of the First World War worked with remarkable unanimity in the matter of awarding decorations.

It never entered into the head of Socrates that he should

engage in politics. He was forbidden by his *daimonion* as he called that inner voice. He never claimed for this *daimonion* any kind of spiritual power, still less of any divine power. A friend of his who asked the oracle at Delphi to say who was the wisest man came back with the oracle's unusually straightforward reply that Socrates was the wisest man. Socrates himself had said that the oracle had made a mistake and set out to find a man wiser than himself. In this pursuit he abandoned metaphysics and astronomical speculation. Pope expressed in a couplet what Socrates set his mind upon:

> Know then thyself, presume not God to scan;
> The proper study of mankind is man.

In the pursuit of that study Socrates showed inflexible moral courage, and when at last it brought him to the threshold of death he faced death with imperturbable humour, simple dignity and genuine compassion for those who had condemned him. He could feel assured that the oracle had not been mistaken and so with a mind at rest he was able with a secure equanimity to fall into a dreamless sleep or migrate to another place.

It is tempting to put forward Pericles as another example of moral courage in ancient Greece, but that would involve too long a digression in evoking the background against which that moral courage was manifested if the modern reader is to understand the choice of Pericles. Indeed, in any discussion of moral courage our estimate of a man's moral courage will always depend on the extent of our familiarity with the background against which it was displayed.

The moral courage of a Socrates can be easily appreciated because if a Socrates of to-day behaved like his predecessor, he would be an extremely unpopular personality with the general public. The ignorance of the public in spite of the Press, in spite of free libraries, in spite of raising the school age for education, in spite of television and broadcasting, still far outweighs its knowledge. A little learning is a dangerous thing but the persistency of the misquotation that a little knowledge is a dangerous thing shows how true that also is. Nevertheless, if a Socrates could interrogate men and women in those walks of life where education is a comparatively recent privilege, it might well be that he would find on the whole a more intelligent response to searching questions than he would find among those for whom education has been a privilege extending much further back. Bernard Shaw observed somewhere that Englishmen got golf instead of wisdom, and it is sadly true that they and their fellows in Scotland and Wales while working hard to exercise their muscles do let their minds grow stiff for lack of exercise. If the mind sags conviction must sag too; if the mind is deprived of fuel all fervour must cool.

The courage of one's opinions should be a first step on the way to moral courage but if those opinions are formed by headlines in the morning papers read in the train on the way to Paddington or Liverpool Street, and refreshed after a day in the office by the headlines in the evening papers, no courage will be needed to express them. And here let a note of optimism be heard. We can believe that the development of television will gradually overcome this prevailing ignorance and help the public to discard the ready-made opinions provided for them. Indeed, this trend is already noticeable and provided that freedom of the screen be demanded and maintained as strongly as freedom of the Press, in another few years from now we should be able to count on a more powerful influence of what can be called self-educated opinion. We may already speculate that if television had existed in 1914 a disastrous war might have been averted, and if television had existed in the nineteen-thirties we may speculate that we should have been willing to get to grips with Hitler much sooner than we did.

And now I begin to play with the idea of Socrates as an Ed Murrow or any other well-established television interviewer all over the world and imagine the missionary value of those searching questions. But perhaps Socrates with his thick lips, bulbous eyes, and splay nose could not be considered photogenic.

Having chosen a Greek from the distant past it is time to look for a great Roman example of moral courage, and it shall be Marcus Atilius Regulus who was the Romans' own most cherished example of what we call moral courage. Yet he is chosen after some hesitation because modern historians refuse to believe that he ever did what he was revered for doing. It is not worth setting out the arguments on both sides. We can be content to stand by Horace's ode. Marcus Atilius Regulus was a Roman general and consul in the first Punic war, and in 256 B.C. was one of the commanders in the naval battle which smashed the Carthaginian fleet at Economus and allowed the Romans to land an army. Success at first was so great that the other consul was recalled to Rome and Regulus was left in sole command. The Carthaginians were so severely defeated at Adys not far from Carthage itself that the Carthaginians sued for peace, but the terms offered by Regulus were so severe that the Carthaginians resolved to carry on the war. Then in 255 B.C. Regulus was utterly defeated and was himself taken prisoner by Xanthippus and his Spartan mercenaries. Regulus remained a prisoner for over five years until after the Carthaginians were defeated at Panormus he was sent to Rome to negotiate a peace and arrange for an exchange of prisoners. He gave his word that if negotiations for peace or the exchange of prisoners came to nothing he would return to Carthage and surrender himself. When he reached Rome he urged the Senate to refuse to consider terms of peace or the exchange of prisoners. Then he insisted on returning to Carthage himself and was tortured to death.

Horace begins his ode with what we Britons can accept as a fine tribute:

> We believe that Jove the thunderer reigns in Heaven:
> on earth Augustus shall be held a god because he has
> added to our empire the Britons.

Then he went on to sing about the troops of Crassus who settled down in wedlock with barbarian wives and grew old in the service of the enemy whose daughters in Parthia they had married; forgetting the Roman name, the toga, and immortal Vesta.

It was to guard against anything happening like that in Carthage that he preferred to let the youthful prisoners perish. On no account must the Senate accept the shameful terms offered by the enemy.

"With my own eyes," he said, "I have seen our standards hung up in Punic shrines; I have seen arms taken from our soldiers without bloodshed; I have seen the hands of citizens bound behind their backs; I have seen the gates of Carthage wide open; I have seen the fields we had ravaged being cultivated again."

And on he went to argue that prisoners redeemed by gold would never fight and that those who had tamely felt the fetters and stood in fear of death would never be of any use in a second war.

"O shame!" he cried. "O mighty Carthage raised higher upon the disgraceful ruins of Italy."

When he had thus exhorted the Senate to refuse the terms of the peace, like one who had lost his civil rights Regulus put away the kisses of his wife and his little children and turned his eyes sternly down towards the ground until the Senate ceased to waver and accepted his advice. When this was agreed he made a swift and glorious departure. Although he knew what tortures awaited him, he pushed aside the kinsmen who tried to block his path and the people who tried to stop his going, pushed them aside "with no more concern than a lawyer whose case had been decided and was seeking recreation at Tarentum from the tedious affairs of his clients."

That Regulus was horribly tortured when he surrendered to his parole in Carthage was the belief in Rome two centuries later, but modern historians may be right in attributing this tradition to apologetic propaganda to excuse the torture which the Romans themselves undoubtedly did inflict on some of their Carthaginian prisoners. The important point is the admiration felt for Regulus in choosing to suffer whatever might happen to him rather than break a Roman's word of honour.

According to Cicero the phrase *civis Romanus sum* was a passport for the protection of a man's life and dignity in any part of the ancient world, and in that sense it was a statement of the power of Rome to punish anybody who maltreated one of her citizens, but *civis Romanus sum* carried with it an immense pride which must not be mortified by any behaviour beneath the dignity of such a claim. Even to-day a Roman will say *Io sono Romano di Roma.* (I am a Roman of Rome.) You never hear a Florentine or a Milanese or a Neapolitan tell you where they come from with such an air of self-congratulation.

By the nineteenth century the Englishman was announcing his nationality with that same air. A Scotsman when in Europe would often stress his nationality, in the hope that Continentals would be able to grasp that they might hope for a human being who would understand their point of view better than an Englishman. The Englishman was not interested in understanding the point of view of Continentals or in their understanding his. He was an Englishman, and as such he expected to be recognised as a privileged person, who felt politely sorry for anybody that was not an Englishman. That his grandchildren would be continually mistaken on the Continent for Americans would have been unimaginable to him.

It may be an idle speculation founded on quite insufficient grounds but I have always indulged in the fancy that Britain inherited much more from the Roman occupation than is realised. The French are a more civilised nation than the Germans probably because Gaul had been conquered by Rome, an advantage which the Germans lacked. May we not claim that the English are more civilised than the Germans for the same reason? After all, the occupation of a country for over four centuries must have left behind it a strong strain of Roman blood. Bloody and ruthless as the Anglo-Saxon invaders were they could not have extirpated the whole of the British population. Indeed, it is obvious by the survival of the Roman manor with its hamlet attached in the area roughly west of London in contrast to the big Anglo-Saxon village in the east that there must have been more mixing of Anglo-Saxon with British blood in the west, and that mixing must have included much Roman blood. The Cornish and the Welsh must have preserved even more Roman blood. To carry this speculation a step further, one could make a specious case out for the opposition to the usurping Lancastrians, to Henry VIII, to the Parliament, and to the Hanoverian dynasty being an atavistic memory of the reverence for the

Roman Emperor. It may be argued that Ireland and the Highlands of Scotland showed an equally instinctive devotion to the divine right of kings, and that there was no Roman blood in either. That is certainly true of Ireland. Yet in Perthshire there is a tradition that Pontius Pilate was born in Fortingall.

It may be all idle speculation, but I cling to my belief that the Englishman of the nineteenth century with his mixture of Roman, Celtic, Danish, Saxon and Norman blood was the heir of Imperial Rome, with a reverence for the law and a respect for his pledged word. Incidentally, until Mussolini abolished the habit all traffic in Rome kept to the left. What was the origin of our keeping traffic to the left in Britain? It is perhaps something more than a coincidence that until Hitler's shadow darkened the scene traffic in Vienna kept to the left; and Vienna was another Imperial city.

There must have been innumerable examples of moral courage in ancient Rome, but none occurs immediately to the mind which is not inextricably mixed up with politics and they are more truly examples of what the Germans call civic courage.

Indeed, as one goes back in history the difficulty of estimating the weight of moral courage involved in any action compared with the physical courage by which it was so often demonstrated grows more and more apparent. There is always the danger, too, of assaying moral courage by contemporary standards. In which Kings of England or Scotland or of the United Kingdom can we recognise outstanding moral courage as we think of it to-day? A satisfactory answer is difficult to find. Some might say that Henry II's act of penance for the murder of Thomas à Becket showed moral courage. That may be true, but the circumstances that called for it are so remote from any similar circumstances we can imagine to-day. The moral courage of Henry VI was nearer to saintliness. Mary Queen of Scots and Elizabeth were both capable of moral courage, but that of Mary never failed her whereas that of Elizabeth failed her completely when she assented to the execution of the Queen of Scots. When the state of the country is considered, Elizabeth's defenders can plausibly enough plead political compulsion for her action. That could equally be pleaded for Charles I's failure to save Strafford or Laud. Yet nobody could find any lack of moral courage in the way he confronted the regicides. Oliver Cromwell was often a moral coward but that cowardice was hidden by his abundant physical bravery. James II was a man of tremendous moral courage, but that moral courage was obscured by what seemed an unreasonable obstinacy. He transmitted some of that moral courage to his son but none at all to his daughters. Physical courage was a characteristic of the Hanoverians with the exception of George IV; but the first outstanding act of moral courage by a sovereign had to wait until King Edward VIII, and his was an expression of moral courage which should have been but was not appreciated by all his subjects.

VI

Abdication from a Throne

ON 12TH DECEMBER, 1937, less than two years before Britain would slide down the slope of safety first into the chasm of the Second World War *The Times* wrote of the Abdication of King Edward VIII on the previous day:

"The nation has treated a great issue worthily, as though moving soberly and steadily, with reluctance but without sentimentality, with searching of heart but without tumult towards a firm conviction of the duty that might be laid upon it. This dignified judgment of a free people was given articulate expression yesterday in the practically unanimous passage of the Abdication Act through both Houses of Parliament in less than three hours... For some time the international esteem for Great Britain has been rising, as foreign policy, and the domestic basis of foreign policy, had been reconstructed on more resolute, confident lines . . . the British people, facing its ordeal under an unprecedented glare of foreign publicity has earned the wonder and admiration of the world . . . not for the first time a sudden emergency has enabled the British nation to prove its native greatness."

That Britannia in patting herself on the back had dropped her trident and let her shield clatter down was not apparent to Geoffrey Dawson, who after lending his editorial support to Stanley Baldwin's fear of rearmament in case he lost a by-election would presently lend the full weight of that support to Neville Chamberlain's policy of appeasement. Yet even he, mouthpiece though he was of men who did all that was possible to prevent the British nation from proving its native greatness, might have spared a word of gratitude to the man who by his own demeanour made it so much easier than it might have been to do so.

Mr. Winston Churchill who a day or two before had been howled down by a hysterical House of Commons when he tried to plead for the King to be given time spoke these words in the course of his speech about the Declaration of Abdication Bill:

> " He (the King) has voluntarily made a sacrifice for the peace and strength of his realm, which go far beyond the bounds required by the Law and Constitution."

At ten o'clock on the night of Friday, 11th December, 1937, H.R.H. Prince Edward broadcast from Windsor Castle a farewell to his people. That farewell was listened to all over the world. No man ever spoke to such a vast audience. In darkness and in daylight, by sea and by land the world listened.

> " At long last I am able to say a few words of my own.
>
> " I have never wanted to withhold anything, but until now it has not been constitutionally possible for me to speak.
>
> " A few hours ago I discharged my last duty as King and Emperor, and now that I have been succeeded by my brother the Duke of York, my first words must be to declare my allegiance to him. This I do with all my heart.
>
> " You all know the reasons which have impelled me to renounce the Throne, but I want you to understand that in making up my mind I did not forget the country or the Empire, which as Prince of Wales, and later as King, I have for twenty-five years tried to serve.
>
> " But you must believe me when I tell you that I have found it impossible to carry the heavy burden of responsibility, and to discharge my duties as King as I would wish to do, without the help and support of the woman I love.
>
> " And I want you to know that the decision I have made has been mine, and mine alone. This was a thing I had to judge entirely for myself. The other person most nearly concerned has tried up to the last to persuade me to take a different course.

"I have made this, the most serious decision of my life, only upon the single thought of what would in the end be best for all.

"This decision has been made less difficult for me by the sure knowledge that my brother with his long training in the public affairs of the country and with his fine qualities, will be able to take my place forthwith, without interruption or injury to the life and progress of the Empire.

"And he has one matchless blessing, enjoyed by so many of you, and not bestowed on me, a happy home with his wife and children.

"During those hard days I have been comforted by Her Majesty, my mother, and my family; the Ministers of the Crown, and in particular Mr. Baldwin, the Prime Minister, have always treated me with full consideration.

"There has never been any constitutional difference between me and them, and between me and Parliament. Bred in the constitutional traditions of my father, I should never have allowed any such issue to arise.

"Ever since I was Prince of Wales, and later on when I occupied the Throne, I have been treated with the greatest kindness by all classes of people wherever I have lived and journeyed throughout the Empire. For that I am very grateful.

"I now quit altogether public affairs, and I lay down my burden. It may be some time before I return to my native land, but I shall always follow the fortunes of the British race and Empire with profound interest, and if at any time in the future I can be found of service to His Majesty in a private station, I shall not fail.

"And now we all have a new King. I wish him and you, his people, happiness and prosperity with all my heart. God bless you all. God save the King!"

In an endeavour to utter that last "God save the King" with all the fervour of his own loyalty, the light, once buoyant voice broke.

Next morning was published a moving message from Queen

Mary to the Nation and Empire in the course of which she said:

"I know that you will realise what it has cost him to come to this decision; and that, remembering the years in which he tried so eagerly to serve and help his country and Empire, you will keep a grateful remembrance of him in your hearts."

Prince Edward of York was born in 1894, and was therefore brought up as a child in the Victorian style, in his case thanks to having an extremely conservative father in the strictest Victorian style. This is important to bear in mind if we are to estimate fairly the moral courage he was one day to display. A childhood passed even in the last decade of the nineteenth century meant a bringing up and education entirely unprepared for the twentieth century, and this was particularly true of the upper classes. Indeed, they were most of them unaware that the twentieth century had arrived until six years after its arrival when the Liberals swept the polls at a General Election, and when even more incredibly fifty-three Labour members sat on the benches of the House of Commons.

Prince Edward's education continued at the Royal Naval Colleges of Osborne and Dartmouth, and that meant it was as yet untouched by the twentieth century. However admirable such an education might be for a future admiral it was by now not really the best education for a future monarch. Later, although his residence at Oxford was not as much hampered by ceremonious restrictions as that of his grandfather had been as Prince of Wales, nevertheless as Prince of Wales himself now he was not perfectly free. From Oxford the Prince went on to serve through the First World War, still conscious of the restrictive etiquette demanded by his royal position and feeling ever more and more anxious to go through the war exactly like all his brother officers in the Grenadier Guards. Then came his tours in Canada, India, Australia, the United States and South America. All agreed that never before had a Prince of Wales done so much to enhance the prestige of the monarchy. And he had done that by demonstrating that it was not an anachronism in the twentieth century. His accession to the Throne in January 1936, just ninety-nine and a half years after Queen Victoria ascended the Throne, was welcomed by the three men whose influence would prevail in bringing his reign to an end eleven months later.

Mr. Stanley Baldwin, the Prime Minister, told the House of Commons what universal goodwill had been the fruit of King Edward's travels as Prince of Wales, and spoke of his broad experience in public affairs and his unique knowledge of the varied conditions under which his subjects lived both in the British Isles and throughout the Empire. In a moment of eloquent enthusiasm Mr. Baldwin declared that the new King had the secret of youth in the prime of age.

Shortly before King George V died the Archbishop of Canterbury at a public dinner had spoken of the new King's manifold public services as Prince of Wales "for all that belongs to our common life, for the sick and not least for the unemployed and for that embassy of Empire, which the Prince fulfils in every part of the world and, I begin to think, in almost every language. . . . It is no exaggeration to say that future historians will look to the Prince's speeches to learn the best that can be said of the industrial, social, and commercial life of his day and generation."

Finally *The Times*, voicing presumably the opinion of its editor, a former member of the same college at Oxford as King Edward, described a number of kingly attributes which included physical courage, "an unerring eye for the distinction between dignity and solemnity, and an interest in all sorts and conditions of people" which "more democrats profess than feel." And then the readers of *The Times* were told to remember that the new King was a bachelor so that "in the life of responsibility, day in day out, which will henceforth be his, he will lack the help and counsel of a consort."

So much for the testimonials. King Edward himself spoke directly to his people for the first time in a broadcast he gave on 1st March, St. David's Day. In his closing words he made crystal clear the spirit of the reign he then hoped could be a happy reign.

> "I am better known to you as the Prince of Wales, as a man who, during the war and since, has had the opportunity of getting to know the people of nearly every country of the

world under all conditions and circumstances. And although I now speak to you as the King, I am still that same man who has that experience and whose constant effort it will be to continue to promote the well-being of his fellow men."

He was to demonstrate conclusively that he was " still that same man " when he proposed to marry the woman with whom he had fallen in love when he was Prince of Wales after she had been granted a divorce from her husband in the autumn of that year 1936.

That divorce had been preceded by a cruise in the Mediterranean that summer when Mrs. Simpson had been one of the guests on board. The gossip in the American and Continental Press which this cruise aroused was not reported in the British Press, but Mr. Baldwin felt that he must make some inquiries, and so before the divorce was heard in Ipswich he paid an informal visit to Fort Belevedere at ten o'clock in the morning. Towards the end of their talk the Prime Minister asked the King if the divorce must really go on. In his own words from *A King's Story* the King replied:

" Mr. Baldwin, I have no right to interfere with the affairs of an individual. It would be wrong were I to attempt to influence Mrs. Simpson just because she happens to be a friend of the King's."

On 13th November King Edward came back from a visit to the Fleet at Portland to find a letter from Major Hardinge, his private secretary, marked *Urgent and Confidential*.

In this letter Hardinge told his master that the silence of the British Press could not be kept much longer, and that the Government's resignation was likely, in which case he had " reason to know " it would be impossible for the King to form a new one.

The Duke of Windsor says that the effect of this letter on him was to make him " resolved to come to grips at once with Mr. Baldwin and the nebulous figures around him." He felt that his private secretary was in sympathy with the point of view of the other side. So he decided to call in Mr. Walter Monkton,[1]

[1] Lord Monkton.

to be his liaison with the Prime Minister in the place of his private secretary who would normally have acted as such. It was the best choice he could have made.

The second meeting between Mr. Baldwin and King Edward took place on 16th November. The decree nisi in favour of Mrs. Simpson by now had been pronounced.

To quote the Duke of Windsor again:

> "I told Mr. Baldwin that marriage had become an indispensable condition to my continued existence. Whether as King or as man, I intended to marry Mrs. Simpson as soon as she was free to marry. If I could marry her as King, well and good, I would be happy and in consequence perhaps a better King. But if, on the other hand, the Government opposed the marriage, as the Prime Minister had given me reason to believe it would, *then I was prepared to go.*"

The next ordeal for the King was to tell Queen Mary what he had told the Prime Minister. He dined with her that same night. The Princess Royal was also at Marlborough House. After dinner he told them of his love for Mrs. Simpson and of his determination to marry her, and of the opposition of the Prime Minister and the Government to the marriage. He became "conscious of their growing consternation that I could even contemplate giving up the Throne of my forebears. My mother had been schooled to put duty, in the strict Victorian sense, before everything else in life. From her invincible virtue and correctness she looked out as from a fortress upon the rest of humanity, with all its tremulous uncertainties and distractions."

Now comes a vital point in the argument whether King Edward VIII's abdication was an act of tremendous moral courage or whether it was a piece of royal wilfulness. He realised that to Queen Mary monarchy was something sacred and that the Sovereign was a personage apart. But he and she had a different idea about duty. Her duty was to kingship; his duty was to his own idea of kingship. He was ready to serve his people and perform the innumerable duties expected of the King as Head of the State; he was not prepared to include among those duties what he believed to be the duty to himself of marrying where his heart was. The King now asked Queen Mary to let him bring Mrs. Simpson to meet her. This to his distress she refused and in that moment he understood more clearly than ever what a strain upon his moral courage it would be to carry through the course of action to which he had dedicated himself.

Having told his mother and his sister what he was proposing to do, he now told his three brothers. The one most involved was the Duke of York because in the event of abdication it would be he who would have to take his elder brother's place as King. The Duke of York dreaded the idea of taking upon himself the burden of kingship, but with the generosity that was so characteristic of him he wrote to tell King Edward how anxious he was for him to be happy and that he of all people could understand what a happy marriage meant. He added that whatever his brother decided to do he was sure that it would be in the best interests of the country and the Empire. From that moment the King saw little of the Royal family until the end. He did not think it would be fair to involve them in the clash between himself and the Government that now seemed inevitable. He set out on his visit to the Welsh coalfields where the miners had not yet recovered from the merciless treatment they had received in the great coal strike of ten years ago.

Lying awake in his sleeping-berth on the way to Wales, he thought about the struggle before him in Whitehall. But in his own words he was at peace with himself. His spiritual struggle was over. He had passed the climax. He had declared himself.

When the King returned to London he saw Sir Samuel Hoare, the First Lord of the Admiralty. Hoare was as smooth as he always was, but he made it clear that the Prime Minister had the Cabinet behind him. Duff Cooper was more optimistic. He pointed out that the King could not marry Mrs. Simpson until the decree nisi was made absolute over five months hence and that therefore the Government could not force him into a decision about a constitutional issue which had not yet arisen. He urged the King to go forward with the Coronation and then later on, to raise the question of marriage when the excitement had died down. King Edward felt that he could not go through with a religious ceremony with sincerity if he was intending to do something of which the Church of which he was the Governor disapproved. He felt that his honour demanded that the question of his marriage should be settled before the Coronation.

The next suggestion came from Mr. Esmond Harmsworth[1] who asked Mrs. Simpson if she would be willing to marry the King morganatically. Mrs. Simpson asked what that meant and it was explained to her that a morganatic marriage was one between a Royal personage and a woman of lower birth. She would be legally married but she would not have her husband's rank and the children of such a marriage could not inherit their father's rank. After a good deal of hesitation King Edward decided that such a solution of the problem was feasible. The suggestion was communicated to Mr. Baldwin by Mr. Esmond Harmsworth who reported that the Prime Minister's reaction had been " surprised, interested and non-committal." However, he had promised to consult the Cabinet.

A day or two later the King sent for Mr. Baldwin to find out his opinion. Mr. Baldwin replied that he had not yet considered it, but as a " horseback opinion " he did not think that Parliament would ever pass the necessary legislation; he asked if the King would like him to examine the proposition formally. Upon the King's assent to this Mr. Baldwin told him that this would mean consulting the Dominion Cabinets as well as the British Cabinet. Did the King want him to do that? The King said " Yes " and his Prime Minister hurried away. He had hardly left the room when the King realised that by asking Mr. Baldwin to consult the British and Dominion Governments he had placed himself in the position of having to accept their advice, and the advice of a Government to its constitutional monarch is tantamount to an order.

The Prime Minister presented the morganatic marriage to the Dominions in a way that ensured their refusal of it. At a meeting on 27th November he told the Cabinet that there were only two choices open to the King. Either the Government

[1] Lord Rothermere.

must accept the King's wife as Queen or if they refused and the King insisted on marrying Mrs. Simpson in spite of the Government's disapproval, there would be no way out of the impasse except abdication.

So far these events behind the scenes had escaped the glare of the Press footlights at home. Then on 1st December the Bishop of Bradford addressing a Diocesan Conference on the Coronation wished that the King "gave more positive signs of his awareness of the need of God's grace." This was taken to be an allusion to his proposed marriage and the Press no longer felt called upon to refrain from letting the public know what was going on. Dr. Blunt denied at the time that his remarks had referred to the marriage and had merely been intended to suggest that the King was lacking in churchmanship. A few months later in Quebec he contradicted himself and declared that he "took the risk because of the danger that silence about the Mrs. Simpson affair was doing to the Crown and Empire." On which side of the Atlantic Dr. Blunt was telling a lie we shall now never know.

The provincial Press started on the day after the Bishop's speech and the London Press followed on twenty-four hours later.

Lord Beaverbrook counselled the King to let him muster the forces of the friendly newspapers to put forward a strong case for the right to marry a woman who has divorced her husband. The King was anxious to do nothing that would split national opinion and jeopardise the position of the Monarchy on what would seem merely as thus presented an issue of his own personal happiness. He was also most anxious to protect Mrs. Simpson against sensational publicity. He may have had an instinctive mistrust of handing over the conduct of his case to Lord Beaverbrook lest it should appear as an opportunity taken by Lord Beaverbrook to get level with Mr. Baldwin who had not so long ago silenced him by a stinging public rebuke.

Soon after what seemed to Lord Beaverbrook too ready a surrender to the forces against the King, the Prime Minister waited on the King to say that the replies of the Dominion Premiers so far received indicated that they were opposed to legislation for a morganatic marriage. He was sure that Parliament would take the same line. The King protested that Parliament had not been consulted. The Prime Minister replied that inquiries he had made had convinced the Cabinet and himself that people would not approve of His Majesty's marriage to Mrs. Simpson. There were three choices before the King. He could abandon the marriage. He could marry against the advice of his Ministers. He could abdicate. The Prime Minister hoped that the King would choose the first. The second was impossible because if he married against the advice of his Ministers he could not hope to remain on the Throne.

Mr. Baldwin might have been impeached for high treason but that lily-livered Parliament elected in 1935 would have acquitted him without doubt, and whoever rose to impeach him would have been howled down as Mr. Winston Churchill was howled down a day or two later.

The King now had the idea of making a direct appeal to his people in a broadcast, and it was considered a wise step for Mrs. Simpson to go abroad. *The Times* led many other papers in hostile comment, though the Rothermere and Beaverbrook Press with the *News Chronicle* came out in support of the morganatic marriage. In that proposed broadcast there were to be two paragraphs which the Duke of Windsor has since published.

> "Neither Mrs. Simpson nor I have any right to insist that she should be Queen. All we desired was that our married happiness should carry with it a proper title and dignity for her befitting my wife.
>
> "Now that I have at last been able to take you into my confidence, I feel it is best to go away for a while so that you may reflect calmly and quietly, but without undue delay, on what I have said. Nothing is nearer to my heart than that I should return; but whatever may befall, I shall always have a deep affection for my country, for the Empire and for you all."

That broadcast was never delivered. Mr. Baldwin told the King that his Ministers could not advise him to make any public statement. He then asked for the King's decision about his marriage without delay, because the prevailing uncertainty was liable to create a dangerous constitutional situation.

Now came another problem for the King to solve. Was he or was he not to encourage the formation of a King's Party? After a "night of soul-searching" while he paced his bedroom floor he decided that it would be wrong to split public opinion because it would damage the British Crown which is "the living symbol of Imperial unity and voluntary allegiance." Abdication was the only course consonant with his duty.

Having notified Mr. Baldwin of his intention to abdicate, the King asked if a Bill could be submitted to Parliament to make Mrs. Simpson's decree nisi absolute at once, so that their marriage could take place without delay and they could be spared a separation of nearly six months which would otherwise be inevitable. Mr. Baldwin thought this was a reasonable request, but that reasonable request was refused.

Mr. Winston Churchill had continued to plead for time.

> "I plead for time and patience. The nation must realise the character of the constitutional issue. There is no question of any conflict between King and Parliament. Parliament has not been consulted in any way, nor allowed to express any opinion.
>
> "The question is whether the King is to be allowed to abdicate upon the advice of the Ministry of the day. No such advice has ever before been tendered to a Sovereign in Parliamentary times. . . .
>
> "If the King refuses to take the advice of his Ministers they are, of course, free to resign. They have no right whatever to put pressure upon him to accept their advice by soliciting beforehand assurances from the Leader of the Opposition that he will not form an alternative Administration in the event of their resignation, and thus confronting the King with an alternative. Again there is cause for time and patience. . . .
>
> "The King has no means of personal access to his Parliament or his people. Between him and them in their office

are the Ministers of the Crown. If they thought it their duty to engage all their power and influence against him, still he must remain silent. All the more must they be careful not to be the judge in their own case, and to show a loyal and Christian patience even at some political embarrassment to themselves."

Mr. Winston Churchill made a last effort to ask for time, but by now Parliament was worried about the effect of any further delay on the Christmas shopping, on the preparations for the Coronation, and on the Stock Exchange. When he faced the House he received a roar of "Sit down!" The mother of Parliaments was in hysterics.

With relief the House heard from the Prime Minister on 9th December that on the following day he would have a definite statement to present and, elated by the prospect of business being as usual almost at once, a thronged House met next day to hear the Speaker read a document signed by the King's own hand which put into words a supreme act of moral courage.

"After long and anxious consideration, I have determined to renounce the Throne to which I succeeded on the death of My father, and I am now communicating this, My final and irrevocable decision. Realising as I do the gravity of this step, I can only hope that I shall have the understanding of My people in the decision I have taken and the reasons which have led Me to take it. I will not enter now into My private feelings, but I would beg that it should be remembered that the burden which constantly rests upon the shoulders of a Sovereign is so heavy that it can only be borne in circumstances different from those in which I now find Myself. I conceive that I am not overlooking the duty that rests on Me to place in the forefront the public interest, when I declare that I am conscious that I can no longer discharge this heavy task with efficiency or with satisfaction to Myself.

"I have accordingly this morning executed an Instrument of Abdication in the terms following:—

"'I, Edward VIII, of Great Britain, Ireland and the

British Dominions beyond the Seas, King, Emperor of India, do hereby declare My irrevocable determination to renounce the Throne for Myself and for My descendants, and My desire that effect should be given to this Instrument of Abdication immediately.

"'In token whereof I have hereunto set My hand this tenth day of December, nineteen hundred and thirty-six, in the presence of the witnesses whose signatures are subscribed.

(Signed) EDWARD, R.I.'

"My execution of this Instrument has been witnessed by My three brothers, Their Royal Highnesses the Duke of York, the Duke of Gloucester and the Duke of Kent.

"I deeply appreciate the spirit which has actuated the appeals which have been made to Me to take a different decision, and I have, before reaching My final determination, most fully pondered over them. But My mind is made up. Moreover, further delay cannot but be most injurious to the people whom I have tried to serve as Prince of Wales and as King and whose future happiness and prosperity are the constant wish of My heart.

"I take My leave of them in the confident hope that the course which I have thought it right to follow is that which is best for the stability of the Throne and Empire and the happiness of My peoples. I am deeply sensible of the consideration which they have always extended to Me both before and after My accession to the Throne and which I know they will extend in full measure to My successor.

"I am most anxious that there should be no delay of any kind in giving effect to the Instrument which I have executed and that all necessary steps should be taken immediately to secure that My lawful successor, My brother, His Royal Highness the Duke of York, should ascend the Throne.

EDWARD, R.I."

Does any other historic document show an act of comparable moral courage in a monarch? King Edward renounced the Throne because in his own words spoken to an audience of many millions he would find it impossible to discharge his duties as King without the help and support of the woman he loved. He had been willing to forgo any demand that his wife should be Queen and was willing to make his marriage morganatic. He was told that morganatic marriages were not recognised in Great Britain and he was forced to choose between marriage and abdication. Yet by denying the Duchess of Windsor equal rank with himself he was given a morganatic marriage. He was careful not to let the country have the least idea that he had any pressure brought to bear upon him in making the choice he did. That is true in a literal sense. Nevertheless, it could be argued that the main object of Stanley Baldwin was to manage the whole affair in such a way as to present himself as a kind of good uncle who had rescued a babe in the wood. He was insistent on the fact that he had never consulted any of his colleagues. He was determined to present himself as a Casabianca standing alone upon the deck of the burning Ship of State. In the admiration with which Mr. Baldwin managed to surround himself he failed to say what he should have said. That was left to Mr. Winston Churchill who told the House which a day or two before had howled him down:

> "No Sovereign has ever conformed more strictly or more faithfully to the letter and spirit of the Constitution than his present Majesty. In fact, he has voluntarily made a sacrifice for the peace and strength of his Realm, which go far beyond the bounds required by the Law and Constitution."

If instead of abdication execution had been the alternative the chief regicides named by history would have been Stanley Baldwin, Geoffrey Dawson and Cosmo Gordon Lang. The country turned against the first when Hitler's war started, unreasonably because in him the dominant mood of the country had been incarnate and public opinion should have kicked itself even harder than it kicked Lord Baldwin of Bewdley, K.G. Public opinion did not turn against Geoffrey Dawson, the editor of *The Times*, as one of the chief architects of appeasement because the vast majority of the people of Great Britain had no idea who the editor of *The Times* was. It was Neville Chamberlain who had been acclaimed much more enthusiastically than ever Stanley Baldwin was against whom public opinion turned. We are left with the behaviour of the third regicide to consider. Whatever might be argued was the duty of the Archbishop of Canterbury to protect the standards of the Church of which he was the spiritual head by opposing the marriage of King Edward VIII to a woman who had divorced two husbands, no Christian could find any argument to justify that broadcast on Sunday morning, 13th December, by the Primate of All England.

Dr. Lang opened with some unctuous flattery of the British people for the way they had passed through "a week of such bewilderment, suspense, and anxiety," and then he turned upon the man who by making up his mind so quickly had relieved the suspense of the Stock Exchange and the anxiety of the Christmas shops.

> "What pathos, nay what tragedy, surrounds the central figure of the swiftly moving scenes. On the 11th day of December 248 years ago, King James II fled from Whitehall. By a strange coincidence on the 11th day of December last week King Edward VIII, after speaking his last words to his people, left Windsor Castle, the centre of all the splendid traditions of his ancestors and throne, and went out in exile. In the darkness he left these shores.
>
> "Seldom if ever has any Sovereign been welcomed by a more enthusiastic loyalty. From God he received a high and sacred trust. Yet by his own will he has abdicated—he has surrendered the trust.
>
> "With characteristic frankness he has told us his motive, it was a craving for private happiness. Strange and sad it must be that for such a motive, however strongly it pressed upon his heart, he should have disappointed hopes so high, and abandoned a trust so great. Even more strange and sad it is that he should have sought his happiness in a manner inconsistent with the Christian principles of marriage, and within a social circle whose standards and ways of life are

alien to all the best instincts and traditions of his people. Yet those who belong to this circle know that to-day they stand rebuked by the judgment of the nation which had loved King Edward. I have shrunk from saying these words. But I have been compelled for the sake of sincerity and truth to say them.

" Yet for one who has known him since childhood, who has felt his charm and admired his gifts, these words cannot be the last. How can we forget the high hopes and promise of his youth, his most genuine care for the poor, the suffering, the unemployed; his years of eager service both at home and across the seas? It is the remembrance of these things that wrings from my heart, the cry—' the pity of it, O, the pity of it.' To the infinite mercy and protecting care of God we commit him now wherever he may be."

The Archbishop then went on to speak of the great qualities of the new King. Here he was impeccable in his phrasing and sentiments. But what an opportunity he lost in not allowing King Edward moral courage so that he could pay an eloquent tribute to the immense moral courage of King George VI in the way he assumed the burden of kingship. It was a different kind of moral courage that was exacted from him because it did not involve the courage of shocking conventional opinion by the step he felt it was his duty to take. Nevertheless, it was for him a great sacrifice of the comparative freedom of his way of life as Duke of York, and no monarch in the long line of English, Scottish and British monarchs fulfilled his task more worthily.

After that slur on the character of a man who could not reply the Archbishop went on to announce:

" My desire is then, if God will help me, to make to the nation a somewhat solemn recall to religion. Who can doubt that in all the events of these memorable days God has been speaking? . . .

" We still call ourselves a Christian nation. But, if the title is to be a reality and not a mere phrase, there must be a renewal in our midst of definite and deliberate allegiance to Christ—to His standards of life, to the principles of His Kingdom."

When the cry was wrung from the heart of the Archbishop of Canterbury—"O, the pity of it," the hearts of good Christians who heard that broadcast were wrung by the same cry because they knew that in his broadcast the Archbishop had dealt a cruel blow to the religion to which he was pleading for a recall.

Some Anglican bishops in their sermons that Sunday morning were as unchristian as their Primate; others were charitable. Discussing that broadcast with me an intimate friend now dead who was an Anglican bishop said to me, "You know there are moments when I wonder if Lang is the Devil." No doubt it was no more than a wry quip and it was said to an old and intimate friend, but that it could be said at all reflected the mortification that some bishops and many priests in the Anglican Church were feeling after that broadcast.

King Edward set a great example when he refused to go through with the religious ceremony of the Coronation because he did not feel justified in concealing his intention to marry the woman he loved if that intention was wrong according to the doctrine of the Church of which he was the temporal Head. To cheapen that gesture by making it appear as if his abdication was the act of a self-willed man ready to shirk his duty in order to indulge himself was ignominious. The comparison of the Duke of Windsor's leaving England with the flight of King James II from Whitehall was infelicitous. King James fled from Whitehall because he wanted to avoid civil war; if he had stayed Lord Craven and his guards would have shot down the Dutch invaders marching along Whitehall. It may have seemed to Archbishop Lang a happy reminder of an earlier triumph of Anglicanism; he forgot that his predecessor Archbishop Sancroft, who had fought more boldly than himself with a King upon the Throne, had preferred to surrender Lambeth itself rather than trim his conscience to deny his King. We may wonder if Archbishop Lang would have had the moral courage to do as much. He went on to speak of the dates as a strange coincidence. He would not have dared to amplify that coincidence, for he would have had to remind his audience that King James II's abandonment of his kingdom had involved the treachery of men of State, the desertion of a King by his own daughters, and the loss to the Church of England of all its holiest bishops and priests. The comparison and the coincidence should have been rejected; they were unworthy of a prelate's charity, scholarship and manners.

The final comment on the Archbishop of Canterbury's recall to religion may be left to Canon Sheppard who had been Dean of Canterbury for the first two or three years of Dr. Lang's primacy. Canon Sheppard invited people to reflect whether "recall to religion" suggested to them "a nation imbued with a passion for righteousness, or merely a nation resolved on respectability."

VII

Memories of D. H. Lawrence

THERE IS A WIDELY SPREAD BELIEF to-day on both sides of the Atlantic that D. H. Lawrence has been an emancipating force in British life and British letters by the exercise of a moral courage which sustained him to fight a lifelong battle for freedom of thought, freedom of expression and freedom of behaviour, the fruits of which were won thirty years after his death by the verdict of a British jury that *Lady Chatterley's Lover* was not an obscene libel.

Before the evidence given by the many witnesses in the case is discussed, it may be worth while taking a look at D. H. Lawrence as he appeared to an exact contemporary whose first novel was published in the same month of the same year as Lawrence's first novel was published.

I first met Lawrence at the end of that fatal August of 1914. I was staying with Martin Secker, my publisher at the time, working feverishly to finish the second volume of *Sinister Street*, but I took a day off to visit Gilbert Cannan who with his wife was living in a converted windmill near Tring. Cannan suggested a visit to D. H. Lawrence who was living not far away at Chesham, and we drove to a modern red brick cottage in Bellingden Lane, which remains vividly in my memory as the ugliest cottage I have ever seen. It stood in a tiny garden crowded with tall nettles the tops of which growing above the window-sill shed a green gloom over the sparsely furnished little sitting-room out of which a curved staircase went up to a couple of rooms above. When Cannan and I arrived Lawrence was on his knees, scrubbing the floor with a pail beside him. With his red moustache and hair and the attractive pink and white complexion of a redhead he looked much younger than his twenty-nine years.

"We've only just got in and the place was filthy," he said. Then rising and wiping his hands he went to the bottom of the staircase and shouted, "Frieda!" There was no answer for a moment or two and then he shouted again twice as loudly, "Frieda!" A pair of legs in ringed black and white stockings came into view at the top of the curved staircase before the body they supported appeared. "Shut that door!" he called. The legs kept on their way. "Frieda, shut that bloody door!" he shouted. She turned back to shut the door and then came down into the sitting-room. There was a slightly proprietary air about Lawrence, who two or three months earlier had been able to marry Frieda, her husband having divorced her after some delay. He had been elated, as he wrote in a letter about this time, by marrying "the daughter of Baron von Richthofen, of the ancient and famous house of Richthofen." Now war had come with Germany, and Lawrence's rage with the war was fed by his having a German wife.

Frieda herself shed a warmth and geniality of welcome as on Lawrence's orders she went out to the little kitchen to prepare tea.

In the course of conversation I told Lawrence that if I could not get into the war I should go back to Capri next month when I had finished the book I was working on.

"I can't face the depressing view of these flat English fields surrounded by their melancholy elms," I told him. He agreed that it was the saddest prospect in the world, and I went on to say that I had a cottage in Capri which I should be glad to lend him if he thought of going back to Italy.

"I'll remember that," he said. "Yes, I'll remember that." And he did remember. In December 1919 came a letter from Lawrence to Capri. He and Frieda had left England and were now in Picinisco, a beautiful mountain village in Southern Italy. He wrote that he had been driven away from England by the melancholy elms, my remark about which five years ago had haunted him ever since. I had said then that I had a spare furnished cottage—was it vacant?—and if it was might he and his wife take advantage of my offer to lend it to them? I had to write back and say that the cottage was not vacant because I had lent it to Francis and Jessica Brett Young. I hoped that the Lawrences would come to Capri nevertheless, for I was sure we could find them cheap and reasonably comfortable accommodation.

So just after Christmas the Lawrences arrived and were pleased with the two rooms and kitchen we had found for them at the top of an old palazzo with a view of the Bay of Naples on one side and of the outspread Mediterranean on the other. All this for just over £3 a month. The charcoal stove gave Lawrence much pleasure because he had mastered the art of cooking on charcoal and enjoyed a demonstration of his skill. A young Roumanian who used to be proud of the way he could fan a *fornello* used to compete with Lawrence. Francis Brett Young and I once came upon them in the middle of an argument about Plotinus, both fanning away so hard that the room was full of the fumes of charcoal and neo-Platonism. Unless we had hurriedly opened the windows, both the philosopher cooks might have been asphyxiated.

Lawrence who had grown a beard looked much older than when I had last seen him, and there is no doubt that this beard was a help to him in developing the messianic belief in himself which was encouraged by his female disciples. In their company his sense of fun (he did not have any sense of humour) was in abeyance because he was for ever teasing their competitive adoration. This was a pity because when he allowed himself to laugh in fun it was the laughter of a child and completely charming.

Frieda Lawrence had a Teutonic mirth, but she could never resist encouraging Lorenzo, as she called him, to pull people to pieces, applauding the sneers with boisterous laughter. With Frieda this eternal "knocking" of everybody was probably the result of those wretched years in England during the war when spy-mania was rampant and when on top of the divorce she was so much on the defensive that attack was the only alternative. Lawrence too had suffered the exasperation of having a really good book *The Rainbow* prosecuted and suppressed by some piddling magistrate.

By 1917 Lawrence was already inclining to play on his messianic attraction for emotionally hungry women. He was always savagely contemptuous of philanderers, but without the least intention of giving himself away by making practical love he used to enjoy the sexual teasing. In a letter to Cecil Gray he was writing that if Jesus had paid more attention to Magdalene and less to his disciples it would have been better.

"As for me and my 'women' I know what they are and aren't and though there is a certain messiness, there is further 'reality.'"

And then he went on to say that his "women" represented, in an impure and unproud, subservient, cringing, bad fashion the threshold of a new underworld of knowledge and being. Cecil Gray wanted an emotional sensuous underworld, like Frieda and the Hebrideans in their songs. Lawrence's "women" wanted an ecstatic subtlety of intellectual underworld like the Greeks.

Lawrence had read a book by John Burnet about the early Greek philosophers—Heraclitus, Parmenides, Anaxagoras, κτλ—and had been much impressed by it. He had found the book among mine in Capri and had taken it away to re-read. I suggested that Socrates who with Lawrence had a *daimonion* thought it was more profitable for the mind to investigate men than to speculate about the underworld, but Socrates was brushed aside like a gnat. One day Lawrence and I were talking about these ancient Greeks on our way to the piazza. Suddenly Lawrence stopped to argue that men must give up thinking with their minds. "What we have to learn is to think here," he exclaimed, the declaration being illustrated by stopping and bending to point a finger at his fly-buttons to the obvious surprise of passers-by.

Frieda did not appear to be the least worried by Lorenzo's "women." She talked about them as a portly, jovial vicar might talk about his church fowls.

"But why won't Lorenzo let me have lace on my underclothes, Mackenzie?" she once asked. "Look at what he makes me wear." And pulling up her skirt above her knees she displayed the austere calico drawers on which Lawrence insisted. He disapproved of "clothes" with all the fervour of a local preacher. In a letter to one of his "women" he wrote that I wore a pale blue suit to match my eyes and a woman's large brown velour hat to match my hair. I did have a blue Harris tweed suit, but the hat was an ordinary brown felt hat with a wide brim to keep the sun out of my eyes.

One morning Lawrence came along to Casa Solitaria before I was up. He eyed me as a roundhead might have eyed a malignant in the days of the Great Rebellion.

"I hate those damned silk pyjamas you wear," he said in the tones of William Prynne reading aloud his *Histriomastrix*.

"I don't hate but I don't particularly like that depressing grey flannel shirt you wear. If you had two silk shirts instead of two grey flannel shirts you'd find them very much easier to wash."

Yet in spite of his disapproving of my appearance which he attributed to the fatal influence of the stage, Lawrence and I much enjoyed each other's company.

"I have never known anybody Lorenzo has liked so much as he likes you," Frieda bubbled. "He thinks it is a splendid idea that you should go to the South Sea Islands together."

Lawrence long remembered that aspiration. When he was on his way from Australia to San Francisco in August 1922 he sent me a postcard from Rarotonga:

> "If you are thinking of coming here, don't. The people are all brown and soft."

This was a pleasanter postcard than one Lawrence sent to Middleton Murry from Capri. He and Frieda came along to Casa Solitaria one morning, both looking extremely cheerful.

"I've just sent a postcard to Jack Murry," Lawrence announced.

"Did you tell him you were enjoying Capri?"

"No. I told him he was a dirty little white worm."

"Isn't that so good for him, Mackenzie?" Frieda gurgled. "I am so pleased Lorenzo has told him that."

He must have written to Katherine Mansfield also that day because a letter of hers published after her death by Middleton Murry tells him that Lawrence in a letter to her had called him "a dirty little worm." At this date Murry was editing the moribund *Athenæum.*

During that winter Lawrence was working at his *Fantasia of the Unconscious* and I lent him my L. C. Smith typewriter of which only the red half of the ribbon was still usable. So the original typescript of this book was in red, which according to the author had been helpful. How was not at all clear.

I have a vivid picture in the mind's eye of that typewriter's return. Most people would have hired a *facchino* to carry it back, for an L. C. Smith Number 2 was a formidable weight. Would that typewriters of such solidity and endurance were made to-day!

Lawrence carried it on his own head all the way from the Piazza to Casa Solitaria, which meant a good mile and a half's walk including some steep steps down to the rough cliff path that led to our villa. Not only did he carry the typewriter on his head but in one hand he held a bottle of Benedictine as a birthday present. This was Lawrence when for an hour or two he was at peace with life, and in such a mood he was Puck and Ariel in one. He eyed the world with delight and seemed a part of the classic scene. On other occasions he could seem as remote from it as a nonconformist chapel on the Acropolis.

During the months before Lawrence arrived in Capri I had been receiving from Chicago each month copies of *The Little Review* in which Joyce's *Ulysses* was being published serially. I lent these copies to Lawrence who was horrified by them and said much the same about *Ulysses* then as he would say to Maria and Aldous Huxley eight years later:

> "My God, what a clumsy *olla putrida* James Joyce is! Nothing but old tags and cabbage-stumps of quotations from the Bible and the rest, stewed in the juice of deliberate journalistic dirty-mindedness—what old and hard-worked staleness masquerading as the all-new!"

Or to another friend:

"James Joyce bores me stiff—too terribly would-be and done-on-purpose, utterly without spontaneity or real life."

As one might expect James Joyce took an equally low view of Lawrence. When *Ulysses* was competing with *Lady Chatterley's Lover* for the attention of salacious tourists as books refused entry by the British Customs, Joyce observed, "This man really writes very badly." And on another occasion wrote of *Lady Chatterley's Lover*: "I read the first two pages of the usual sloppy English, and Stuart Gilbert read me a lyrical bit about nudism in the wood and the end which is a piece of propaganda in favour of something which outside of D. H. L.'s country, at any rate, makes all the propaganda for itself."

I see a gloomy Lawrence. He is wearing a covert-coat, only the top of which is fastened so that it swings open to reveal an austere triangle of the clothes underneath. He is not carrying a bottle of Benedictine this time but a string-bag in which there is an orange and a banana and under his arm are the copies of *The Little Review* I had lent him. "This *Ulysses* muck is more disgusting than Casanova," he proclaimed. "I *must* show that it can be done without muck.

I have always fancied that Lady Chatterley and her lover were conceived at that moment. Certainly this reading of *Ulysses* had fired Lawrence to enumerate more theories of sex than I had yet heard from him. One thing that was worrying him particularly was his inability to attain consummation simultaneously with his partner. I pointed out that this was always a rare and happy coincidence but he became gloomier and gloomier. Failure to achieve this coincidence must mean a love as yet imperfect. Then he went on to say that on reflection he believed that the nearest he had ever come to perfect love was in his youth when he had loved a young coalminer. On and on he went until at last I said:

"If you are determined to show that you can describe the sexual act in detail without shocking people . . ."

"I want to shock them," he interrupted.

"I was using the word conventionally, without embarrassing people . . ."

He broke in again with his talk about the need for people to think with their genital organs instead of their minds, on and on about the Etruscans who he was convinced without the faintest justification from archæology or history were a people that thought with their genital organs, on and on about the sexual act until at last I had to stop the sermon.

"Listen, Lawrence, there's one thing you've got to bear in mind when you write about the sexual act. Except to the two people who are indulging in it the sexual act is a comic operation. Like love-letters read out in court during a breach of promise action."

Lawrence gazed at me with an agonised expression and his pale face grew paler. Then he hurried away with the string-bag to eat his lunch in solitude. He did not come to see me until next day, when he told me that perhaps I was right. This made him grimly determined to prove to the world that the world must observe the sexual act with reverence.

There is no doubt that the circumstances of the time helped to unbalance Lawrence. One could imagine nobody less fitted to withstand the strain of that First World War under the most favourable conditions; but for Lawrence married to a German wife, pressed for money and in poor health, the war annihilated reality. It plunged him into a miasma of morbid dreams. And then, as if he were not already suffering enough, his book, *The Rainbow*, was seized by the police in 1915, the futility of which action was shown when a few years later the novel was re-issued by another publisher, Martin Secker, without any alteration. The effect on Lawrence was disastrous, and the constipated booby of officialdom responsible for this action deserved a public purging. The attack on the book was led by that journalistic scavenger, James Douglas, who a few years later led another attack on that pathetic but wearisome book *The Well of Loneliness* to which attack the ineffable Sir W. Joynson-Hicks as Home Secretary gave his blessing. I challenged James Douglas to a debate with me about *The Well of Loneliness* in a broadcast, but after accepting he funked it at the very last minute with the excuse of indisposition.

What most embittered Lawrence in the shameful business of *The Rainbow* was the failure of any prominent author to come to his aid, and it does cast a reflection upon the state of mind to which the war had reduced men like John Galsworthy and Arnold Bennett that not an effective word was said on Lawrence's behalf. The whole malodorous business was carried through with a hole-in-the-corner pruriency that disgraced English justice.

When Martin Secker was about to publish *Women in Love* Philip Morrell offered to finance Peter Warlock in a libel action because he was furious with an alleged portrait of his wife, Lady Ottoline, in the book. In fact Lawrence's caricatures of various people in his novels sometimes deserved to be jumped on, but by now Lawrence was incapable of perceiving in those threats of libel actions anything except deliberate persecution. On top of that the volume of poems published in Italy was forbidden ingress to Great Britain, and when finally the police closed an exhibition of his pictures at a London gallery his sense of martyrdom became acute. By the time *Lady Chatterley's Lover* was published any sense of proportion left to him had vanished.

Norman Douglas wrote of him:

" Being inwardly consumed and tormented, he never clarified his outlook. Lawrence had neither poise nor reserve. Nor had he a trace of humour. He had courage. He knew what would be the consequences if a notorious work of his should now be published: a howl of execration. He went ahead. I think the writings of Lawrence have done good; his influence was needed by a large class of our fellow-creatures. He has done good negatively, as a warning to thinkers and on occasion to writers; positively, because his work is in the nature of a beneficent tabu-shattering bomb. An American friend tells me that Lawrence's romances have been of incalculable service to genteel society out there. The same applies to genteel society in England. Scholars and men of the world will not find much inspiration in these novels. Lawrence opened a little window for the bourgeoisie. That is his life work."

"And of course it was the lavatory window he opened," Douglas used to chuckle.

These words should be heeded by those who have not yet been able to explain coherently what Lawrence was after and have exalted his ethics above his æsthetics and his metaphysics above both, without giving us a clear exposition of what his ethics or metaphysics were. The important fact that Lawrence hammered an entirely new beauty out of the English language has been lost sight of in an effort to extract from his hotch-potch philosophy compounded of undigested early Greek theories and medieval heresies a practical gospel for to-day. As already pointed out, Lawrence himself succumbed to this messianic atmosphere with which a number of devotees, mostly women, surrounded him and his egopathy sometimes bordered on megalomania. His anti-Christian obsession was based on a personal jealousy of Jesus Christ. This may sound absurd; but it is related of Byron that he was jealous of Shakespeare and the limits of egocentricity, once it be completely surrendered to, may lie anywhere. We have had a terrifying example of that in the career of Hitler. As early as 1920 when Lawrence was walking with me along the Via Tragara in Capri, he stopped and proclaimed twice:

"There's not going to be another war."

Then, snatching my stick and striking the wall by the edge of the road, he shouted at the top of his voice:

"*I* won't have another war."

His mind was as much hag-ridden by sex as that of John Knox. This preoccupation could make him misjudge the simplest human action. It even led him round the world in search of a people that could think genitally instead of mentally. His interpretation of human nature was based on a mixture of hyperæsthesia about himself and an inability to believe that the most innocent child was not an accomplished hussy. Hence he was always banishing people from his life because they were presumed to have shown malice towards himself or because they had disturbed his austerity by what he believed to be blandishments of manner or attire. So long as Lawrence restricted his self-expression to poems the genius that inflamed him sometimes burned with a dazzling concentrated light; but when in a novel he tried to illuminate with the flame groups of people, the effect was too often grotesque, for many of these emanations of Lawrence's own moods incarnate in externally recognisable contemporaries lack any life of their own.

When one of Lawrence's disciples produces an intelligible code of behaviour from the gospel embedded in the lovely matrix of his work it will be time to contemplate hailing him as a messiah. During the last thirty years there has been a small amount of good æsthetic criticism and an exhaustive accumulation of biographical material; the interpretations and expositions of Lawrence's message have been most of them pitiable verbiage which, lacking the magic of the master's style, has hindered rather than helped the appreciation of the imperishable qualities in his work. Orpheus met his fate at the hands of infuriated mænads, and in the years soon after he died Lawrence's renown looked like suffering an equal fate from their kindly intentions. Shelley was spared this competitive dissection by women, and it is much easier to sustain a comparison between Lawrence and Shelley than that between Lawrence and Blake which some of his critics profess to discern.

The prosecution of Penguin Books for publishing *Lady Chatterley's Lover* in its unexpurgated form and the failure of the prosecution to secure a verdict from a jury of men and women has been a victory of immense importance for the freedom of the Press. Incidentally, although the freedom of the Press may include the freedom of newspapers its real meaning is the freedom of the printing-press to publish anything without censorship.

After several publishers of high repute were prosecuted for publishing novels called obscene libels in the phraseology of the Common Law, in which the result seemed to hang on the amount of common sense which the presiding judge possessed, the Society of Authors decided that something must be done to bring the Common Law more up to date and at last after a five-year struggle some of the recommendations by the committee chaired by Sir Alan Herbert were accepted by the Government, and in 1959 an Act of Parliament was passed in which there was one vital clause which prevented the suppression of a book " if it is proved that publication of the article in question is justified as being for the public good on the ground that it is in the interests of science, literature, art, or learning, or of other objects of general concern."

This meant that the Defence could call experts to testify accordingly and equally of course the Prosecution to contradict such testimony.

So when *Lady Chatterley's Lover* was on trial at the Old Bailey in October 1960 thirty-five experts went into the witness-box to testify in favour of the book whereas the Crown were apparently unable to find a single expert to testify against it. Mr. Gerald Gardiner, Q.C., handled these experts with masterly skill. What Milton had achieved 315 years earlier with his *Areopagitica* to establish that " promiscuous reading is necessary to the constitution of human virtue " Mr. Gerald Gardiner achieved again. With Milton he could have said " give me the liberty to know, to utter, and to argue freely according to conscience, above all liberties."

The irony of it was that this great victory should have been won not by *The Rainbow* but by *Lady Chatterley's Lover* and that in 1960 thirty-five experts with as many more in reserve should have had the mutually buttressed moral courage to speak out for *Lady Chatterley's Lover* whereas in 1915 not a single well-known author had had the moral courage to denounce the disgraceful proceedings against that much greater book *The Rainbow*.

Nearly thirty years ago I wrote of *Lady Chatterley's Lover* a few words that seem to me as true to-day as when I wrote them:[1]

" *Lady Chatterley's Lover* was unworthy of Lawrence's genius. When the scenes in which certain words never hitherto

[1] *Literature in My Time.*

printed in a serious work of English literature were removed the book became something not unlike a novelette, in which here and there some magical phrase that only Lawrence could have written lights up the tedious unreality of people and place. Was anything of value gained by printing those words expurgated from the public edition of the book? The question of what is and what is not obscene language is obviously unanswerable in any absolute sense; but the belief of some that Lawrence by printing the words he did performed a useful operation on clogged minds is unsupported by any evidence."

I had not had in 1933 the benefit of reading the evidence of those experts in 1960.

"When a word has become associated with obscenity through its uses as an expletive, the restoration of it to literature with the full implications of its meaning serves no kind of purpose, and Lawrence's solemn printing of words which, however familiar in *speech*, are only written on the walls of public lavatories was either comic or pathetic or both. Women, in their recent race to catch up with men in everything, have accepted Lawrence's portentious parade of obscene monosyllables as a direct tip from the masculine stable. They do not apparently realise that it would be an unwarrantable piece of impudence for one man to use such words in the presence of another man unless he were assured of a social, intellectual and amicable equality that would prevent his freedom of speech from being misunderstood. Women do not find it difficult nowadays to behave like men, but they often find it extremely difficult to behave like gentlemen. They are apt to lack that particular sensitiveness of the male to the taboo; not unnaturally, since for countless generations of humanity so many taboos were directed against themselves. Probably Lawrence himself was actuated by a desire to break some of these masculine taboos; but the taboos he perceived most readily were the taboos of another class whose difference he resented. Yet no man was more securely bound by the taboos of his own class. It may or may not be an ethical advantage to destroy all manners, but if manners are to be destroyed, let the destruction be general. To obliterate the relics of feudalism and chivalry and retain the relics of a bourgeois puritanism is unprofitable. Probably Lawrence shocked himself when he wrote the expurgated passages in *Lady Chatterley's Lover.* This emotion would have deceived him into supposing he was administering a salutary shock to his readers.

"From the moment that women established themselves as the potential equals of men in opportunity the necessity to uphold the doctrine of romantic love vanished. It was only when women escaped from the conventional epithet of the 'fair sex' that the emotions hitherto given a moral significance by terms like love and passion and lust were all merged in sex. It may be observed that even such an adjective as erotic with its exclusively masculine suggestion has almost vanished.

"From the days of Eve women have always faced sexual facts with more courage and realism than men. Therefore as soon as the pretence of having to shelter women from the knowledge which the male had to confront as the inevitable concomitant of experience became superfluous a freedom of expression both in speech and in writing came into general practice, which, particularly in Britain and America, was intensified by the repression of the nineteenth century. It is noteworthy that in France where the matriarchal position of women had been more secure than anywhere else in the world, novelists and dramatists had enjoyed what in Victorian England was regarded as licence, even if from time to time the State had proceeded against books for offences against public morals. Yet on such occasions there was never any suggestion that the book could do particular harm to women, whereas in England the outraged moralists always protested like seamen that they were thinking of the women and children first."

As told already Lawrence hated the instalments of *Ulysses* that were first printed in *The Little Review* and circulated, when they were not being seized by the United States police. When in 1922 *Ulysses* appeared complete in an edition published in Paris by Sylvia Beach, Lawrence was gnawed by jealousy and envy until he could demonstrate that he was able to use words as boldly as Joyce and at the same time claim for his freedom of expression that it was the purifying freedom of one who had a gospel to preach and not the corrupting freedom he condemned in Joyce.

When over forty years ago *The Little Review* ventured to assert that *Ulysses* was a major work of literature as significant as the *Divina Commedia* of Dante, the claim seemed preposterous to the point of imbecility, and I should have laughed at anybody who had told me that forty years later I should commit myself to recognising it as the major work of fiction this century has witnessed. I should still find it imbecile to compare *Ulysses* with the *Divina Commedia*; I prefer to class Joyce with Rabelais. Yet an even better comparison may be with Goethe. Indeed, *Ulysses* is *Faust* rewritten in terms of to-day and the most convincing proof ever penned in fiction of the possibility of human damnation. Such a revelation could only have been made by an Irishman and a Catholic. It is to be noted that Lawrence made his character Michaelis an Irishman when he produced a kind of greensick Michael Arlen to make the first attempt at assuaging Lady Chatterley's longing to be loved.

When Lawrence sought to strip the ultimate veil from sexual intercourse (I apologise to the bold boys of *The Guardian*, *The Spectator* and *The Observer* for not using the gerund of their canonised four-letter word) the effect was as painfully embarrassing as when an old maid suddenly goes mad and begins to shriek obscenities. That was the result of the provincial Anglo-Saxon revolting against provincial puritanism. It is the shadow of Lucifer which broods over a work like *Ulysses*; the only shadow over *Lady Chatterley's Lover* is cast by a little tin Bethel.

In watching the mythopoeic process at work on Lawrence's personality my judgment about this book may be prejudiced by my personal knowledge of him. The ultimate truth of Lawrence as an artist must be the truth that his devotees learn from him, and if he is capable of inspiring a faith, no amount of scepticism on the part of the unconverted will affect it one way or the other.

It is the intellectual fashion of to-day to deromanticise the past before 1914 but the present should deny itself the joy of romanticising its own human products. The future may find that the psychological maze in which we have temporarily lost ourselves was an unnecessary complication of human motives. The older I grow the more I am inclined to agree with Balzac that there are only about a dozen fundamentally different characters in western man and that human conduct is a much simpler affair than we like to suppose. Material progress has moved forward at such a pace that civilisation finds itself bewildered, and this bewilderment confuses human behaviour. Hence the appearance of complicacy our behaviour now presents. What this age needs are writers who can have cut on their tombstones Stendhal's epitaph, "He lived, he loved, he wrote." Too many of our present intelligentsia can only manage to write.

The need for Penguin Books to win a verdict against the Director of Public Prosecutions was imperative, but the testimony of one witness after another for the Defence spread through the court-room of the Old Bailey like a fog. The mental obfuscation of Lawrence was lighted even at its darkest by an emotional phosphorescence like that shed by a glow-worm in a midnight lane, but it was not powerful enough to illuminate that fog of anxious admiration voiced by self-conscious progressives. Lord Gage in the course of the debate in the House of Lords described it perfectly as "all the anxious endeavour which has gone into defending what is just a rather bad book in only bad taste."

VIII

The case of Lady Chatterley's Lover

THE FIRST WITNESS FOR THE DEFENCE was Mr. Graham Hough, a Lecturer in English and Fellow of Christ's College, Cambridge. He had been Professor of English in the University of Malaya and had been a prisoner of war in the hands of the Japanese for three years; he had written a study of D. H. Lawrence called *The Dark Sun.*

Mr. Hough had first read *Lady Chatterley's Lover* in 1940 and said that Lawrence was generally recognised to be one of the most important novelists of this century. He did not think that would be seriously disputed. He then went on with a reckless credulity to say he had heard it authoritatively stated that over 800 books had been written about Lawrence, in other words that books about Lawrence had been coming out once a fortnight for thirty years. I am reminded of a broadcast printed in *The Listener* some years ago in which the speaker said he had heard it authoritatively stated that Sir Winston Churchill had the largest vocabulary of any living Englishman. It was estimated to be 100,000 words. This meant that Sir Winston Churchill used about 40,000 more words than could be found in the *Concise Oxford Dictionary.*

Mr. Hough thought that the true meaning of *Lady Chatterley's Lover* was to be found in "an attempt to give a sympathetic understanding of a very painful and intricate and difficult situation."

Lawrence's compassion for the unhappy Sir Clifford who had been paralysed in the lower half of his body by a war wound is not discernible. The intricacy of the situation is that Lady Chatterley who was not a virgin when she married him is in search of sexual satisfaction. This she cannot obtain from Michaelis the Irishman whose performance in bed recalled Lawrence's problem posed to me at Capri forty years ago. Then she finds a first-class performer in her husband's gamekeeper and decides that life with Mellors will suit her better than looking after an incapacitated husband.

Mr. Gardiner asked skilfully if Mr. Hough would agree that the book "sets upon a pedestal promiscuous and adulterous intercourse." That enabled Mr. Hough to tell the jury that Lawrence condemned promiscuous intercourse and remind them that adultery had preoccupied a great deal of fiction since the time of Helen of Troy. He then insisted that the variations on the sexual theme were intended to "show the development of Connie Chatterley's awareness of her own nature," or in other words that the appetite grows with eating.

Mr. Hough was then asked about the four-letter words and was encouraged to give a little lecture on the reason for their being necessary.

"In Lawrence's view there is no proper language to talk about sexual matters. They are either discussed in clinical terms, which deprive them of all emotional content, or they are discussed in words that are normally thought to be coarse and obscene. He thinks that this results in a secretive and morbid attitude towards sex, and he wishes to find the language in which it can be discussed openly and not irreverently, and to do this he tries to redeem the normally obscene words."

One is reminded of the story of the lunatic whose behaviour was so sane that a visitor to the asylum could not understand why he was there.

"Oh, it's because I am trying to bring back into use words that people think rude and one of the fellows here has to go round behind me and rub them out as fast as I chalk them up. But I'm too clever for him," the lunatic added, with a chuckle.

"Just now I'm two F's ahead and I've just chalked C on your back."

Mr. Hough was cross-examined by Mr. Griffith-Jones for the Prosecution. He was asked if he had heard of Katherine Ann Porter and replied that she was a very distinguished American short-story writer.

Counsel went on to quote from an essay in *Encounter* written by her:

> "When I first read *Lady Chatterley's Lover*, thirty years ago, I thought it a dreary, sad performance with some passages of unintentional, hilarious low comedy, one scene at least simply beyond belief in a book written with such inflamed apostolic solemnity."

Mr. Hough on being asked if he got that impression when he first read the book replied that it was an eccentric opinion.

Mr. Griffith-Jones read some more of Katherine Ann Porter's essay.

> "Nowhere in this sad history can you see anything but a long, dull grey, monotonous chain of days, lightened now and then by a sexual bout. I can't hear any music, or poetry, or the voices of friends or children. There is no wine, no food, no sleep, no refreshment, no laughter, no rest and quiet —no love. I remember then that this is the fevered day-dream of a dying man sitting under his umbrella pines in Italy indulging his sexual fantasies."

Mr. Hough found this a fatuous criticism. I who knew Lawrence, which Mr. Hough did not, find it all too painfully just, but in fairness to Mr. Hough it must be added that he was not prepared to defend the scene at the club between Mellors and Lady Chatterley's father.

"Do you think any future generation reading that conversation would get anything approaching an accurate picture of the kind of way in which Royal Academicians conducted their conversation?" Mr. Griffith-Jones asked.

"No, sir, I do not. I think this is a disastrously bad passage, and I said so quite plainly in my book years ago. I think it is the one utterly, disastrously bad passage in the book."

Mr. Gardiner in re-examination took the opportunity of putting right with the jury any possibly unfavourable influence Katherine Anne Porter's remarks might have had. So he read what Archibald MacLeish, an ex-Librarian of Congress, had written about *Lady Chatterley's Lover* in which we were dared at our own risk to deny that the book was "one of the most important works of the century, or to express an opinion about the literature of our own time or about the spiritual history that literature expresses without making his peace in one way or another with D. H. Lawrence and with this work."

Katherine Anne Porter took the risk and put this puritan flapdoodle in the wastepaper basket: Mr. Graham Hough swallowed it.

Miss Helen Gardner, Reader in Renaissance English Literature at Oxford and a Fellow of the British Academy, followed Mr. Hough. She found that by the time she had finished the book Lawrence's four-letter words were the only ones that could be used in the context. She felt that Lawrence had redeemed the words from "low and vulgar association." Indeed, she thought that by the last page of the book one of the words had "taken on great depth of meaning." So presumably the next time Miss Gardner hears it as an expletive she will be shocked not by its vulgarity but by its profanity.

"What do you gather from the book itself was Lawrence's intention in using four-letter words?"

"I think his intention was to make us feel that the sexual act was not shameful, and the word used in its original sense therefore was not shameful either."

But who until the Puritans infected Merrie England ever did suppose that the sexual act was shameful? Did Chaucer when he used "swive"—a good Anglo-Saxon five-letter word not a bastard Latinism like Miss Gardner's revered four-letter word—suppose that he was using a word associated with a shameful act?

Under the influence of Lawrence's ability to give a spiritual value to his four-letter words Miss Gardner declared that the passages in which they appeared were "among the greatest things that Lawrence wrote."

"I think these passages do succeed, far beyond expectation, in doing something extraordinarily difficult, which very few other writers have really attempted with such courage and devotion, and that is an attempt to put into words experiences that are really very difficult to verbalise."

In 1750 John Cleland had the courage to attempt such verbalisation in *Fanny Hill*, for which he was summoned before the Privy Council. He pleaded poverty and was not punished. Lord Granville who was present at the council meeting allowed Cleland £100 a year to put his talents to better use. The book was not suppressed and the bookseller who issued it made £10,000 out of John Cleland's courage, which was certainly not inspired by any desire to give spiritual value to four-letter words.

Miss Gardner was followed by Mrs. Joan Bennett, Lecturer in English at Cambridge and Fellow of Girton College. She insisted that the parts of the book not about sex were not padding. According to her Lawrence was interested in social questions and the relationship between "upper classes, middle classes, and working classes."

Lawrence was either wondering at his achievement in becoming a friend of Lady Ottoline Morrell and Lady Cynthia Asquith and in marrying a German aristocrat or he was rebuking himself for having succumbed to such wonder. He felt compelled to caricature the upper classes in order to demonstrate to the world his own superiority. Beethoven on one occasion was furious with Goethe for taking off his hat and bowing to an archduke and archduchess. Lawrence hated Goethe and we had two or three arguments about a man whom I revere. Some of the witnesses for the Defence seemed to think that *Lady Chatterley's Lover* was on a level with the Ninth Symphony, and so Lawrence's bad manners were as easily forgiven as those of Beethoven. It did not occur to them that Sir Clifford Chatterley who had lost his manhood in fighting for his country, whose elder brother had been killed in action and who was therefore the last of a long line without any hope of an heir should have been a subject for compassion not a target for Lawrence's own inverted snobbery. His picture of Wragley Hall and its owner is worthless as literature because Lawrence himself was incapable of the necessary feat of creative imagination. One of the reasons why *Lady Chatterley's Lover* has taken in so many American critics is their unfamiliarity with the social background in England. If Lawrence had tried to present a comparable social background in the United States his incompetence to do so would have been ridiculed. However, Mrs. Bennett with one son, three daughters and eight grandchildren was prepared to maintain that it would be educative for young students to read *Lady Chatterley's Lover.*

That last question and reply trapped the Prosecution into an error of tactics, for which we must be grateful to Mr. Gardiner because whatever may be our opinion of the book and the detergents used by the witnesses for the Defence to add brightness and whiteness it would have been a disaster for the future of English letters if Penguin Books had lost the case.

The mistake made by Mr. Griffith-Jones was to press Mrs. Bennett on the educative value for young people of a book about adultery. This enabled her to put forward common-sense views about marriage which the jury would understand. Whether the book was to be condemned for what could be put forward as a strictly moral attitude to marriage the jury had their doubts.

In his re-examination Mr. Gardiner asked if it was clear from the book that the husband *told* her to go and have a child by another man.

"Yes," said Mrs. Bennett, and then aimed a Parthian shot at counsel for the Prosecution. "Lawrence's own marriage lasted the whole of his life." And Mr. Griffith-Jones was not quick enough to shoot back, "After he had gone off with another man's wife." That might have set the jury wondering whether Lawrence's attitude to marriage was so moral after all.

Dame Rebecca West was not prepared to say that *Lady*

Chatterley's Lover was a great book but she considered that in spite of its many faults it could be called a good book. She stepped on dangerous ground when she called Lawrence " a very practical and realistic man " who saw the danger of the " vast urban populations " being " taken in the direction of evil by their obedience to leaders such as Hitler." Lawrence's doctrine that the blood was more important than the mind was uncomfortably like Hitler's revivalism. He was in favour of fascism at first, but while he was watching a Fascist procession in Florence one of the Fascist militia trod on his toe when he was keeping back the crowd to give the procession room, and this made Lawrence so indignant that he turned against fascism. He would probably have been taken in by Hitler at first like Wyndham Lewis and Dr. Buchman.

Dame Rebecca was followed by Dr. John Robinson, the Bishop of Woolwich, who was asked what, if any, were the ethical merits of the book. This led to an argument between Mr. Gardiner and Mr. Griffith-Jones, the latter maintaining that the Defence was only entitled to call witnesses to testify to the literary merits of the book. In the end the Judge ruled in favour of the Defence.

The Bishop maintained that Lawrence regarded the sex relationship as something essentially sacred and went on to quote Archbishop William Temple's observation that Christians did not make jokes about sex for the same reason that they do not make jokes about Holy Communion, not because it is sordid but because it is sacred. The Bishop thought that Lawrence tried to portray the sex relationship as in a real sense an act of holy communion. " For him flesh was completely sacramental. His description of sexual relations cannot be taken out of the context of the whole, to me, quite astonishing sensitivity to the beauty and value of all human relationships. Some of his descriptions of nature in the book seem to me to be extraordinarily beautiful and delicate and portraying an attitude to the whole organic world of which he saw sex as the culmination." We may wonder if Dr. Robinson will find *Lady Chatterley's Lover* of verbal use if he be called upon to translate the Song of

Solomon for the New English Bible. Why not? The vulgarisation of the New Testament has already been achieved.

Under the Bishop's eloquence the four-letter words took on a kind of liturgical meekness and he was not prepared to advocate that they or the descriptions of sexual intercourse should be expurgated. Indeed, he felt that such an expurgation would suggest that Lawrence had written them in a sordid spirit. He found the last ten pages of the book "a most moving advocate for chastity." Mr. Griffith-Jones in cross-examination failed to ask him whether the old Latin tag *post coitum homo tristis est* was equally moving.

In his re-examination Mr. Gardiner asked the Bishop if this was a book which in his view Christians ought to read.

"Yes, I think it is. Because I think what Lawrence was trying to do . . ."

The Bishop was denied an opportunity of any more sacramental comparisons because the Prosecution objected to the question, and the Judge sustained the objection. It was too late, however. The papers that evening would carry headlines A BOOK ALL CHRISTIANS SHOULD READ, and not surprisingly the Archbishop of Canterbury was as little amused as Queen Victoria would have been by such a recommendation.

Dr. Vivian Pinto, the Professor of English at Nottingham University, was the next witness. To him Mr. Gardiner read various passages with four-letter words galore, all of which Dr. Pinto praised, and we can feel sure that the good manners and good taste of Nottingham students are safe in Dr. Pinto's hands.

"It has been said that the only variation in the description of sexual intercourse is in the place. Do you agree with that?"

"No, I think there are very subtle differences, a great many variations."

As Professor of English Dr. Pinto is not likely to lecture on Aretino, but he would obviously be well qualified to do so. He went on to make a ludicrous comparison between Lawrence's

Mrs. Bolton and Dickens's Mrs. Gamp, and one asks on a note of apprehension what Dr. Pinto is teaching the young people at Nottingham about Dickens.

Now came an extract from Lawrence's essay *Apropos of Lady Chatterley's Lover* which was read by Mr. Gardiner after Dr. Pinto had called it "one of his finest pieces of critical writing."

To my fancy in trying to feel my way through this reek of words the charcoal was filling the room again with fumes as it did when Lawrence was arguing about neo-Platonism with the young Roumanian at Capri once upon a time.

> "And in spite of all antagonism I put forth this novel as an honest healthy book, necessary for us to-day. The words that shock so much at first don't shock at all after a while. Is this because the mind is depraved by habit? Not a bit. It is that the words merely shocked the eye, they never shocked the mind at all. . . . We are to-day as human beings, evolved and cultured far beyond the taboos which are inherent in our culture. . . . The evocation of the so-called obscene words must have been very dangerous to the dim-minded, obscure, violent natures of the Middle Ages, and perhaps are still too strong for slow-minded, half-evoked lower natures to-day. But real culture makes us give to a word only those mental and imaginative reactions which belong to the mind, and saves us from violent and indiscriminate physical reactions which may wreck social decency."

The picture of Lawrence bending over in the piazza of Capri to point at his fly-buttons and declare that we must learn to think there may be remembered as Lawrence proceeds.

> "In the past man was too weak-minded, or crude-minded, to contemplate his own physical body and physical functions, without getting all mixed up with physical reactions that overpowered him. It is no longer so. Culture and civilisation have taught us to separate the reactions. We now know the act does not necessarily follow on the thought."

All this clotted nonsense is being churned out by Lawrence because he was himself in a sexual mess up and unable to satisfy his wife's exuberance. He forgot or probably never knew that the ancient Greeks did not corrupt language and turn words into obscenity by using them for oaths. The Greeks had an exact word for every form of sexual emotion and expression: not only that but they had a great store of double-meanings on which their comic poets could always draw with perfect appropriateness. However, when Mr. Gardiner read out that long passage from *Apropos of Lady Chatterley's Lover* from which a few lines have been quoted above Dr. Pinto nodded with appreciation.

"That was the passage I had in mind," he declared sagely, and as the evidence of these literary experts is being extracted by counsel I am reminded of the last time I saw H. G. Wells; it was in 1946, hardly two months before he died. Suddenly in the middle of an outburst of despair about the state of mankind he said:

"This fellow Lawrence. I think that book of his, *Sons and Lovers*, was pretty good. But what did he want to go to Arabia for?"

I could not bring myself to tell H. G. that he was confusing the two Lawrences, each a man of genius but with no other link between them, because I did not want to make a great man aware that I knew his mind was failing. So I proceeded to create a mythical figure like a chimera for H. G. and myself to speculate about. Yet that chimera of the two Lawrences in one evoked by me on that sunny summer afternoon in Hanover Terrace, Regent's Park, was not a whit less credible than this mystical D. H. Lawrence evoked by witnesses at the Old Bailey who claimed to speak with authority about his work.

It is a relief to turn from the evidence of experts, literary and ethical, to that of Sir William Emrys Williams and Sir Allen Lane. Sir William spoke of Lawrence's courageous attempt to present sex, but as much or more moral courage was demanded for Penguin Books to challenge the attitude of the Director of Public Prosecutions to a trial of strength over the new Obscene Publications Act.

Prebendary Hopkinson thought the book would be "important and valuable for his daughters to read." This obviously shook the Judge who may have been relieved when the Prebendary added that only one of his children, to his knowledge, had read the book so far and that he had found it rather dull, which suggests that the son has more discernment than his father.

Mr. Richard Hoggart, Senior Lecturer in English Literature at Leicester University, declared that *Lady Chatterley's Lover* was " highly virtuous and if anything puritanical." This obviously shook Mr. Justice Byrne again, but Mr. Hoggart maintained that Lawrence was a " British nonconformist Puritan."

With this we may agree without necessarily regarding such a mental condition as something admirable. Mr. Hoggart stuck sturdily to his esteem for puritans, at one point stressing " an intense sense of responsibility for one's conscience " as the distinguishing feature of British puritanism, and in his answers to the questions put to him sharpened the disquiet some of us feel about the value of " Eng. Lit." as education at the Universities.

Mr. Francis Cammaerts said nothing to allay that disquiet. The son of the distinguished Belgian poet should not have made the mistake of supposing that Lawrence's four-letter words are Anglo-Saxon. He found *Lady Chatterley's Lover* the " only book that treated the sexual relationship between human beings in a really serious way " from *Genesis* onwards we may presume.

Miss Sarah Beryl Jones, Classics Mistress at Keighley Girls' Grammar School, mentioned that most girls did not want to read books like *Lady Chatterley's Lover*. And of course she was right. The reason is that women are more realistic than men.

The cloud of witnesses grew cloudier and cloudier in testifying to Lawrence's puritan status. It was a relief from this portentous cloud of priggishness when Miss Anne Scott-James gave bright simple answers to the usual questions, and when Mr. J. W. Lambert had the honesty to admit that one of the reasons why he read *Lady Chatterley's Lover* at school was its reputation as a dirty book.

The Rev. Donald Tytler, Director of Religious Education in the Birmingham Diocese, found the book of " moral and educational value." In his examination Mr. Gardiner read

Lawrence's tribute to true marriage from *A propos of Lady Chatterley* in the course of which he wrote:

"A marriage is no marriage that is not basically and permanently phallic."

Mr. Gardiner then asked Mr. Tytler if the word "phallic" had always had a sacred connotation.

"I don't know that it has *always* had a sacred connotation," Mr. Tytler replied, "but like many words taken over from a pagan world, it has been baptised by Christians and made into a sacred word."

So are we to assume that instead of vegetable marrows ithyphalli will be a feature of harvest festivals in the Birmingham Diocese under the stimulating educational influence of Mr. Tytler?

The testimony came to an end, for the Prosecution called no witnesses. Perhaps the Prosecution was intimidated by hearing that Mr. Gardiner had another thirty-five witnesses in reserve. In any case by now the Director of Public Prosecutions must have realised what a blunder he had made in taking proceedings against *Lady Chatterley's Lover*. The Prosecution had given up hope of a verdict, but expected a disagreement by the jury in which event the case would probably be abandoned. However, after three hours' argument among themselves the jury found for the defendants, and this verdict was due to the remarkable skill with which Mr. Gerald Gardiner had handled the witnesses and the sober eloquence with which he had addressed the jury. Mr. Justice Byrne summed up as sensibly as the Obscene Publications Act 1959 allows the intrusion of common sense. The new Act is a great improvement, but the Defence is hampered by it in a case like this and, although after three hours' consideration the jury finally acquitted Penguin Books of an obscene publication, one may be allowed to doubt whether any counsel except Mr. Gerald Gardiner would have secured that acquittal. The most that seemed possible to hope for was the inability of the jury to reach agreement. It is a pity that the jury's discussion could not be recorded. This would have been of immensely greater value than the testimony of the witnesses for the Defence in estimating the significance of *Lady Chatterley's Lover*. The occasionally hysterical puritanism of the latter was a disservice to manners whatever may have been its putative service to morals.

It was of course essential that these witnesses should testify to the literary merit of the book. The representatives of Penguin Books argued with complete justification that Lawrence's contribution to the novel could not be considered fairly presented to readers if *Lady Chatterley's Lover* were omitted; it was part of a canon. They were equally justified in refusing to publish the book in its expurgated form.

Two or three of the literary experts were boldly prepared to call *Lady Chatterley's Lover* one of Lawrence's greatest books, but most of them more discreetly refused to do this. When I was asked if I was prepared to testify I replied that I should be willing to say that Lawrence wrote the book under the impression that he was writing a moral tract but I should have to declare that as a piece of literature compared with Lawrence's best novels it was contemptible. That opinion I have held for thirty years and on re-reading the book that opinion has been confirmed. The literary judgments of one or two of those professors and lecturers in Eng. Lit. have filled me with a deep pessimism about the value of a University education to-day. If what we heard in court is to be accepted as the standard opinion of professors and lecturers, while we may still hope to see classical scholars in the future there seems little prospect that the schools of English Literature will produce anything but young men and young women crammed with predigested courses, dehydrated information, tinned opinion, and desiccated taste.

What concerns the present discussion is whether Lawrence's attitude to life was an example of moral courage with a particular manifestation of it in the writing of *Lady Chatterley's Lover*, whether the witnesses for the Defence displayed moral courage in testifying publicly, and whether the publication of the book was an act of moral courage.

The last question can be answered with an affirmative. True there was no risk of public opprobrium and loss of face but merely of loss of pocket. Nevertheless, it was a challenge to the conventional servility of public opinion on which the Law relies and one asks why Mr. Justice Byrne declined to give a reason for his refusal to make an order as to the costs. It seems unjust that Penguin Books should have to pay about £13,000 to show the Director of Public Prosecutions what an Act of Parliament means. Penguin Books had had reason to hope that there would be no prosecution in view of the fact that a year before a United States Federal Court had decided that *Lady Chatterley's Lover* was not an obscene book. Penguin Books had failed to appreciate how much of the ass can still obstinately retain its nature in the English Law.

And what of the moral courage of the witnesses, of the ladies, one or two of them maiden ladies, who were prepared to argue that Lawrence had given a spiritual value to those four-letter words which even Lady Chatterley herself heard for the first time. Do these ladies really want to bring them into polite usage? And can novelists in future assume that they can call a spade a spade with impunity? Mr. Gardiner did not seem to think so, for he warned the jury:

> "There is one thing about which I want to be quite plain, because in my submission it is of some importance not only that you should realise this but that everybody should realise it. It is this: that no one should think that if the use of these words for this special purpose, by this particular author, in this particular book, is legitimate, it will follow that these words can be used by any scribbler writing any kind of novel."

The bold boys of *The Observer, The Guardian* and *The Spectator* did not heed Mr. Gardiner's warning and were censured by the Press Council in consequence. *The Times* was not so brave. The consternation in Printing House Square once upon a time when a disgruntled typesetter anxious to get back on his employers scattered four-letter words through the speeches of various Ministers of the Crown in the report of a Parliamentary Debate may not have been forgotten, nor the frenzied efforts to rescue from circulation the copies of that first edition.

It seems impossible to discern a demonstration of moral courage in the evidence of those witnesses for the Defence because beyond a few ribald gibes they had nothing to fear. Indeed, as we listened to those thirty-five witnesses with another thirty-five in reserve and Mr. Gardiner's superlative skill in creating an atmosphere of respect almost of reverence for their professed opinions it would almost have been an act of moral courage to express disagreement with them.

And what of Lawrence himself? Should he be cited as an example of moral courage?

When people call Lawrence a genius they presumably mean that he was ruled by an inward compulsion of which a typical example is the *daimonion* that inspired Socrates. Blake, Bunyan and Burns are instances of such a genius in our literature. This genius may be creative or destructive, and Lawrence's genius was destructive. He created nothing: he destroyed much. That he hoped to create something out of his genius may be true but it was a hope continuously thwarted by his own imaginative impotence. He would talk for hours about the need to find a place in the world where the life he wanted to rescue from the collapse of humanity could be lived, but when he was asked to expound the principles of such a life he was incapable of formulating them. He argued much about the Christian faith but his paranoiac jealousy of Jesus Christ made such argument a waste of intellect and emotion. He hated the notion of loving his neighbour as himself because he was entirely obsessed by himself. He could criticise others but nobody must criticise him. He must express himself without regard for the feelings of anybody else, and by a strange magic he could always find disciples who would put up with anything from him. In some ways there was a similarity between him and Hitler. Fortunately he was able to express himself to his own satisfaction and to the admiration of others as an artist. Hitler was no artist and therefore his genius became a practically destructive force.

Lawrence convinced himself that *Lady Chatterley's Lover* was his final and finest effort to inspire western men with the will to shake off the fetters with which industrialism had bound them and find freedom in the sexual act. They must cease to be cephalic and become phallic. There were times when he sought for the noble savage as naïvely as Jean-Jacques Rousseau and other times when the past overlaid him. That was the effect Monte Cassino had on him when he visited it and sent me a postcard to say he would like to destroy it. If he had lived another ten years he would have seen his wish granted. Lawrence's resentment of Monte Cassino was the same resentment he had of people with a background or with ancestors. He delights in mocking the unfortunate baronet, married to that woman whom Dame Rebecca West once compared to a stale spongecake, because he could not have an heir. He once told me to consider the advantages I had enjoyed compared with his own.

"My dear Lawrence, I carry with me what for a novelist to-day are the impedimenta of a public-school and University education. You are free of such impedimenta. You can stay in a house and enjoy its hospitality and you will be forgiven if a year later you write a book in which you hold up your host to ridicule. You can do what suits you when it suits you, and if you can't do it at the moment you want to because you are short of cash you can take it out of the society that doesn't pay you as well for your books as you think you ought to be paid."

The picture of Mellors the gamekeeper is a picture of Lawrence as physically he would have liked to be. The nagging problem ever at the back of his mind was his inability to satisfy his wife sexually. He was angered by anybody who told a ribald story, but he was for ever discovering signs of sexuality even in children. He was haunted, indeed harried, by sex and he could not lay the ghost of it. He could not bear to be wrong and for that reason he would not correct or tinker with his work. If he was not satisfied with a book he had written he rewrote the whole book. The blame was on his genius or dæmon or familiar spirit, which was made to pay for having misled him.

Another reason for writing *Lady Chatterley's Lover* was his determination somehow to snatch from the head of James Joyce the laurel wreaths that were being woven from leaves gathered in the shrubberies of Bloomsbury. The resentment against James Joyce of which I had seen the beginning when he read parts of *Ulysses* in those numbers of *The Little Review* grew deeper with the years, and when the two books were competing in Paris for the patronage of concupiscent tourists and when the name Joyce was mentioned, it was like calling Rats! to a terrier.

Lawrence had abundant cause to rage against the suppression of *The Rainbow* and abundant reason to complain of the lack of support he received from his fellow-writers. In justice to them the younger writers were many of them away on active service. He could be excused for believing himself an object of persecution when another idiotic magistrate closed the gallery in which his pictures were on show, on the grounds of their indecency. It is difficult not to fancy that Lawrence wrote *Lady Chatterley's Lover* in a spirit of defiance, but if as the admirers of the book claim it is the supreme inspiration of Lawrence's genius many will cite it as an example of moral courage. Yet some of us will retain our doubts about this. Some of us realise by now that if Lawrence had been charged with committing a nuisance by the statue of Eros in Piccadilly he would have found devotees to argue that it was a splendid gesture of moral courage to show up a cowardly society which resorted to using underground lavatories instead of performing a natural function in public.

In so far as moral courage always implies a minority, sometimes a very small minority, who will approve of whatever speech or action it has inspired, one can allow that the writing and publication of *Lady Chatterley's Lover* demanded moral courage from the author. Nevertheless, it is to be remembered that, although he protested, often in extravagant language, what torture it was causing him to expurgate the book, he did agree to its being published thus expurgated, which if the passages of the book excised were as important as he believed them to be was a surrender by him to insincerity.

Yet if Lawrence had been asked whether it had taken courage to write and publish the book he would have been angry because such a question would have seemed to imply the possibility of his being subject to ordinary human weakness. In estimating the degree of moral courage in words or deeds the amount of megalomania involved must always be reckoned. Lawrence believed himself to be infallible, and therefore everybody was out of step except our Johnny.

In the review *Encounter* a deep-piercing criticism of *Lady Chatterley's Lover* by Mr. Colin Welch boldly suggested that the inspiration of the book was the witchcraft of the Old Religion. He could not agree that it was in the puritan tradition, but we may remember that witchcraft flourished as a result of puritanism's oppression of the soul. Mr. Welch did not intend to suggest by witchcraft that Lawrence was playing with magic; he merely meant that he was preaching the phallus-worship of the old fertility rites. Not that Lawrence was aware of doing this. He was an unconscious throwback to those trying to escape from the dark toils of puritanism. Between Lawrence's female disciples and a coven of witches there was a remote kinship. If the Old Religion be left out of it, Lawrence was not merely passionately anti-Christian, but equally contemptuous of the Christian concept of God. In one letter he wrote of a picture he wanted to paint showing God being pelted out of Eden by Adam and Eve, and in his book *The Man Who Died* he felt he had shown how foolish it was to suppose that he was less of a messiah than Jesus Christ.

What must also be understood about Lawrence's mystical phallicism is his discovery that it was a social equaliser. Nobody had less reason to bother about class, but it forever tormented him and this was why Lady Chatterley had to be the wife of a baronet. It may be significant that many young men who have benefited by the larger opportunities provided by the Welfare State get from Lawrence a reassurance about their own status. When one contrasts Lawrence with Robert Burns the comparative feebleness of Lawrence is apparent. Burns who spent much sweeter hours among the lasses than Lawrence ever spent was never worried about class, and he was able to endow a nation with self-respect without that morbid egopathy which never ceased to trouble Lawrence's spirit. Moreover, Burns had a virility which was denied to Lawrence whose only perfect love affair according to himself had been with a young miner.

Lady Chatterley's Lover cannot be called an obscene book by any intelligent reader, but the imbecility of the decision to prosecute it has merely been successful in making it an obscene book for a vast number of readers. A few dons and clergymen and bluestockings have been made to appear ludicrous in the eyes of a vast unintelligent public because in order to counter the charge of obscenity they have had to maintain that the book really did succeed in imparting the moral precepts that Lawrence believed he was offering to " a tragic age " as a means of salvation. If one of the dons had had the courage to defend the four-letter words because they were the words that a man drawn as the author drew Mellors would use, instead of trying to argue that Lawrence was preoccupied with the prevention of cruelty to words, what a deal of humbug we should have been spared. Yet probably the only way to win the case was to humbug the jury, and it was vital to win the case for the sake of the future of English literature. It was not a victory for moral courage, although probably every witness believed he or she was showing as much moral courage in proclaiming it to be a primer of life for young people as Lawrence had displayed by writing what in several letters he called an " improper " book, suggesting alas, to everybody who knew him that curious little high-pitched titter of his as he said it. Let Sir William Emrys Williams have the last word in a letter he wrote to *Encounter*:

> " The most frustrating feeling I had during the case was that it was being conducted before the wrong tribunal. . . . I am sick to death of the kind of Chatterley discussion we have all had to put up with in the last few weeks, and although I am obviously glad that we at Penguin's won the verdict, I take no pleasure in the actual form of the contest."

IX

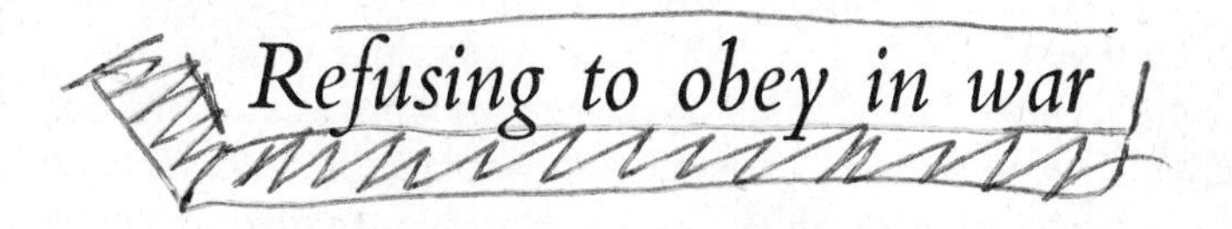

Refusing to obey in war

ONE OF THE HARDEST TESTS of a man's moral courage is his ability to face the disapproval even of his friends for an action which strikes at all the traditions of his class but which nevertheless he feels compelled to take in order to be at ease with his own conscience.

Such an action was taken by William Douglas Home, a younger brother of Lord Home, the Secretary of State for Foreign Affairs, in August 1944. After Eton and New College, Oxford from which he was twice rusticated, that is to say sent down for what was left of term, he made up his mind to be a playwright and had had one play produced with some success before the war came, and another produced not long before the phoney war came to an end, the run of which stopped when Hitler attacked the Netherlands.

Douglas Home was a strong supporter of Neville Chamberlain's policy of appeasement because he believed that German decency would reassert itself if what they thought was the injustice of Versailles was wiped out and that Hitler and his Nazis would fade from the scene. He admired what he felt was Chamberlain's great courage in going to see Hitler and he felt that Munich was a credit to British policy not a disgraceful betrayal of Czechoslovakia. In an autobiography called *Half Term Report*, which was published in 1954 when he was forty-two years of age, he makes no attempt to hedge about his feelings when he was twenty-six, and such honesty of mind is typical.

When his call-up papers came he considered asking to be exempted from military service as a conscientious objector, but he decided that he was not as much a conscientious objector as a political objector, whose exemption was not provided for. He did not feel that he could claim exemption on religious grounds. Nor did he feel that he could conscientiously volunteer for non-combatant service because by volunteering he would be agreeing with a war of which politically he disapproved.

So he wrote to the Labour Exchange which had sent him his call-up papers and told them that he must accept them because there was no provision for political objectors. At the same time he wanted to make it clear that he was opposed to prolonging the war to a bitter end, that he favoured a peace by negotiation and that he believed British war aims should be plainly stated. Finally he announced that while he should try to do his best as a soldier, he could not be relied upon in all circumstances. We learn without surprise that Douglas Home received no reply to this letter.

After two or three months as a conscript Private Douglas Home was told that he had been picked for O.C.T.U. training. He decided that if he had to be a soldier he might as well be an officer, and presently he was posted to the Brigade of Guards squad at Sandhurst. He had felt more or less at ease with his unit down in Devonshire in the company of simple chaps not in the least interested in politics and with nothing but domestic problems to worry them. When the invasion alarm in the West of England and throughout Scotland was started on that September day in 1940 by the vicar of a Cornish parish ringing his church bells at the sight of a local fishing fleet, the regiment was called to action stations. For twenty-four hours Douglas Home lay in a wood with a Bren gun trained on a bridge, and during that time was at peace with himself because if the Germans really were invading the country he longed to defend it.

On that September night the most westerly Home Guard company in Great Britain defending the Isle of Barra in the Outer Hebrides slept in their beds because the telegram with the code-word *Cromwell* which was the signal to man the beaches and keep Hitler from landing was held up by a suspicious clerk in the Inverness post office and did not arrive until next day accompanied by another signal to say that the invasion was a Boojum.

Douglas Home after his time at Sandhurst was not considered a suitable officer for the Brigade of Guards, much to his relief, and went back to his old regiment in Devonshire where presently the order came that they were to be mechanised and become part of the Royal Armoured Corps.

In the course of his training with Churchill tanks Douglas Home managed to get leave three times from the War Office to contest by-elections; the first was as an Independent for the Cathcart Division of Glasgow. His campaign lasted only three days, but he came second in the poll to the Unionist candidate with over 3000 votes. Not long after this he stood again, for the Windsor Division, and with three weeks in which to canvas the constituency and address five meetings a night he was defeated by the Conservative candidate, an old school friend, but he polled over 10,000 votes.

Then in January 1943 came the Casablanca meeting when President Roosevelt and Mr. Churchill declared that the only terms offered to the Germans would be unconditional surrender. This was a shock to Douglas Home who felt that such terms put an end to any hope of securing "a stable political future" for the world.

During that year Douglas Home became increasingly exasperated by "the constant attempt of our politicians and the Press to point out to the German officers and men where their duty lay. I found the argument that all good Germans would refuse to fight, and lay down their arms, particularly nauseous. . . . I felt, with increasing despair, that in their attempts to undermine the patriotism of German soldiers our politicians were suggesting with unbearable cynicism and criminal immorality a course of conduct which in their own services, they would regard as being reprehensible."

So continued throughout the year what Douglas Home calls "the rising temperature of my emotional reactions." At last in April 1944, hearing of a by-election in the Clay Cross Division of Derbyshire he decided to stand as an Atlantic Charter candidate and was granted permission by the military authorities. His platform was that the "Atlantic Charter declaration had been jettisoned by politicians who relied on unconditional surrender in its stead."

The response of the electors in a Labour stronghold was not encouraging; this time Douglas Home lost his deposit.

We may surmise that by now the colonel of the regiment was tired of having a squadron officer arguing about the wrong of Unconditional Surrender. At any rate, he put Douglas Home in command of the reserve squadron which meant a minimum of activity when the regiment landed in Normandy and left him time to brood over the folly of Unconditional Surrender. This was confirmed when he heard the way that the enemy was fighting on the assumption that they would be given no quarter if they surrendered and therefore died rather than let themselves be taken prisoner. The news of the July plot to kill Hitler strengthened Douglas Home's belief that the policy of unconditional surrender was a disastrous blunder. He felt sure that besides those German officers who gave their lives in an effort to overthrow Hitler there must be many many more with less desperate courage who would respond to an offer of peace on reasonable terms.

For the last eighteen months Douglas Home had longed to resign his commission and revert to the rank of private in order to divest himself of as much responsibility as even a junior officer bears. He had refrained from this step because he had been afraid that people might think he had done so as a way of trying to dodge the Second Front. Now he felt he could ask to resign his commission without exposing himself to that gibe. He wrote to the colonel giving his political reasons for the request; his letter was ignored for a fortnight. So he wrote another and this time he sent a copy of it to the Press. A fortnight later the colonel sent for him and asked if he had written the letter which had appeared above his name in the *Maidenhead Advertiser*.

"You shouldn't do it," he was told and the interview was ended.

At this point some readers may be feeling that Douglas Home was a difficult, contrary chap who had been given too much latitude to open his mouth wide and had been allowed to break all the rules of soldierly behaviour with remarkable leniency. The test of his willingness to stand by his words at whatever cost to himself was at hand. The proof of the pudding would be in the eating and a damned unpleasant pudding it was going to be proved.

That evening an Intelligence officer told Douglas Home that something had happened right up his street. To quote Douglas Home's own report of that brief conversation:

" 'The German general in Le Havre has asked to evacuate all the civilians.'

" 'Good,' said I.

" 'But we've refused to let him.'

" 'Why?' I asked.

" He shrugged. 'Not time,' he said.

" 'Not time,' I cried. 'The battle isn't for three days, is it?'

" 'No,' said he. 'That's why I said it was up your street.' "

Later that night the adjutant told Douglas Home that the colonel had ordered him to proceed to C Squadron to act as liaison officer. Turning over in his mind that conversation with the Intelligence officer, Douglas Home realised how right he had been to say that something had happened right up his street. There was a German general trying to save the lives of thousands of men, women and children in a great French city and here were we refusing to listen to such a humane proposal.

When Douglas Home reached the harbour of C Squadron in the morning the quiet atmosphere confirmed the fact that the attack on Havre would not start for three days, and it was obvious that there was time for the whole civilian population to walk out of Havre and pass through the Allied lines to safety.

But the German general's request was refused, and when he asked for time to move all the civilians into a special quarter of the town to escape the bombing, even that was refused.

Douglas Home, recalling our exhortations to the officers and men of the German Army to disobey orders of which they disapproved, knew what would be said to a British officer who disobeyed an order because he disapproved of its morality. It would be a crime. And what would be the penalty?

That night on his camp-bed among piles of apples in the loft of a farmhouse Douglas Home lay awake, contemplating the alternatives before his conscience. In his own words:

"Faced with what I considered to be an immoral order, I must either obey it and abandon what I had conceived to be the humanitarian fight that I had waged so long—thus proving myself afraid to practise what I preached, or I must disobey it and face the unknown fate that would be mine."

Then he fell asleep, and woke in the morning about half-past five with his mind clear, his purpose firm. He drove in a jeep to Regimental Headquarters, and then as he was driving indecision returned and it took seven circuits of a field of roots before he finally made up his mind to do what he felt was for him the right thing to do.

The colonel was shaving when Douglas Home arrived and these questions surged through his mind as he waited a moment or two before he spoke:

Is one man, in the name of patriotism, always to be allowed to override the man of peace? Is opposition to an immoral order in war always to be suppressed by the irrelevant arguments that to oppose is to be unpatriotic, to work for peace is to be a traitor, to disobey an order is to be a coward? Or would there be a gleam of hope for the future if one man, ignoring all these irrelevancies, were to stand by his convictions, refuse to obey an immoral order, and leave it to the future to decide if he were right or wrong?

"I told the colonel my decision. He stopped shaving, swore, and called his second-in-command."

The colonel then asked in the presence of the second-in-command whether Douglas Home would carry out his order, and on his refusal he was told to return to C Squadron and look after the transport. Douglas Home replied that having refused to take part in the battle as liaison officer he could not take any other part in it.

The junior officer who had disobeyed an order felt that his commanding officer might expose himself to censure from above by not putting him under arrest. This he told the colonel, but the colonel refused to listen and told him to go back to C Squadron and wait there for further orders.

The next day Douglas Home sat with the sergeant-major of the squadron who had taken his place in charge of the transport. The battle for Le Havre began and lasted five hours. There were no casualties in Douglas Home's regiment and very few casualties among any of the Allied troops. According to the Press in England 12,000 civilians were killed during the preliminary bombardment from the air. One can feel hopefully sure that this was an exaggeration, but even if only 1200 men, women and children were killed they were 1200 lives sacrificed needlessly.

Then Douglas Home wrote a letter to the Press, to explain what he had done and why he had done it.

> "That letter landed me in Wormwood Scrubbs. Time and again, I have been called a fool for writing it. Time and again, I have heard people say that if I had not written it, I would not have been sent to prison or cashiered. Time and again I have been told that my military superiors had very likely decided that, even if my action was not justified (and perhaps they even thought it was), it was at least to be expected of me in a situation of that kind. And, time and again, I have tried to explain that my personal position was not my chief concern. I was, at that time, on fire with crusading zeal. I wanted, above everything, to advertise my action, not from an exhibitionist motive (as my enemies no doubt alleged), but because the voice within me shouted to be heard. I hated the smug hypocrisy of politicians and the one-sided propaganda devoted to blackguarding our enemies. And I hoped that an exposure of the situation at Le Havre would help to make the public see that all our propaganda was one-sided and dishonest and inevitably calculated to prolong the war. And so the letter, unbeknown to the colonel (for I thought he might have stopped it) went."

The publication of that letter left the War Office with no alternative but to bring Douglas Home before a court-martial. He had one consolation and that was to hear that on the day his letter had been published the German general at Calais had asked permission from the Allied commander after the battle for Calais had begun to evacuate the civilians, and this permission had been granted. It might have been a coincidence but Douglas Home could reasonably hope that it was not.

The court-martial held at Ghent could hardly have returned any verdict but guilty of disobeying an order; Captain William Douglas Home was cashiered and sentenced to twelve months' imprisonment with hard labour. This sentence was served in the gaols of Wormwood Scrubbs and Wakefield.

If Douglas Home had not paid for his opinions and the expression of them by going to prison he might have been dismissed by his critics as nothing more than a vain and self-opinionated young man. As it was, while they could still criticise his action, none of them could deny that he was morally courageous. For all he knew he might have been sentenced to be shot. Doubtless it was an improbable sentence in what are more enlightened or degenerate times according to one's outlook. Nevertheless, however remote, death was a contingency. In any case a year in prison for a man of his background was a formidable ordeal to face.

When I had to face an Old Bailey trial my counsel persuaded me to plead guilty because if I pleaded not guilty and were found guilty the Judge might send me to prison, and reminded me that nine months in Wormwood Scrubbs was not a pleasant experience. On the other hand if I would plead guilty he was able to guarantee that the penalty would only be a fine. I remember telling this to Lady Oxford who begged me to choose prison because I should be able to write such a good book about it. I hope, if I had believed that my going to prison would successfully rouse the public to the wrong done to British justice by the abuse of the power of hearing the vital evidence against an accused man *in camera*, I should have had the moral courage to accept the risk of prison. I lacked that belief and therefore I accepted the bargain that justice offered. Incidentally it may be observed that none of the evidence in the spy case of March 1961 was heard *in camera* and that recent agents with only initials to disguise them from the Press were prominent in open court. No doubt the reason for this publicity was the anxiety of the counter-espionage experts to advertise their skill, now that at last they had a spy case according to Cocker.

It may be doubted whether Douglas Home would have been sent to prison if he had not flouted the military authorities by writing that letter to the *Maidenhead Advertiser*. However, he was courageous enough to carry his refusal to obey an order given to him on active service to its logical conclusion. He believed passionately, rightly or wrongly, that the war was being prolonged by the battle-cry of No Surrender, and at whatever the cost to himself and his career he had the moral courage to be true to his convictions.

Coincidence ruled that about the same time as Douglas Home was challenging authority, another Scot of about the same age was challenging authority to the point of going to prison. This was Douglas Young, a noteworthy Greek scholar and a poet of delightful ingenuity. He had been at New College, Oxford, after Douglas Home because he had been at St. Andrews first. When lecturer in Greek at Aberdeen in 1938 he joined the Scottish National Party which had been welded (or perhaps kneaded would be a more accurate verb) out of various associations devoted to the advocacy of Home Rule for Scotland. The only aim on which all the members of the National Party agreed was the need for a Scottish Parliament.

In 1937 a resolution was passed that in the event of another world war members of the Scottish National Party should refuse to serve in the British Forces unless and until Scotland had recovered her own Government. Douglas Young recognised that this was a strong resolution but was much encouraged by such evidence of an ability to face facts. Most of the resolutions passed by the Scottish National Party at their conferences were concerned with local grievances and failed to see Scotland's national position in relation to the international situation.

In all British wars after the Treaty of Union the Scottish losses were comparatively much heavier than those of the English regiments, because most of the English troops excelled in defensive tactics and the Scottish troops excelled in attack. In the eighteenth century it had been an approved policy to expend as many Highland regiments as possible in order to help in the depopulation of what was still considered a possible centre of unrest. The same policy was pursued with the Irish troops. The Highlands could hardly be considered a threat by the time of the Peninsular War but the tradition lingered. Indeed, it continued into the First World War when costly attacks inflicted disproportionately heavy casualties on the Scottish regiments. Apart from that during the years after the First World War Scotland had suffered economically much more severely than England and it should have been obvious to any Nationalist that the onset of war would make it more than ever necessary for Scotland to exert some control over her own affairs.

Douglas Young who had been shaken by what seemed to him the cynical treatment of the Czechs which culminated in the Munich agreement felt more strongly than ever that Scotland should have the same equality of rights within the British Commonwealth as the Dominions. Such rights should include the enlistment and control of Scotland's own forces.

By the spring of 1939 the need for conscription was being debated, and in Scotland Nationalists began to ask themselves whether conscription could be constitutionally applied to Scotland by the terms of the Treaty of Union. Douglas Young was asked this question by a heckler at a May Day demonstration in Aberdeen, and he replied that it was constitutionally *ultra vires* for the United Kingdom Parliament to conscribe Scots for foreign service. Having once expressed this opinion publicly, Douglas Young felt that he could not retract it unless he found himself out-reasoned in argument. Indeed, the more he pondered over the terms of the Treaty of Union the more positive he became that this opinion was right.

Douglas Young was away in Greece when Hitler invaded Poland, and when he returned to Britain a fortnight later he went to Oxford and inquired at a recruiting centre if there was anything he could do. He was then told that being over twenty-five he was in a reserved occupation and could therefore do nothing. This was the first Douglas Young had heard about conscription and he at once made up his mind to oppose it in Scotland, a decision which was strengthened by the timidity of the British Government over applying conscription in Northern Ireland.

Back in Scotland Douglas Young found nationalist opinion divided. Some wanted to oppose the war on pacifist grounds; others were in sympathy with the attitude of the Independent Labour Party; others were wanting to volunteer to fight for the Finns against Russia. The general opinion was that although theoretically Scotland was entitled to determine for herself how conscription should be applied nothing could be done now to assert her right practically and the only thing to do was to fall in at the orders of the British Government. Douglas Young was not prepared to fall in. He considered that it was his duty to resist unconstitutional conscription whether for military service or as was now threatened for industrial work. By the spring of 1942 Scottish workers were being compelled to go and work in the Midlands and elsewhere in England where naturally with the Whitehall bureaucracy in charge the big English industrialists were getting most of the new factories. Scottish opinion became restive but the restiveness was not carried beyond words; Douglas Young decided to cut the cackle and get to the horses. When his age group was dereserved in bureaucratic English and he received his call-up papers he refused to obey the order to submit himself for the medical examination demanded.

This meant a summons to appear in a sheriff court where Douglas Young, six feet six inches tall, thin and bearded, argued with an elderly Sheriff that the Treaty of Union had conveyed no power to the Parliament of the United Kingdom to conscribe the Scots for foreign service. The Sheriff, who must have thought that he had something like a totem pole before him, congratulated Douglas Young on the able presentation of his case and then, expressing regret, sentenced him to twelve months' imprisonment. Young appealed to the High Court of Justiciary and was released on bail until his case came up.

While the appeal was pending Douglas Young by a small majority was elected Chairman of the Council of the Scottish National Party at the Annual Conference.

Then came the appeal when for an hour and a half their lordships listened to Douglas Young arguing that the National Service Act was:

(i) contrary to the Common Law of Scotland, as was proved by references to a number of statutes and other constitutional actings;

(ii) contrary to the Scoto-Anglic Treaty of Union which constituted the United Kingdom of Great Britain and the British Parliament;

(iii) unknown to the Law of Scotland, being a statute of a foreign state, *viz.*, the Kingdom of England;

(iv) a fundamental nullity, being a pretended statute of what is now a legal non-entity, *viz.*, the so-called Great Britain, which is deficient in the qualifications of a legal personality by International Law.

The court in dismissing the appeal paid no attention to any of the contentions put forward by the appellant but instead, no doubt because they found it easier to answer, invented for the appellant a contention he had never put forward and solemnly refuted it. This was that all the acts of the Imperial Parliament since 1707 were null and void and of no effect. This imaginary proposition they had no hesitation in rejecting. The court's handling of the case was criticised by many Scots lawyers, but cautiously in private; the court with equal caution forbade the publication of the case in the law reports which suggests that the Judges did not relish any publicity for a performance hardly up to the high level of Scottish justice.

After Douglas Young came out of the prison of Saughton on the outskirts of Edinburgh there was a by-election in Kirkcaldy Burgh, and himself a Fifer he was adopted as candidate by the Scottish Nationalists. His opponents were a local Labour town councillor supporting the Coalition Government and a pacifist standing as a Christian Socialist. Fifty-two per cent of the voters supported the Coalition candidate, forty-two per cent voted for Douglas Young.

The Scotsman commented:

> "There is here something the Government and the Scottish Office must take note of. Mr. Douglas Young is a fervid Scottish Nationalist who refused from conviction to obey the law of a Government whose authority to conscribe Scotsmen he denied. Kirkcaldy Burgh's electors, instead of ridiculing his constitutional claim, went to the polls and voted for him in large numbers."

Presently Douglas Young drafted a statement of Scotland's claim to Dominion status which the National Party Council submitted to the Dominion Premiers, all of whom except Mr. Curtin, the Australian Premier, declared themselves in favour of such a claim. Whether this annoyed Mr. Ernest Bevin is not clear, but the Ministry of Labour pestered Douglas Young to apply for a job and when he refused to pay attention to the order he was brought up before another sheriff court.

Ernest Bevin had by now become unreasonable under the effect of dictatorial responsibility. I had had occasion to challenge his bull-headedness earlier. In the spring of 1941 there was a scare about the possibility of a German landing in Scotland. I received a sealed envelope in which was enclosed another sealed envelope and finally in a third sealed envelope an order to say that if Barra was attacked I was to hold the island to the last man and the last round for twenty-four hours. By the same post my driver Kenneth MacCormick, a sergeant in the Home Guard, was called up for the R.A.F. with orders to report to Music Hall, Edinburgh. I wrote to Music Hall, Edinburgh, to say that it was impossible to release Sergeant MacCormick at present because he was the only man on the island who knew how to put cars out of action and how to keep the telephone working. At the same time I wrote to Ernest Bevin to ask him to let the R.A.F. know that in view of the orders I had received from Northern Highland Command Sergeant MacCormick's call-up must be postponed. Replies came from R.A.F., Music

Hall, and from the Ministry of Labour to say that Mr. [*sic*] MacCormick must report in Edinburgh. I informed the R.A.F. that under my orders Sergeant MacCormick would not present himself at Music Hall until I thought he could leave the island of Barra without impairing the efficiency of the Home Guard, and I notified Mr. Bevin that he would be personally responsible if I was hindered in taking suitable steps to hold the island of Barra for twenty-four hours because the Ministry of Labour insisted on removing a man I considered indispensable to carry out a military order. Back came replies from Music Hall, Edinburgh, and Whitehall. The R.A.F. were pained by the attitude I had adopted about Mr. [*sic*] MacCormick because if he did not present himself at Music Hall, Edinburgh, by such and such a date the R.A.F. would be under the disagreeable necessity of having to send Air Force Police to arrest him. The Ministry of Labour wrote to say that the Minister of Labour could not possibly accept personal responsibility for anything that happened in Barra.

To the R.A.F. threat I replied with a counter-threat: if Air Force Police arrived in Barra to arrest Sergeant MacCormick I should immediately arrest the Air Force Police for trying to obstruct me in carrying out a military order. To the Ministry of Labour I replied that the Minister was a servant of the public not as he seemed to suppose its master and it was idle for him to disclaim any personal responsibility in the matter because if anything went wrong in Barra and I survived I would pin the responsibility to him publicly when the war was over. I added that I was so shocked by the attitude of the Ministry of Labour and the R.A.F. that I was sending copies of the whole correspondence to the Prime Minister. There was a silence for ten days at the end of which I received a letter from the Prime Minister's private secretary to say that Mr. Churchill sympathised with my difficulties but that he did not feel he could intervene. By the same post came a letter from the Ministry of Labour to say that Mr. MacCormick's call-up had been deferred for six months.

Ernest Bevin had been much irritated by criticism of his

high-handed way of moving Scottish workers down to England, and he welcomed an opportunity to assert himself over Douglas Young, who was sentenced to the maximum of three months' imprisonment. The scholar appealed on two grounds:

(i) that authorisation of the regulation he was charged with contravening was beyond the powers conveyed to the United Kingdom Parliament by the Treaty of Union;

(ii) alternatively, that even if that were not so, the Minister of Labour and his officers had no authority to ignore Article XVIII of the Treaty of Union in giving effect to the regulation.

With a sad show of pusillanimity another set of Scots judges refused to hear the appeal and committed the appellant to gaol. Caledonia douce and mild is no fit nurse for a poetic child like Douglas Young, and anyway this is not the place to argue about the legal rights and wrongs of his case. It would be equally inappropriate to argue whether William Douglas Home was right or wrong in his view about unconditional surrender. The point is that both he and Douglas Young were prepared to carry their beliefs far beyond inconvenience, the acceptation of which Sir James FitzJames Stephen recognised as a test of moral courage in the definition quoted earlier.

Both Douglas Home and Douglas Young knew that their actions in time of war would excite strong disapproval from their fellows. This was particularly so in the case of Douglas Home. Every class has its conventions but none is narrower than the aristocratic convention of behaviour.

In time of war the expression either by word or action of what seems in the geared-up state of popular opinion unpatriotic criticism is always a difficult decision for the individual to take. Towards the end of November in 1917 the Marquess of Lansdowne sent a letter to *The Times* in which he advocated a negotiated peace with the Central Powers. This letter the editor of *The Times* refused to print and it appeared instead in the *Daily Telegraph*. The outcry was clamorous and that such a statesman-like proposal could be received with such a baying and barking and yapping by a pack of outraged patriots seems to-day fantastic.

The Government issued a semi-official communiqué to declare that Lord Lansdowne had not mentioned his letter beforehand to any Member of the Government. Mr. Asquith who was suspected by some of having prompted Lord Lansdowne had to make it clear in a speech at Birmingham that he had no knowledge of the letter until he saw it in the Press and that he had no responsibility, direct or indirect, for its terms.

Mr. Lloyd George who not so many years earlier had been reviled as a pro-Boer because he had tried to promote sanity over the South African War was now severe on Lord Lansdowne. Speaking at a dinner given by the Benchers of Gray's Inn, the Prime Minister declared it was a great misfortune that if Lord Lansdowne meant to say exactly the same thing as President Wilson he did not carry out that intention. He did not feel that the extreme pacifist was dangerous but he must solemnly warn the nation against the men who thought that there was a half-way house between defeat and victory. "To end a war entered upon in order to enforce a treaty, without reparation for the infringement of that treaty, merely by entering into a new and more comprehensive treaty, would indeed be a farce in the setting of a tragedy."

And so the hell of Passchendaele was prolonged. The Bolshevik Revolution raged. The dark dreams of an insignificant egopath were given nurture and allowed to become significant. The civilisation of Europe was imperilled, and many more thousands died. Perhaps William Douglas Home should have realised that what Lord Lansdowne had failed to achieve by moral courage in 1917 he was unlikely to achieve in 1944.

If it demands moral courage to take a stand by word or action in the middle of a mundane war it demands just as much to support a minority which because it is a minority is driven to fight in a way that shocks people. What those in the majority never seem able to grasp is that if a minority is driven to fight for its cause the majority is responsible for the horrors that inevitably ensue. The blame for what happened in Ireland rests on a British Government determined to beat a weaker nation to its knees. It seemed a hideous outrage to quiet folk across the

Irish Channel when they read of British officers pulled out of bed and shot in front of their wives. It was forgotten that to quiet folk in Ireland it seemed a hideous outrage when young men who had taken part in the Easter Rising of 1916 were shot by orders of a British general in consignments. If the yellow press had existed in the time of William Wallace or William Tell their murderous exploits would have roused as much loathing as those of Sinn Feiners or E.O.K.A. terrorists.

A man to whose moral courage a tribute must be paid was the late Earl of Longford. He never failed to speak out for Ireland at a time when it was considered a social crime to defend the Irish rebels. He was doubly courageous because his background in Ireland was that of the traditional Ascendancy and the Irish themselves for some time could not bring themselves to believe that he was sincere in his devotion to an Ireland which had won her independence. However, he was able to express that devotion in a practical way, and enjoyed, what not all who display moral courage enjoy, full recognition of his patriotism.

How different was the fate of Roger Casement whose display of moral courage was rewarded by the quicklime of a felon's grave in Pentonville.

The story of Roger Casement is unpleasant reading for those who cherish the illusion either that British justice is never influenced by the prevailing climate of emotional opinion or that British fair play can be taken for granted.

Roger Casement after a valuable life of consular service was knighted and retired on a pension. He belonged to an Ulster family and, although his mother was Catholic, he himself was brought up as a Protestant. Even when he was still an official under the Foreign Office he dreamed of an independent Ireland and after the outbreak of the First World War he went to Germany and tried to persuade Irish prisoners-of-war to let themselves be formed into an Irish Brigade to fight under German command. This Casement himself strongly denied at the trial, and it may well be that he had in his mind to trick the Germans over this. Certainly the Germans were inclined to regard him with suspicion. Then getting to hear of the imminence of the prepared rising in Ireland he felt that it was his duty to warn his fellow-countrymen of the impossibility of such a rebellion being successful. So he persuaded the Germans to land him in Ireland from a submarine which was escorting a vessel loaded with arms for the insurgents. As so often with French attempts to support Ireland or Scotland in the past the enterprise was a fiasco, the vessel with the arms being sunk and Casement himself captured by the police on the coast of Kerry and sent from there first to Dublin and then to London. On Easter Sunday he was taken to Scotland Yard and questioned by Sir Basil Thomson as he would become, the Assistant Commissioner of Metropolitan Police, who specialised in spy-catching during the war and Captain Reginald Hall, the Director of the Intelligence Division at the Admiralty, afterwards Admiral Sir Reginald Hall.

In the course of this interrogation Casement said: "Some Irishmen are afraid to act, but I was not afraid to commit high treason and I am not endeavouring to shield myself at all. I face all the consequences. All I ask you to believe is that I have done nothing dishonourable, which you will one day learn. I have done nothing treacherous to my country. I have committed perhaps many follies in endeavouring to help my country according to what I thought was best, and in this last act of mine in going back to Ireland I came with my eyes wide open and knowing exactly what I was going to do, knowing that you were bound to catch me. Knowing all the circumstances, I came from a sense of duty, in which if I dared to tell you the fact, you would be the first to agree with me."

Casement was alluding to the rising which was to happen next day and of the imminence of which obviously Thomson and the D.I.D. were ignorant. The reputations of both of them for omniscience were always ludicrously inflated.

While the interrogation at Scotland Yard was going on, the police went to Casement's old rooms in Ebury Street and removed some trunks he had left behind when he gave up the lodgings. In one of these trunks were the five volumes of diaries by the contents of which Thomson was deeply shocked.

His own behaviour in Hyde Park nine years later hardly suggested such sensitive purity.

On Easter Monday the rising started, and when the news reached Scotland Yard Casement was pressed for information about the leaders; but they could extract nothing from him.

On the following day the newly elected member for East Herts, the unspeakable Pemberton Billing, asked Mr. Asquith at question time in the House of Commons, to the accompaniment of loud cheers, whether it was true that Sir Roger Casement had been brought to London and whether he could "give the House and the nation an assurance that the traitor will be shot forthwith."

That afternoon Thomson was summoned to a conference with Sir F. E. Smith, the Attorney-General, to be told that the Cabinet had decided on a civil trial for high treason. Thomson, Hall, and the naval and military authorities wanted a court-martial, and in the hope of persuading the Government to agree to this Thomson had Casement transferred from Brixton to the Tower of London.

The wretched Casement was now shut in a cell with two soldiers to guard him day and night. The window except for a single pane of glass was boarded up. The sentry outside had to look in through this all the time, and the electric light was never turned off night and day. He was deprived of writing materials and not allowed to communicate even with a lawyer. His clothes, which were those in which he had waded ashore in Kerry, were filthy. His tie, bootlaces and braces were taken from him as a precaution against suicide. He had to shuffle about in laceless boots holding up his trousers with his hands. To crown it the cell was verminous and the prisoner's arms, neck and back were swollen by the bugs feeding on him.

In this condition he was kept for over a fortnight while the authorities argued whether he was to have a civil trial or a trial by court-martial.

At last on 15th May Gavan Duffy, the solicitor acting for Casement, persuaded the authorities to transfer the prisoner to Brixton to await his trial in the High Court. Thomson and Hall were disappointed but they decided to prejudice the case against Casement by the despicable device of having Photostats made of those portions of the diaries that were most likely to shock people. These they showed to British journalists, and what they thought more usefully to American journalists.

The trial began on 26th June and lasted three days. It was clear from the start that Casement did not have a chance of being acquitted. There was irony in the fact that the Attorney-General when he was "Galloper" Smith just before the war had done nothing to discourage the Orange stalwarts from appealing to Germany for help to defend Ulster against Home Rule. It may be doubted if the weight of guilt for the outbreak of the First World War that may rest on Unionist shoulders is even yet comprehended. There is no doubt whatever that if the Germans had not supposed that Great Britain was preoccupied with Irish troubles they might have paused long enough for the tragedy to be averted.

After the verdict of guilty, Casement was asked if he had anything to say before sentence was pronounced. Towards the end of a moving and eloquent speech he taunted F. E. Smith with the prospect of becoming Lord Chancellor one day with these words:

> "The difference between us was that the Unionist champions chose a path they felt would lead to the woolsack; while I went a road I knew must lead to the dock. And the events prove we were both right. The difference between us was that my 'treason' was based on a ruthless sincerity that forced me to attempt in time and season to carry out in action what I said in word, whereas their treason lay in verbal incitements that they knew need never be made good. And so, I am prouder to stand here to-day in the traitor's dock to answer this impeachment than to fill the place of my right honourable accusers."

The future Lord Birkenhead was obviously flicked on the raw by this taunt, and with a curious loss of dignity muttered in an audible aside, "Change places with him? Nothing doing!" He was a great man, was F. E. Smith, but he was a small man at that moment when he rose and ostentatiously walked out of the court with his hands in his pockets.

The Lord Chief Justice who was supported by Mr. Justice Avory and Mr. Justice Horridge pronounced the death sentence, at the end of which Mr. Justice Avory deprived of the pleasure he always seemed to take in sentencing a man to death managed to associate himself with it by saying " Amen! "

Casement's appeal as expected was dismissed and the Attorney-General refused his fiat for an appeal to the House of Lords.

Meanwhile, photostats of the pages from the diaries were being sedulously circulated both in the United Kingdom and in the United States. The Assistant Commissioner of the Metropolitan Police and the D.I.D., deprived of their court-martial, were determined to discourage any petitions for a reprieve by making possible signatories chary of helping to save the life of a pervert. The names of Sir Basil Thomson and Admiral Sir Reginald Hall need not be tainted with any suspicion of circulating forgeries engineered by themselves: there can be little doubt that Casement wrote the entries himself and that unless he was indulging himself in erotic fantasies, which is not improbable, he did behave in such a way as to suggest perversion on the edge of insanity. Nevertheless, the use made of those diaries to secure a man's death remains a filthy blot on officialdom.

It is a relief to find forty well-known and honourable names at the foot of a petition which was drafted by Clement Shorter and presented to the Prime Minister by Sir Arthur Conan Doyle, a man of outstanding moral courage. Another petition to Mr. Asquith was drawn up by Bernard Shaw who did not sign it himself because he feared that his name at the bottom of it might prejudice the chance of getting certain other signatures. This is an indication of the pro-German cloud over Bernard Shaw at this date which was noted earlier.

Shaw brought his common sense to bear on the matter. He took advantage of the slight revulsion in Britain against the shooting in cold blood of young rebels who had surrendered to superior forces. The execution of James Connolly who had been severely wounded and was carried out strapped in a chair to be shot had sickened even some of the bitterest enemies of Ireland. So Shaw's petition pointed out to the Government that if Casement was hanged they would make a martyr of a man who had never been a national hero.

Petitions came from America in spite of the circulation of the diaries by British Intelligence agents in the United States.

While the case was *sub judice* the Press had been debarred from alluding to the homosexual revelations in the diaries, but as soon as Casement had been sentenced to death the *Daily Express* next morning described Casement as an "extremely degenerate traitor." On the day before Casement's appeal was heard the *Weekly Dispatch* observed:

> "Roger Casement's diary is being greatly discussed at the present time, and people are wondering whether Mr. Clement Shorter, who is raising an appeal for the reprieve of Casement has perused that remarkable document, and also Sir Arthur Conan Doyle."

Dr. H. Montgomery Hyde in his admirable introduction to the new edition of the Casement case in *Notable British Trials* says:

> "There is no doubt that the petitions, particularly Sir Arthur Conan Doyle's, would have attracted the signatures of some influential people, had it not been for the effect exercised by the diaries at this time. It is known for instance that Dr. Randall Davidson, the Archbishop of Canterbury, Dr. Hensley Henson, the Bishop[1] of Durham (who is said to have been shown a typed copy by King George V) and the Irish Nationalist leader, John Redmond (who was shown what he called this 'loathsome' matter by Augustine Birrell, the Chief Secretary for Ireland) all refused to sign petitions for Casement's reprieve in consequence of what they saw and accepted as true."

Now appears one of those dark bureaucratic figures who wield so much power behind the scenes. This was Sir Ernley Blackwell, the Legal Assistant Under-Secretary at the Home Office, who was asked to draw up a memorandum to help the Cabinet to decide whether the Royal prerogative should be sought on the ground

[1] He was in fact Dean of Durham at this date.

of insanity. Blackwell consulted Thomson who gave him copies of the diaries. In this memorandum Blackwell enlarged on the subject of homosexuality in what might have struck a suspicious mind as being curiously well-informed for a bachelor of close on fifty who would remain a bachelor until he was sixty-eight. In a second memorandum Blackwell wound up by writing: "So far as I can judge, it would be far wiser from every point of view to allow the law to take its course and by judicious means to use these diaries to prevent Casement attaining martyrdom."

Blackwell showed these memorandums to Thomson but told him that with such a weak Cabinet he did not know what the result would be. He was worried because Lord Crewe had circulated a letter from Miss Eva Gore-Booth, a sister of Countess Markiewicz who had been sentenced to death but reprieved for her part in the Easter Rising, in which it was asserted that Casement's object in going over to Ireland was to stop the rebellion. This had worried some of the "waverers" in the Cabinet, but in the end they surrendered to the popular desire for Casement to die.

What is distressing is to hear that Mr. Asquith approved of the effort to win over America by representing Casement as a homosexual whose life was not worth saving. True this statement rests on the authority of Sir Basil Thomson whose accuracy was always uncertain and whose veracity could never be relied upon. Thomson alleged that he had been told by one of the staff of the American Embassy that on 1st August two days before the execution Walter Page, the Ambassador, was dining at No. 10 Downing Street and that Asquith wanted to show him the diary. The Ambassador said he had already been given photographs of it, no doubt by Captain Hall through the American Naval Attaché. "Excellent," Asquith is said to have exclaimed, "and you need not be particular about keeping it to yourself."

Surely this story cannot be true, for it is difficult to believe that Asquith the day after such behaviour would write to Miss Gertrude Bannister the courteous letter he did write to her. She and her sister were Casement's nearest relatives in England and they had spent all they could of money and devoted energy on his defence. Miss Gertrude Bannister had made a personal appeal to the Prime Minister and he had promised to let her know the result of the final Cabinet meeting.

With his own hand he wrote: "It is with sincere pain (and only in compliance with your request) that I inform you that, after very full consideration, the Cabinet to-day came to the conclusion that there was not sufficient grounds for a reprieve. I need not assure you that I wish it had been possible for them to arrive at a different decision."

Another disagreeable thing to hear is that Cardinal Bourne refused a faculty to Father Cary, the Pentonville chaplain, to reconcile Casement to the Catholic Church until the condemned man signed an apology "expressing sorrow for any scandal he might have caused by his acts, public or private." This Casement "in all humility" declined to do, and here we must admire the moral courage that made him refuse to deny his country in the hour of his approaching death.

Father Cary took the right accorded to all priests of reconciling to the Church a dying man and heard Casement's confession, after which the condemned man put on paper his last reflections and hopes. That piece of paper was impounded by the prison authorities on the instructions of that sere Scottish bureaucrat, Sir Ernley Blackwell, but before it was seized Father McCarroll, the other Catholic chaplain, made a hurried copy of the document next morning; and this with a few unavoidable gaps reached Casement's friends.

Casement died bravely. Ellis the hangman declared he was the bravest man it fell to his unhappy lot to execute. The Government refused to let Ireland have his remains; they were put in quicklime beside the graves of murderers. Sir Ernley Blackwell in the name of the Home Secretary insisted that "the law requires that the body shall be buried within the walls of the prison." Gavan Duffy argued that this did not apply to an execution for high treason, but to this day the leatherbottoms of the Home Office have refused to let what is left of an unhappy patriot be taken back to the land for which he died.

There may be some who will refuse to admit that Roger Casement was an example of moral courage, but surely there must be many who will agree that his treatment was a fine display of moral cowardice. Yet will there be so many? A similar display of moral cowardice in the face of popular opinion was given when William Joyce was hanged after the last war for treason, although he was not a British subject. The public wanted Lord Haw-Haw to be hanged.

X

The man behind Sherlock Holmes

NOT MANY MEN IN THIS CENTURY have shown as much consistent moral courage as the creator of Sherlock Holmes and Dr. Watson showed right through the seventy years of his valuable life. His father was an architect who had become deputy to the head of Her Majesty's Office of Works in Edinburgh at a salary of £220 which by some thirty years later had been raised to £256. Charles Altamont Doyle came of an old Irish Catholic family of landed gentry, and was a brother of "Dicky" Doyle who was responsible for that long-loved cover of *Punch* which was done away with not so long ago to dispel any notion that *Punch* was old-fashioned. In 1855 he married Mary Foley who was then seventeen; four years later Arthur Conan Doyle was born in Picardy Place, Edinburgh, not a quarter of a mile away from the room in which these words are being written. Conan Doyle's grandfather, John Doyle, was a political caricaturist famous under the initials H. B. who had left behind in Ireland an estate ruined by the penal laws against Catholics and become a prominent figure in London society and upper Bohemia.

Conan Doyle was educated at Stonyhurst which the severe Jesuit discipline made a tough school for youth in those days. From Stonyhurst he went on to Edinburgh University where he took his degree in medicine in 1881. After a voyage as ship's surgeon in a steamship to the west coast of Africa he had to make up his mind about the future. He had no money of his own and without that the prospect for a young doctor in those days was not too bright. A letter came from his aunt who was living with her brother Richard in John Doyle's old house in Regent's Park to suggest that he should pay them a visit to discuss his future. If he wanted the financial help of these relations he felt he must let them know he had lost his faith. Sincerity always ruled Conan Doyle and he could not bring himself to accept help under false pretences. He wrote to his aunt to tell her that he had become an agnostic and that being the case it would not be fair to expect any help in his career from his family.

Perhaps only Irish Catholics will be able to appreciate fully the courageous sincerity of that young man of twenty-three.

Presently Conan Doyle's aunt wrote to say how much upset they all were over the news in his letter. Had he not been a little bit too impetuous? Was he so completely sure that he had lost his faith? Why did he not come down to London and talk matters over? In the dining-room of John Doyle's house round the table at which had sat so many famous figures of the first half of the nineteenth century from Walter Scott onwards Conan Doyle faced his aunt and two of his uncles. All of them were childless, all of them were anxious to help somebody to carry on the Doyle tradition which, whatever success might have come through the arts, was built upon the Catholic Church. For that Church their ancestors had given up all worldly advantages. What help could they conscientiously offer to one who was ready to betray the Faith? Conan Doyle pointed out that if he practised as a Catholic doctor he would be taking money for professing to believe in something in which he no longer did believe. He asked his uncles if they would do such a thing.

An argument about faith began. To the uncles it seemed the merest perversity of the young man that he would not have faith. Conan Doyle said they were talking as if faith could be attained by will-power. They must realise that he was incapable of accepting the Catholic religion. He was asked what he intended to do. He replied that he might go to sea again but that more probably he would try to get a house-surgeon's job at a hospital.

So he and his relatives parted; he seldom saw them again. When his Uncle Richard died the dining-room table at Cambridge Terrace was left to his Aunt Annette and when she died it was left to him. That dining-room table was deeply cherished by Conan Doyle. Not everybody has a dining-room table round which have sat most of the famous poets, novelists, painters and statesmen of half a century.

It will seem paradoxical to some to praise a man's moral courage in avowing himself an agnostic. Nevertheless, for an Irish Catholic or a Scottish Wee Free to avow his agnosticism demands an uncompromising sincerity which is not granted to many. That compulsion to proclaim the truth as Conan Doyle saw it was displayed in a variety of ways and for a variety of causes all through his life. He was unable to believe in any formal religion and even when he became absorbed in spiritualism in his latter days he would not attach to it a religious significance. For him the investigation of spiritualistic phenomena was a scientific investigation in which the object was to establish the truth.

Although Conan Doyle had renounced formal religion, he felt the need for a moral code in obedience to which he determined to regulate his life. He found this code in the rule of behaviour to which a medieval knight subscribed and a breach of which carried with it dishonour. Conan Doyle read widely about the Middle Ages when he was gathering material for his romance *The White Company*. Nobody was ever more suitably knighted than Conan Doyle; throughout his life he was chivalrous to women, he had no fear of powerful people or institutions, he fought injustice with his time and his purse; above all he never refused his help to those in need of it.

Conan Doyle will always be remembered as the creator of the most famous character in the world of fiction, and it is worth while to recall the burly Sherlock Holmes with a moustache of real life who worked as hard to solve a mystery as the lean clean-shaven Sherlock Holmes himself in the pages of a story, worked moreover not for a fee or even for his expenses but purely because his sense of justice and devotion to truth had been affronted, and because somebody was in great trouble.

From February to August in the year 1903 horses, cows and sheep were being horribly mutilated by what was presumably a madman in the fields round the village of Great Wyrley, some twenty miles from Birmingham. At the same time the police were receiving letters signed by various faked or forged names in which they were mocked for their incompetence. They were the same kind of letters as the police in Whitechapel had received from the maniac Jack the Ripper. They all revelled in the horrible details of the mutilations, and the writer of them claimed that he was the member of a gang which was intending by next November to start ripping up little girls in the same way as the animals. It is to be noted that in the first letter the police received there were several enthusiastic references to a life on the sea, but these were not repeated in later letters.

On the night of 17th August twenty policemen were patrolling the district and three of them were watching a field, going across which at half past six on the following morning a boy on his way to work came upon a pony from the neighbouring colliery lying in a stream of blood. The poor brute's belly had been ripped up by a sharp knife and it had bled almost to death. The boy shouted for help and the three policemen who had been watching the field came hurrying up followed presently by others. This was the eighth mutilation since February, all of which it is to be noted must have been performed by somebody who knew how to handle animals.

Inspector Campbell of the Staffordshire County Constabulary believed he knew who was guilty of the mutilations and he decided to arrest him. The suspect was the son of the Rev. Shapurji Edalji, a Parsee clergyman who for nearly thirty years had been vicar of Great Wyrley. He had married an Englishwoman by whom he had had three children. George, the eldest of these, was twenty-seven years old and practised as a solicitor in Birmingham. He lived at home, catching an early train every morning and returning home at half past six. He had taken an honours degree in law at Birmingham University, had been awarded several prizes by the Law Society, and had written a book on railway law. It might have been supposed, even by an exceptionally dull inspector, that this was the last person likely to wander about at night mutilating horses, cattle and sheep, but George Edalji was very dark and he had bulging eyes, and there was also what had happened between 1892 and 1895.

What happened then was that when George Edalji was at Rugeley School there had been a plague of anonymous letters in the neighbourhood, most of which were sent to the Rev. Shapurji Edalji. These letters were slipped in under the vicarage door; they did not come by post. In them the vicar's wife and daughter were abused, but mostly the abuse was for his eldest son George. Then bogus advertisements signed with the vicar's name appeared in newspapers, and postcards signed with his name were sent to various clergymen in different parts of the country. The vicar of a church in Essex was surprised to receive one morning the following postcard:

> Unless you apologise at once and by telegram for the outrageous hints you give in your sermons concerning my chastity, I shall expose your adultery and rape.
>
> S. EDALJI

Besides these letters and postcards various unpleasant "jokes" were played on the Edaljis. Their lawn was strewn with the contents of dustbins, and once a large key, belonging to Walsall Grammar School, was left on the vicarage doorstep. One offensive letter, nominally signed by a boy at the grammar school, was sent to the headmaster, but inquiries showed that the boy could not possibly be the author of the letter. Finally a bogus advertisement in the name of S. Edalji appeared in a Blackpool paper in December 1895, after which the nuisance which had lasted for three years stopped. In February 1903 began the mutilation of cattle by some instrument which made a long wound, causing a lot of blood to flow but not deep enough to kill the animal.

For some reason unfathomable, unless an ignorant prejudice against coloured people was its inspiration, the Chief Constable of Staffordshire, Captain the Hon. George Augustus Anson, got into his head that the writer of the letters signed S. Edalji was the vicar's eldest son, and from time to time he pestered the unfortunate vicar about this. It was useless to point out that George had never been to Walsall Grammar School, useless to protest that letters had been pushed under the door when George Edalji was in the house. The Chief Constable was convinced that the boy was the author of those letters, and continued to believe this after he left school to go to the university. When the Walsall Grammar School key was found on the doorstep of the vicarage the Chief Constable went so far as to write:

"I may say at once that I shall not pretend to believe any protestations of ignorance which your son may make about the key." Later he declared that he hoped to get him "a dose of penal servitude." However, the Chief Constable even with the help of the local police whom he had persuaded of George Edalji's guilt could not find a tittle of evidence, and after the letters ceased in December 1895 the Edalji family were left in peace.

When the mutilations began seven years later Captain Anson immediately decided that George Edalji was the culprit, brought special constables into the district and gave orders for the vicarage to be watched every night. Those orders were given before the anonymous letters started again. In one of these the madman wrote about a particularly skilful member of the gang:

> "He has got eagle eyes, and his ears is as sharp as a razor, and he is as fleet of foot as a fox, and as noiseless, and he crawls on all fours up to the poor beasts."

Eagle eyes? George Edalji had bulging eyes. Yes, he was certainly the offender, the sapient Captain Anson decided.

Then the letters began to accuse George Edalji of being a leading member of the gang:

> "Mr. Edalji is going to Brum . . . about how it's to be carried on with so many detectives about and I believe they are going to do some cows in the day-time instead of at night."

Now Captain Anson was presumably not mentally deficient. He had been Chief Constable of Staffordshire since 1888. He was a brother of a local magnate, the Earl of Lichfield. Yet by some process of idiotic reasoning he was convinced that George Edalji had written these letters to accuse himself. Not only did Captain Anson convince himself; he also convinced the police, and Inspector Campbell could feel sure of his chief's approbation when after the discovery of the maimed and dying pony on 18th August he arrived at the vicarage at eight o'clock that morning. George Edalji had left the house nearly an hour ago to catch his train to Birmingham. Mrs. Edalji and her daughter were at breakfast. Inspector Campbell told her to show him her son's clothing, and any weapon he possessed. Then they searched the house, but the only weapon they could find was a case of four razors belonging to the vicar, which were later proved chemically to be free of any trace of blood. However, they did find a pair of George Edalji's boots stained with black mud: the soil in the field where the pony had been mutilated was a reddish-yellow clay. They also found a pair of serge trousers stained with black mud round the bottom of them; they then found an old house-coat, the sleeve of which had some dark stains which Inspector Campbell hoped optimistically might have been made by the spurting blood of the slashed pony. He asserted that the coat was damp, which the vicar denied. He then declared that he could see horse-hairs on the coat. The vicar took the coat to the window and asked the inspector to show him a single horse-hair.

The police took the coat. Meanwhile, the pony had been put out of its misery and a strip of its hide was cut off. This strip was put in a bundle with George Edalji's clothes. The result of this disgraceful carelessness, which may or may not have been intentional, was that the police-doctor on examining the coat was able to find twenty-nine horse-hairs on it. He reported that the stains on the coat, with one possible exception, were food stains.

Later on that day George Edalji was arrested in his Birmingham office. On his way to the police station he said he had been expecting for some time to be arrested. Of course the wretched man had been aware of the cruel rumours flying around thanks to Captain Anson's attitude. This remark was noted down and it was used at the trial as evidence of poor Edalji's guilty conscience.

Under questioning at the police station he said that he returned home from his office at 6.30 p.m. on 17th August. He did some work, and later walked along the main road to the bootmaker in Bridgtown, where he arrived shortly after 8.30 p.m. He was then wearing a blue serge coat and trousers. Knowing that supper would not be ready before 9.30 he walked for a while. This accounted for the black mud on his trousers. After supper he went to bed. He slept in the same bedroom as his father, and had been sleeping there for seventeen years. He left the bedroom at 6.40 next morning to catch his train.

The night of 17th August had been wild and wet between midnight and dawn. George Edalji's father who suffered from lumbago had been awake most of the night. He testified that he always kept the bedroom door locked and that he must have known if his son had gone out of the room.

The populace was hostile to Edalji. The maimings had naturally roused much indignation, and the mere fact of his arrest was enough to rouse mob emotion. On the way in a cab to appear before the magistrates at Cannock an angry crowd attacked the vehicle and pulled the door off its hinges.

One of the Birmingham papers reported that the most widely held explanation for Edalji's behaviour was that he had been sacrificing the animals to heathen gods. This kind of ignorant gossip was not proceeded against for contempt of court. It may have been the Chief Constable's own theory; his credulity was uncurbed.

On 20th October, 1903, George Edalji was tried at the Staffordshire Quarter Sessions before a county justice whom Shakespeare would have recognised as Justice Shallow. He was so ignorant of the law that a barrister had to be engaged to advise him.

When the Cannock magistrates committed Edalji to trial the police had argued that the crime was committed between 8 and 9.30 p.m. Unfortunately for this theory witnesses came forward to testify to having seen the accused on the way to and from the bootmaker's, and the bootmaker testified to the time of his arrival. Moreover, when the pony was discovered in the morning it was still bleeding and a veterinary surgeon testified that the wound could not have been inflicted before 2.30 a.m. at the earliest.

So when the case was put before a jury the Prosecution claimed that the crime had been committed between 2 a.m. and 3 a.m. Edalji must have got out of the vicar's bedroom unnoticed by his father, dodged the police watching the house, walked half a mile and crossed the railway line, maimed the pony and returned home by a roundabout way through the fields.

Sergeant Robinson testified that, although there had been six constables watching the vicarage on the previous night, he could not be sure how many were watching it on the night of the 17th. The feeling of the jury was that the night had been too wet and stormy for the constables to hang around the vicarage in such weather, thereby giving Edalji an opportunity to get away unobserved.

Next, a constable testified that he had looked around the place where the pony had been maimed, and had picked out from the numerous footprints of sightseers what he thought were likely to be the footprints of the accused. So he had taken Edalji's boot with the black mud on it and pressed it into the soil beside one of these likely prints, getting yellowish-red clay on that boot for the first time. After this he measured the impression made and judged it to be the same as the other impressions he had picked out as likely.

"Were those footprints photographed?" asked the defence.

"No, sir."

"Was a cast made of them?"

"No, sir."

"Then where is the evidence? Why didn't you dig up a clod of earth, so as to get a perfect impression?"

"Well, sir, the ground was too soft in one place and too hard in another."

"But how did you measure the footprints?"

"With bits of stick, sir. And a straw."

Yet this farcical evidence impressed the jury, some of whose heads must have been as hard and others as soft as the ground the constable failed to dig up.

Then that handwriting expert, Gurrin, testified that in his opinion Edalji had written the letters accusing himself of cattle maiming. Gurrin's "expert" testimony had already sent Adolf Beck to prison in 1896: it was now to help in sending another innocent man to prison.

The jury found George Edalji guilty and Justice Shallow, after indignantly denying that the case should have been heard in London on account of the local prejudice, sentenced Edalji to penal servitude for seven years.

While this unfortunate man was awaiting trial another horse was maimed, but the prosecution told the jury that this must have been more work by the Wyrley Gang of whose doings they had heard in the letters written by the prisoner. A month later when Edalji was in Lewes Gaol another anonymous letter in his handwriting according to the expert Gurrin was sent, and yet another horse was mutilated. Meanwhile, in Lewes Gaol, Edalji was set to work making nose-bags for horses.

After the conviction a petition signed by ten thousand people including several hundred lawyers was sent to the Home Office asking for the evidence to be reconsidered, but Akers-Douglas who was then Home Secretary did nothing. A friend of Edalji, R. D. Yelverton, a former Chief Justice of the Bahamas, continued to put forward the arguments for reconsideration of the case, and after Edalji had been transferred to Portland enlisted the help of the weekly newspaper *Truth*. Then suddenly one day after he had served three years of his sentence Edalji was told that he had been released under police supervision. He had been struck off the roll of solicitors. He did not know what he was to do. So he appealed to Conan Doyle.

Conan Doyle worked on Edalji's case from December 1906 to the following August. During this time he did no work of his own. He paid all the expenses involved. And he discovered who was really guilty of the crime of which Edalji had been accused and found guilty. He did not meet Edalji himself until early in January 1907. He had made an opportunity to meet him in the foyer of the Grand Hotel, Charing Cross. Conan Doyle was a little late and when he arrived he saw a dark man reading a paper which he was holding close to his eyes sideways.

Conan Doyle went forward and (we hear the very tones of Sherlock Holmes) " You are Mr. Edalji," he said. " Don't you suffer from astigmatic myopia? Don't you wear glasses?"

Edalji told him that he had consulted two oculists without success. They had been unable to fit him with glasses that were any use. Conan Doyle asked him if this point had not been raised at his trial.

Edalji replied that he had wanted to call an optician as a witness, but his legal advisers had insisted that the evidence against him was too palpably ridiculous for that to be necessary.

Conan Doyle realised that at night Edalji would be incapable of finding his way about in any place not absolutely familiar to him, but he wished to make sure that Edalji was not shamming near blindness. So he sent him to a well-known oculist, who reported that the myopia was even worse than Conan Doyle had supposed.

On 11th January, 1907, the first instalment of *The Case of Mr. George Edalji* was published in the *Daily Telegraph*. Conan Doyle tore the evidence to shreds, and then he turned on the Chief Constable. It was easy to excuse the feelings of uneducated countrymen towards the dark Edalji. It was not so easy to excuse the Chief Constable, an English gentleman who had disliked Edalji since 1892 and who had infected with his own prejudice the whole of the police force under his control.

One might have thought that after Conan Doyle's scathing exposure of his behaviour the authorities would have judged it wise to remove Captain the Hon. George Augustus Anson from his post. Not at all. He remained Chief Constable of Staffordshire until 1929. He was made a M.V.O. in this very year of 1907. He was made a C.B.E. in 1925. Finally he was made a K.C.B. in 1937, after which the Hon. Sir George Augustus Anson lived for another twenty years to reach the age of ninety. Probably in that life full of years and honours it never occurred to him to reproach himself for having destroyed the happiness of a family and almost ruined the life of a young man because that young man's skin was dark. The skin of the Hon. Sir George Anson, K.C.B., C.B.E., M.V.O., may not have been dark but it was certainly pachydermatous.

Mercifully public opinion was more sensitive to injustice than the Chief Constable of Staffordshire, and Conan Doyle's articles in the *Daily Telegraph* made a sensation.

What the public wanted to know was why George Edalji had been set free if he was still to be treated as guilty. The moribund Unionist Government had by now been replaced by a Liberal Government in which Herbert Gladstone was Home Secretary. Gladstone promised an investigation, but pointed out the difficulties by which such an investigation would be faced. Although a Court of Criminal Appeal had been under consideration for some time, it had not yet been instituted. The problem was how to reopen the case. Finally the time-honoured device to postpone the need for a bureaucratic or political decision was resorted to. The Home Secretary would appoint a committee of three to meet in private, examine the case, and recommend a course of action. Half a century later another Home Secretary would use the same tactics to avoid extending compassion to what was left of the mortal remains of an unjustly hanged man because such compassion might seem to imply that the judge, the prosecution and the police had blackened one of Justice's blinded eyes.

Conan Doyle did not protest against the delay involved by the Home Secretary's decision. He was now being Sherlock Holmes and was hot on the trail of the man who really was guilty of those bestial outrages.

On 29th January he wrote to his mother:

"The case I have against my quarry is already very strong. But I have five separate lines of inquiry on foot by which I hope to make it overwhelming. It will be a great stroke if I can lay him by the heels!"

The quarry evidently alarmed by the secret visits of Sherlock Holmes to the Wyrley neighbourhood, started to write letters to Conan Doyle.

"I know from a detective of Scotland Yard that if you write

to Gladstone and say you find Edalji is guilty after all they will make you a lord next year. Is it not better to be a lord than to run the risk of losing kidneys and liver. Think of all the ghoolish [*sic*] murders that are committed. Why then should you escape?"

And again:

"There was no education to be got at Walsall where that bloody swine [*here he named the headmaster of the Grammar School who had received one of those letters between* 1892 *and* 1895] was high school boss. He got the bloody bullet after the Governors were sent letters about him. Ha, ha."

And again:

"The proof of what I tell you is the writing he put in the papers when they loosed him out of prison where he ought to have been kept along with his dad and all black and yellow-faced Jews. . . . Nobody could copy his writing like that you blind fool."

"On the evidence of handwriting," Conan Doyle wrote, "I have come to one conclusion. I contend that the anonymous letters of 1892 to 1895 were the work of two persons: one a decently educated man, the other a foul-mouthed semi-literate boy. I contend that the anonymous letters of 1903 were written by that same foul-mouthed boy, then grown into a man in his twenties. On further evidence I contend that Foulmouth not only wrote the letters, but did the mutilations.

"Let us take the facts in the Wyrley mystery . . . and see what inferences we can draw from them.

"One point is so obvious that I wonder it has escaped notice. This is the extraordinarily long gap between the two sets of letters. Letters, childish hoaxes, abound up to late December of '95. Then, for nearly seven years, *nobody* gets an abusive letter. To me this did not suggest that the culprit had changed his whole character and habits overnight, reverting to them with equal malice in 1903. It suggested absence; that someone had been away during that time.

"Away where? Look at the very first letter in the outburst of 1903. In it the writer makes no less than three glowing allusions to the sea. He recommended an apprentice's life at sea; his mind was full of it. Taken in conjunction with the long absence, may we suppose that he has gone to sea and recently returned? . . . Where are we to look first for traces of this hypothetical person? Surely in the records of Walsall Grammar School."

To the Home Office Conan Doyle wrote:

> "My first step in the inquiry lay at Walsall. I must inquire whether there had been at the school, during the early nineties, a boy who (*a*) had a particular grudge against the headmaster, (*b*) was innately vicious, and (*c*) subsequently went to sea. I took this obvious step. And I got on the track of my man at once."

Between February and April Sherlock Holmes worked hard and with the testimony of each witness appended, he presented the Home Office with an unanswerable indictment against somebody whose name was not published and who was never charged. This creature had gone to sea as an apprentice in December 1895 and returned to Great Wyrley early in 1903. For ten months of 1902 he had served in a cattle-ship and had stolen a horse-lancet on board, of which Conan Doyle obtained possession. He showed that the guilty creature's elder brother had had a share in the 1892 letters.

The Special Commission appointed by the Home Secretary to examine the evidence in the trial consisted of Sir Albert de Rutzen, Sir Arthur Wilson and the Rt. Hon. J. L. Wharton, P.C. On 17th May their report was published.

The Commissioners reported that the conviction of George Edalji for feloniously maiming a horse was unsatisfactory, but that the Home Office would not have been warranted in interfering with it. They saw no reason to doubt that Edalji had written the anonymous letters. "Assuming him to be an innocent man he had to some extent brought his troubles on himself."

The Home Secretary then announced that he had decided to recommend Mr. Edalji for a free pardon, but that the case was not one for compensation.

In other words the white face of Captain the Hon. George Augustus Anson must be saved at the expense of George Edalji's brown face. And one reason for this was that Sir Albert de Rutzen's aunt was the first Countess of Lichfield and that she was the Chief Constable's grandmother. De Rutzen who had been London's Chief Magistrate was seventy-six when he examined the evidence in this disgraceful case but it is easier to presume that kinship rather than senescence was responsible for his betraying the Law he had served all his life.

The Home Secretary's announcement was not well received by the House of Commons where many awkward questions were asked. More serious as criticism of him was the restoration of Edalji to the roll of solicitors by the Law Society. The *Daily Telegraph* opened a subscription for him. Conan Doyle challenged the Home Office about the letters. The Home Office referred Conan Doyle to the Commissioners' report: "These letters can have only a very remote bearing on whether Edalji was rightly convicted in 1903."

I ask again a question I asked in a book [1] written by Wilfred Macartney who in 1928 was sentenced by Lord Chief Justice Hewart to ten years' penal servitude for some farcical "spying." The Baldwin Government was anxious to save its face over the fiasco of the Arcos Raid on the Russian Trade Delegation and therefore had to stage a bogyman trial. "What are these bureaucrats of the Home Office? Are they human beings who have won a place in the Civil Service by a competitive examination? Or are they pterodactyls fossilised by their own arteries?"

As mentioned in the previous chapter Conan Doyle had tried to obtain a reprieve for Roger Casement and by doing so had shown himself indifferent to hostile public opinion. Nearly twenty years later when public opinion about Casement had long recovered from war hysteria the Home Office refused the request of Mr. de Valera for the body of Roger Casement to be brought back to Ireland from that cold vile monument of nineteenth-century crassness and cruelty. The request was re-

[1] *Walls Have Mouths*, of which I wrote the prologue, epilogue and comments on various chapters.

fused because it was "the custom not to interfere with graves."

Conan Doyle, unimpressed and undiscouraged by Whitehall whitewash, set to work again with more articles in the *Daily Telegraph* under the title *Who wrote the letters?* Somehow he got hold of specimens of the handwriting of the two brothers whom he had named to the Home Office and sent these with the letters he had received from the same source to Dr. Lindsay Johnson, the leading European authority on handwriting who had given evidence for Dreyfus. His own opinion was confirmed by Lindsay Johnson. It had no effect on the Home Office. They refused to admit that there was any case against the principal culprit who was still writing these insane letters at intervals until 1913. Perhaps if Sherlock Holmes had not managed to get possession of his horse-lancet he would still have been maiming animals.

At the end of August in that year 1907 the Bill for the establishment of a Court of Criminal Appeal was finally passed, and Conan Doyle could consider it a wedding-present for his second marriage which took place three weeks later, for there is no doubt that the Edalji case coming on top of the Adolf Beck case was largely influential in overcoming conservative opposition to such a long needed Bill.

Conan Doyle had felt compassion for the unhappy Eurasian whose life had been shattered because a Chief Constable had taken a dislike to him, and whose future was left uncertain because the Chief Constable's reputation had to be preserved even if it involved the sacrifice of an individual of a lower caste.

Conan Doyle's attempt to right the wrong done to Oscar Slater was not inspired by compassion; he thought that Slater was a bad lot. Nevertheless, his study of the evidence convinced him that Slater was innocent of murdering Miss Marion Gilchrist, on the evening of 21st December, 1908 in Glasgow. When Oscar Slater was tried in the High Court of Justiciary in Edinburgh, sitting in the same cramped dock as that in which Madeleine Smith had sat just fifty-two years before, he was obviously so sure of the absurdity of the charge against him that he had not the slightest expectation of being found guilty. He listened unmoved to the tub-thumping speech of the Lord Advocate. This was Mr. Alexander Ure, K.C., who would one day become Lord Justice General with the title Lord Strathclyde. His speech stuffed with false statements and unfulfilled promises was a blot on Scottish advocacy, and he lacked even the decency to remain in Court when he had finished his vicious effort to take away a man's life. In the autumn of that same year he was accused by A. J. Balfour of telling a "frigid and calculated lie" at a political meeting. He told several fervid lies in the course of trying to put the rope round Oscar Slater's neck.

Slater heard without embarrassment the Lord Advocate tell the jury that a man who was capable of living on the immoral earnings of a prostitute was capable of murdering and robbing a lady, eighty-two years old. He heard the judge, Lord Guthrie, maundering on about his private life and then telling the jury that they must not let that influence their verdict. He remained in the dock during the jury's absence for an hour and ten minutes, looking completely at ease. But when the verdict of guilty was returned he called out to the judge, "My Lord, may I say one word? Will you allow me to speak?"

The judge told him to sit down while the torturing process of recording the verdict and sentence was slowly carried through. Then in a broken voice Slater cried:

"My Lord, my father and mother are poor old people. I came on my own account to this country, I came over to defend my right. I know nothing about the affair. You are convicting an innocent man."

The judge told the prisoner's counsel to advise his client to reserve anything he had got to say for the Crown authorities.

Then the bewildered and unhappy German Jew cried out again:

"My Lord, what shall I say? I came over from America, knowing nothing of the affair, to Scotland to get a fair judgment. I know nothing about the affair, absolutely nothing. I never heard the name. I know nothing about the affair. I do not know how I could be connected with the affair.

I came from America on my own account. I can say no more."

That outburst was so clearly the outburst of an innocent man that the jury (and six of the fifteen had voted against a verdict of guilty) were obviously uncomfortable. Moreover, the Glasgow Press which had been indulging in a debauch of sensational rumours, including even one that Miss Gilchrist was Oscar Slater's mother, now began to criticise the piffling identifications on which the Crown relied to prove Slater's guilt. Public opinion was dissatisfied. A petition for a reprieve was launched and signed by 20,000 people. The execution had been fixed for 27th May. On the morning of 25th May the sentence of death was commuted to penal servitude for life.

Slater's lawyer conscious of what Conan Doyle had done for Edalji sent him the very careful memorial he had written on the case, acting on which after consulting with Lord Guthrie the judge, Lord Pentland, the Secretary of State for Scotland, had reprieved Slater. Conan Doyle read this memorial and was convinced by it that Slater might be innocent. Then in April 1910 the trial of Oscar Slater was published in the *Notable Scottish Trials* series under the superlative editorship of William Roughead. Conan Doyle studied the complete evidence and after pondering over it came to the conclusion that Slater *was* innocent. He started a campaign in the Press and in 1912 his booklet *The Case of Oscar Slater* was published. In this he asked if the theft of jewels had been the murderer's object? The evidence suggested that he was really looking for some document, possibly a will. The stolen brooch which had taken the Glasgow police to New York had been a false clue and Slater's anxiety to be extradited was an indication of his innocence. And how had Slater got into Miss Gilchrist's flat? Either he must have been admitted by Miss Gilchrist herself or he must have had duplicate keys of the two patent locks.

Sherlock Holmes's deductions were in his best vein; but they were merely deductions, and the authorities were not disturbed.

In March 1914 when Conan Doyle was on the other side of the Atlantic, Detective-Lieutenant J. T. Trench of the Glasgow police, whose conscience had been tormenting him ever since he had been one of the police officers who investigated and gave evidence in the Slater case, could stand it no longer and confided to David Cook, a Glasgow solicitor, that evidence vital to Slater's defence had been suppressed by the police. Helen Lambie, Miss Gilchrist's maid, who was the chief witness in the identification of Slater had recognised the man in the flat and told a female relation of the murdered woman who it was.

The Scottish Secretary, Mr. McKinnon Wood, unwillingly consented to an inquiry but made a tragic farce of it by ordering it to be held in secret, refusing to allow the prisoner or his agent to be present, and worst of all by insisting that the witnesses were not to be sworn. Mr. Gardner Millar, K.C., the Sheriff of Lanarkshire, was appointed to conduct the inquiry and make the report upon it. It was unfortunate for Oscar Slater that the inquiry was not in the hands of a former Sheriff of Lanarkshire, Sir Archibald Alison. He would never have been afraid to speak out for justice. In 1862 he had saved the life of Jessie McLachlan who had been condemned to death for a murder committed by a wicked old man of eighty-seven. In his *Autobiography* he wrote:

> "There is no event in my life to which I look back with more pleasure than the hand I had in her deliverance; and that the best and most elaborate law paper I ever wrote was composed in my seventieth year, to shield a prisoner threatened with death for what would in the circumstances have been a judicial murder."

Gardner Millar's report was published in June 1914 as a Government White Paper, a galaxy of asterisks taking the place of vital evidence it was considered wiser to expunge. After all, the Sheriff of Lanarkshire had been Legal Secretary to the Lord Advocate who was now the Lord Justice General. It would not conduce to respect for the High Court of Justiciary if the public should suspect what is the equivalent of the Lord Chief Justice in England of having connived at the suppression of evidence to secure a conviction. It would be more comfortable for everybody except the prisoner if a German Jew remained where he was. So Mr. McKinnon Wood, the Secretary of State for Scotland, was able to announce he was satisfied that no case had been established to justify him in advising any interference with the sentence.

In the report of the secret inquiry Trench's revelation was thus disposed of:

> " At 7.15 on the night of the murder Lambie came up to the house of a Miss Birrell, a relative of the deceased, and said—' Oh, Miss Birrell, Miss Gilchrist has been murdered. I saw the man who did it. I think it was A. B. I'm sure it was A. B.' Lambie told the same to Detectives Pyper and Dorman. Shown a sketch of Slater on 3rd January, 1909, Lambie failed to recognise it. Asked by Detective Trench if A. B. was not the man, she replied—' It's gey funny if it wasn't him I saw.' This rested on the statement of Trench. Neither Miss Birrell nor Lambie nor the other officers confirmed it."

None of them was on oath it will be remembered.

The most disgraceful feature of the Slater case apart from the flaunting of justice in the trial itself was the treatment of Detective-Lieutenant John Thomson Trench. He was suspended a couple of weeks after the White Paper and the Chief Constable of Glasgow reported him to the Glasgow magistrates for a breach of discipline in communicating to Mr. Cook the lawyer what had been lying so heavily upon his conscience for five years. In spite of Trench's being able to show the letter from the Scottish Secretary asking for his information in writing, the magistrates sacked Trench from the Glasgow Police. He appealed to McKinnon Wood who ignored his letter. At the age of forty-five Trench enlisted in the Royal Scots Fusiliers and having been in the Black Watch before he joined the police was appointed Provost Sergeant of Stirling. The regiment was due to sail with the 52nd Lowland Division for Gallipoli on 14th May, 1915. The day before he sailed he was arrested by the Glasgow police on a charge of receiving stolen jewellery. At the same time Mr. Cook, the lawyer in whom he had confided, was arrested on the same charge, which went back to 19th January of the previous year.

Luckily for Trench when he was at last brought to trial on 17th August the Lord Justice Clerk was in charge of the case, not the Lord Justice General. He made some severe comments on the way the case had been handled by the Crown and practically directed the jury to find the two accused not guilty. This they did to the applause of the spectators in court. Trench rejoined his regiment and served in France with the rank of quartermaster-sergeant, but this man of such integrity and moral courage was greatly affected by the persecution he had suffered and died at the age of fifty in the following year. Two years later David Cook, who had been equally affected, died also.

When Conan Doyle came back to England soon after the issue of the Government White Paper he realised that A. B. who was a close relative of Miss Gilchrist was the murderer and that his speculation about the will was probably correct. For another thirteen years Conan Doyle never ceased to badger the authorities on Slater's behalf. In 1925 the Secretary for Scotland again found no justification for his advising interference with the sentence.

Then in 1927 William Park, a Glasgow journalist who had been a friend of Trench, wrote *The Truth about Oscar Slater*.

> "Dedicated to the memory of the late Lieutenant John T. Trench, King's Medallist, Glasgow, who, as a public officer of the police force, actuated by an inspiring sense of justice sacrificed his career and his pension in a personal attempt to rescue from a life's detention in prison, and with a desire to save others from the risk of a similar cruel fate, a man whom he believed on his conscience to have been wrongfully convicted in the Scottish High Court of Justiciary, and for which noble act he was dismissed and ruined."

Park's book for the first time told the public what Trench's evidence had been without asterisks. The murderer was a nephew of Miss Gilchrist who was going to leave her money to the daughter of an illegitimate daughter of her own.[1] This confirmed Conan Doyle's theory that the murderer had wanted

[1] It is possible that two nephews were involved. This solution is well argued by Mr. Jack House in his recently published book, *A Square Mile of Murder* (Chambers), which gives many more details about the Oscar Slater case.

a will not jewellery. The English Press took up the case with severe criticism of Scottish legal procedure. Sir John Gilmour, the Scottish Secretary, in order to avoid having to hold another inquiry decided in November 1927 to release Slater after serving nearly nineteen years of penal servitude for a crime he never committed.

Conan Doyle now provided money to press for an appeal. Further evidence was tendered and in July 1928 the sentence was quashed by the Court of Criminal Appeal, Oscar Slater being awarded £6000 to compensate him for losing nearly nineteen years of his life.

A new Lord Justice General presided over the appeal. Fortunately for Slater Lord Strathclyde was now on his death-bed. The verdict of the Court of Appeal did its best to whitewash him by abstaining from criticism of his lethal speech at the trial and made the grounds for quashing the verdict a misdirection by old Lord Guthrie who was dead. The Scottish Office took advantage of the way the verdict of the appeal was expressed to deduct £1500 from the £6000 of compensation for the cost of the appeal. Such meanness will serve as a classic example of the soul-destroying indifference of bureaucracy. Evidently there were as many pterodactyls in the Scottish Office fossilised by their arteries as there are in the Home Office.

At the time when the Dreyfus Affair was splitting France in two the British Press oozed self-righteousness, and boasted that it could never happen here. The Edalji and the Oscar Slater cases showed that it could happen both in England and in Scotland.

These two *Adventures of Conan Doyle* by Sherlock Holmes have been told in some detail because not only do they illustrate the tenacity of purpose which is one aspect of moral courage but also because they display the moral cowardice to which bureaucracy, or indeed any kind of officialdom, is continuously prone. Conan Doyle was neither a trouble-maker nor an *enfant terrible*, but he had a rigid code of conduct, all the more rigid because it lacked religious backing, and throughout his life he never betrayed that code. Conan Doyle died not much more than a year after his sixteen-year struggle with his pen and his purse in obtaining justice for a poor devil of a German Jew with a bad reputation for sexual morality, the prime of whose life had been robbed from him by what we now call the Establishment, had at last been successful.

Will it take Ludovic Kennedy as long to obtain a free pardon for a hanged man so that what remains of him bodily may be removed from a felon's grave in Pentonville and given burial in consecrated ground? Will it take another forty-five years before what remains of Roger Casement's body is given burial in the land for whose freedom he died?

I had just asked those two questions with my pen when by a damnable coincidence I switched on the six o'clock news to hear it announced that Mr. Butler found himself unable to grant a public inquiry into the case of Timothy Evans or a free pardon or to allow his remains to be moved from Pentonville. So the moral cowardice of bureaucracy and of politicians overruled by bureaucracy remains what it has been ever since Henry VII invented the Civil Service. Mr. Butler is a man with a civilised outlook, and has shown great moral courage in holding out against the primitive minds in Parliament who believe that corporal punishment is a cure for wickedness and a deterrent from crime. He has fought as hard as he has been allowed to fight in order to abolish capital punishment. Is Mr. Butler afraid that if he admits a mistake was made in hanging Timothy Evans he will be accused of trying to prejudice public opinion about capital punishment?

It is time to turn away from the contemplation of the moral cowardice of politicians, judges, civil servants, chief constables and jacks-in-office to refresh the mind with a few examples of moral courage displayed by simple people unpreoccupied with saving face or with self-advancement.

XI

Just ordinary people

FROM TIME TO TIME the critics of television in the Press have a crack at the B.B.C. programme *This Is Your Life* which attracts a weekly audience estimated to be about ten million. One will suggest that the public are growing tired of it or that, at any rate, if the public are not growing tired of it they ought to be because the critic himself is growing tired of it. Another will suggest that the public are wearying of Eamonn Andrews whose slickness of presentation and the way he puts the subjects quickly at ease after they have recovered from the first shock of surprise is too slick, and one or two of these critics will hint that it's time somebody else took the place of Eamonn Andrews if the B.B.C. are determined to keep on with *This Is Your Life*. Such critics do not of course express a positive opinion that they would make excellent successors to Eamonn Andrews but faintly in the tone of their criticism such a notion steals through. It does not seem to occur to such critics that men like Eamonn Andrews, Ed Murrow, Richard Dimbleby and the late much lamented Gilbert Harding could not draw their immense audiences unless the public were aware of the sincerity at the back of such men and that mere slickness is not enough to make a man a household face.

The critics of *This Is Your Life* go further. They profess to pity the victims of it for the embarrassment the abrupt publicity must cause them, and they even feel sorry for the embarrassment of an audience unfairly compelled to display its own emotion over the simple goodness of ordinary people. Can it really be embarrassing to be made aware of how many good people there are in this world after the reading of our daily paper has drawn our attention to the number of bad people that there are?

The life of Henry Starling, a porter in Billingsgate fish-market, was one of those examples of simple courage and goodness.

Henry Starling was born in Edmonton in 1906, the third son in a humble family of seven children. His father volunteered for Kitchener's Army at the beginning of 1915, which meant that his wife and family would have £1 a week on which to live while the war lasted. Mrs. Starling was then expecting her youngest boy and owing to some delay in the Army Pay Department no money at all arrived for five weeks, which meant that Mrs. Starling had to pawn everything she possessed including the sheets from her own bed to get food. Two years later her husband was killed in action.

At fourteen Henry Starling found a job at a small wage in a factory where they made attaché cases. At eighteen he fell in love with a girl of his own age who for three years had been blind. In 1926 they became engaged, but when Henry Starling asked his boss for a rise in order that he might get married he was given the sack instead. Business was bad; unemployment was increasing; the dole queues were lengthening. Things were pretty difficult in Marigold Street, Rotherhithe, where the Starlings lived. Fred Fosbeary, whose sister Maud was engaged to Henry Starling, came out of the army and got engaged to Henry's sister Daisy. There was no work to be found.

In the programme Fred Fosbeary declared that if it had not been for Henry's optimism he would have lost heart in that grim time.

To quote him:

"As soon as these was a sniff of any work going, Henry was on to it like a bird. He'd be the first to learn if there were barges wanted unloading. If there was a fall of snow, well, that was good news because we was hired to sweep it away. Old Henry never gave up hope. Always wanted to be up and doing. I remember he'd walk four miles to the dock to get a hundredweight of coke and bring it home on his back."

Seven difficult years went by, until in the winter of 1933 Henry Starling managed to find himself with some fairly regular casual work. He and Maud were to be married on Christmas Day. Then on Christmas Eve for a wedding present he got the sack. However, this time he was determined that a seven-year engagement was long enough. He and Maud were married.

Mrs. Starling was asked what was her first week's housekeeping money to pay the rent and feed her husband and herself. To quote her:

"It was two and sevenpence. I gave Henry the penny back, and he put it in the gas-meter. The second week it was seven and ninepence; and the week after that it was the other way round—nine and sevenpence. We'd rented two rooms in Raymouth Street, Rotherhithe, but we were very lucky in our landlord. Mr. Weller got Henry a temporary job with his brother who was a builder."

It was not until 1939 that Henry Starling obtained a steady job in Leadenhall Market with regular wages. At last he was able to save and plan for the future. And then came the war, with all the destruction it brought to the homes of poor people in the East End. In September 1940 the Starlings were bombed out of their place in Rotherhithe and went over to Fred and Daisy Fosbeary's. To quote Mrs. Starling again, and let it be remembered she is blind:

"Next morning I was very worried about my cat, Whisky —so back we went for him. When we got there, they told us, 'You can't go in there,' but Henry said, 'Well, we're going in.' We weren't there five minutes when the warning went. So I picked up old Whisky and we went back to my brother's. We were there about a fortnight when they got worse damage than what we'd had. The windows were blown in right on top of us while we were in bed. Well, there was nothing else for it—back we had to go to *our* place. I'll never forget it. We looked *so* funny. There was my brother with the twins in a push-chair. There was someone else looking after the dog. I had Whisky in my arms. Henry had another push-chair with three cases in it—and of course he had to hold on to me with one arm. And Daisy was in between us with little Eileen in the bassinette. And there we were dodging the hose-pipes, and the dog chasing the firemen, and nearly being run in for it!'

Then Henry joined the Gunners and was sent up to Yorkshire for many months until at last he was posted to a gun-site in the London area and was able to see his wife more often.

Horace Lee who was on a gun with Henry Starling testified to him:

"One of the best. A real cockney. He used to think Yorkshire people were foreigners. We used to share our two bob a day, and I'd go and spend many a week-end leave with Henry and Maud. And the cat. It's a funny thing about that cat. It really used to know when there was an air raid going to start. As soon as old Whisky got fidgety we knew there was something up. Why, we've even put off a visit to the pictures because of it. And sure enough he was always right. Yes, I had some wonderful times with old Henry and Maud. They're grand. I don't think you could find a more loving couple anywhere."

When the war was over Henry Starling obtained a regular job as a porter in Billingsgate Fish Market and he has found and earned the security his moral stamina deserves. The Starlings had no children of their own, but two members of the Blind Friends' Social Club came forward to say that their lives had been happier thanks to Henry and Maud Starling, who herself had been blind since she was fifteen years old.

The words spoken by Eamonn Andrews at the end expressed what some millions of viewers must have been feeling:

"Henry Starling, and you, Mrs. Starling, believe me, have been most welcome here on our stage and, we're sure, in the homes of our audience." Then turning to that audience he said:

"We have recalled no great achievements, but you have seen the affection and loyalty that are the mainspring of this jolly and unremarkable family, typical of thousands of others. Henry

Starling is at once one and all those people, and we leave him, as we found him, working happily in Billingsgate Market. There he goes now, unnoticed, one of the many thousands of cheerful, ordinary people whom we hope we have saluted through you, Henry Starling."

Henry Starling may not have given a display of moral courage by seeking truth and justice at the cost of his own popularity but we must not overlook that quieter aspect of moral courage which consists in going through life doing one's best.

It was difficult to decide whether two or three of the "lives" chosen as aspects of moral courage should not more accurately have been called examples of physical courage, and this set me off again wondering about that definition of moral courage by Sir James Stephen cited in the *Oxford English Dictionary*: "Moral courage is readiness to expose oneself to suffering or inconvenience which does not affect the body." Certainly we should always have to concede moral courage when a man acts or speaks without regard to the consequences for his career, his position or his good name, but surely we must allow that often what may need physical courage to sustain demands high moral courage to face what may ensue from displaying it. Every deliberate martyr has required moral courage as well as physical. Every man who has done what he has considered it right to do has had to face the risk of being let down by his physical courage, which is a risk that needs moral courage to accept.

In due course we shall be relating the moral courage of those Germans who resisted the evil beliefs of the Nazis. That needed physical courage because there was no mercy for those who resisted those evil beliefs. At the same time, the will to resist was founded upon moral courage. Put the other way it was not necessarily physical cowardice that led so many Germans to display moral cowardice. The force of public opinion is often more deterring than the force of arms.

So, although well aware of the demand upon the physical courage of the examples chosen from the subjects of *This Is Your Life*, they are chosen primarily as illustrations of moral courage.

Sergeant Charles Coward of the Royal Artillery was recalled to his old regiment at the beginning of the Second World War and was taken prisoner after the hand-to-hand fighting at Calais when he was wounded in the leg and head by a German hand-grenade. In the course of his time as a prisoner of war he made over half a dozen attempts to escape but was always recaptured. At last he was sent to a prisoner-of-war camp just outside the entrance to Auschwitz where he heard the horrifying tales of what went on in that infamous concentration camp. Coward without talking about it made up his mind to do what he could to help the victims. He was an accomplished scrounger and he managed to exchange cigarettes and chocolates for the bodies of dead Jews who had been working as slave labour in the I. G. Farben factory. Somehow these bodies were smuggled out of the factory and hidden in a ditch beside the road leading to Birkenau, which was the camp with the gas-chambers and crematoriums. Coward would then wait until the next batch of Jews were being marched along the road to the gas-chambers. If he had four bodies in the ditch then four men in the extermination party would somehow be warned in advance to drop out on the road and roll into the ditch, from which they were to push the dead bodies on to the road. The guards always marched at the head of the column and when they reached the gas-chambers there was a count. Four being missing, a search party would be sent back along the road when the four dead bodies would be found and thus the four missing Jews would be accounted for. This work of giving a chance of escape to the Nazi victims went on at intervals without the Germans having any suspicion of what Coward was doing.

Then came a signal act of courage. In 1943 Coward heard a rumour that a British naval officer was being held prisoner in the extermination camp and he smuggled himself into that hell in the hope of being able to help him to escape. Coward did not succeed in finding the prisoner but he did see what was going on in the camp and after the war he gave evidence about Auschwitz at the Nuremberg Trials.

Just after Christmas 1944 the I. G. Farben factory was

bombed twice by the Americans and three times by the Russians. Thirty-nine British prisoners of war were killed. Early in 1945 when the advancing Russian army was sweeping across Poland the British prisoners had hopes of freedom, but sudden orders came for them to be moved and they were marched some 500 miles to Hanover by which time they were in a bad way. However, Sergeant Charles Coward was determined to escape again and at last he was successful, being picked up by American troops and flown back to England a few days later.

Not only did he testify at the Nuremberg Trials, but in 1951 he volunteered to give evidence at a German trial in Frankfurt.

Norbert Wollheim, a German Jew living in Berlin, was arrested by the Nazis in March 1943. On the platform of the railway station at Auschwitz he was separated from his wife and three-year-old son, neither of whom he ever saw again. Wollheim was employed as a slave-labourer in the I. G. Farben factory until January 1945, and after the war he brought an action against the I. G. Farben Company for maltreatment. This was a test case and opened the way for thousands of others, some of which are still pending.

To Charles Coward the German court set on record this tribute:

> "As a Chamber of the German Court, we regret that the German defendants and witnesses were so lacking in courage, and so debased in morale. It was left to a British prisoner of war to show them what moral courage means and involves."

One feels inclined to say that critics who sneer at a programme which can tell a story like that are as "debased in morale" as those German defendants.

The Second World War provided no more tales of courage than every war before it, but being nearer to the present and therefore more easily imagined by a vast contemporary audience, it is natural that the series *This Is Your Life* should search among its chronicles for examples of courage that can hold their own with the heroic tales of the past.

Alfred Southon escaped from a prisoner-of-war camp in Italy in September 1943 and for a year fought side by side with the Italian partisans who represented that Italy which in the days of the risorgimento had captured so many British hearts, so many who could say with Browning, " Open my heart, and you shall see graved inside of it Italy."

On 8th November, 1944, Alfred Southon and thirty-eight partisans decided it was necessary to escape from Italy into France because the Germans were becoming more and more active in the area in which they were fighting as the Allies were pushing northward. It was for them either escape or certain obliteration.

After two days of Alpine climbing Southon found himself trying to shelter from a fierce blizzard under an overhanging rock. With him was another escaped British prisoner of war. All the party except two Italians had thought it wise to press on through the blinding snow in the hope of getting help. Southon's companion was fast growing weaker, and Southon himself knew he must keep him awake and this he desperately tried to do. At the end of the third day no food was left and Southon's legs and feet were numb. Carlo and Giuseppe, the two Italian partisans who had stayed behind, had by now pressed on like the others to seek help or find shelter.

By the end of the fifth day Southon's blistered hands began to bleed, and suddenly his companion, driven crazy by hunger, attacked him. Then on the seventh day Southon's companion died and he was alone in the snow, still just alive, 8700 feet up in the Galisia Pass. Two more days went by. His only hope was that his thirty-seven comrades had reached a place from which they would be able to send help. He mercifully did not know that nearly all of them were already dead. From time to time he would try to shout for help into the savage teeth of the blizzard. By now Southon's fingers were black, and in his agony he began to fancy that he could hear voices. On the tenth day these voices became real, and with what was left to him of strength Southon shouted for help.

Gildo Bianchetti, an Alpine guide, who used to lead groups of partisans from Italy into France, was exploring a path when he met Aldo Grossotti who told him that as he was descending the mountain he thought he had heard someone cry out. Bianchetti told him it must have been imagination, and then one of his own companions declared he could hear a voice calling. They went towards it and at last discovered Southon. He was now completely black and his hair was pasted with snow. One of the men who found him said the only thing that made them think he was alive was that his teeth were shining. Beside Southon was the dead body of his companion. His rescuers did not think it was possible to keep Southon alive; it was his twenty-fifth birthday when they found him. All night they massaged him and as his circulation came back he suffered an agony of pain. At last he was taken to a hospital at Aix-les-Bains, where he heard that every single one of those who had started with him to cross the mountains had perished in the blizzard. He was the sole survivor. Then he had to face the news that both his legs must be amputated and that he must lose all the fingers of his right hand. Back in England, he was in hospital for many months, and after he had been out of hospital for eight months he had to endure the ordeal of re-amputation.

So far this may seem a story of fantastic physical courage. There was, indeed, an abundance of that, but now Southon had to draw upon an equal abundance of moral courage. He was determined not to become a useless survivor of that fearful ordeal. With artificial legs and no fingers on his right hand he set out to get a job and in doing that job to drive a car. He married and had a son. When one hears the story of a man like Alfred Southon it is difficult not to feel a little impatient of people who can make life miserable for themselves and for other people by that self-pity which seems to be a malady that is on the increase with material progress.

There are many other stories of courage that might be told from that heartening series *This Is Your Life*. There is the tale of Mrs. Bloom who was married when the Japanese were closing in on Singapore. She and her husband were separated after the surrender for three and a half years, she to go with four hundred women and children into Changi Gaol, he to an internment camp. For nearly two years Mrs. Bloom devoted herself to keeping up morale in various ways, and then came the Kempe Tai, the Japanese secret police, who suspected that messages were somehow being sent out of Changi to the Allies. The gaol was ransacked for clues, and in Mrs. Bloom's cell the secret police found some Christmas cards in Braille which Mrs. Bloom was making for the blind children in the gaol. At last the Japanese thought they had found something to justify their absurd suspicions. Mrs. Bloom was taken off for a brutal interrogation at the end of which she was shut in a wooden cage with fifteen men and made to sit cross-legged for fourteen hours a day on a stone floor without moving or speaking. This ordeal lasted for five months before she was sent back to Changi.

When the war came to an end, Dr. Bloom and his wife returned to England with nothing except the clothes they stood in.

In September 1946 a little girl was born to them, and perhaps as the result of those years of semi-starvation and that ghastly ordeal in the wooden cage that little girl was born deaf. This gave to Mrs. Bloom's courage a fresh challenge, which was not only to get the best out of life for her own child but also for all deaf children, too many of whom, alas, are left shut off in that silence.

Miss Dorothy Brodie, the Headmistress of the Ackmar School for Deaf Children, paid Mrs. Bloom this tribute:

> " She has been Chairman of our Care Committee for the last two years, and what a difference she made from the moment she joined us. Energy and effort are not enough when one is working for deaf children. One must have understanding *and* compassion. Mrs. Bloom knew that deaf children because of the demands they make upon one's time and patience can so easily become neglected. When she entered the silent world of her own daughter she learned what was needed to make that world as happy and normal as possible. And what she had learned she was able to make others understand, especially the parents of other deaf children. They need to be taught just as much as their children."

Once upon a time Mrs. Bloom edited a paper in Changi

Gaol; it was called *Pow-wow*, and it was one of the ways in which she helped to keep up the morale of the other occupants. Now she edits a quarterly called *Talk* which is the magazine of the National Deaf Children's Society and sums up in its title what should be the aim of every teacher and every mother, and that is to make the deaf child talk.

It was once my privilege to sit next Miss Helen Keller at lunch on the occasion of her receiving an honorary degree from Glasgow University. Helen Keller became deaf, dumb and blind when 19 months old. She was accompanied by the devoted friend who had performed the miracle of teaching her to speak. The tone of her voice as Miss Keller rose to thank the university for the honour she had received is still in my ears from thirty years ago and reflection upon that miracle of courage and patience has been for me a moral refreshment ever since.

Surely one may feel that the sight of Mrs. Bloom's young daughter Virginia on television and the sound of her voice must have been a moral refreshment for many in that great audience of ten million.

Another moving story of courage was that of Madame Anne Brusselmans, a Belgian lady with a husband and two small children who lived in a flat over the offices of the Gas Company in Brussels. There during the five years of the German occupation she sheltered many airmen in her own flat or as *chef logeur* in the Belgian resistance arranged for their shelter elsewhere until the escape route was ready. She also conducted them herself for the first part of the journey along the Comet Line. This was a thread of escape stretching for 900 miles from Brussels, through Belgium and France, over the Pyrenees into Spain. Over 600 airmen who had been shot down passed along it safely. Two hundred and twenty-seven Belgian and French patriots were shot by the Germans for helping those airmen on the way to safety.

Major Henry Sarnow of the United States Air Force flew from Chicago to add his tribute to the courage of Madame Brusselmans. Major Sarnow was hidden for five weeks in her own flat. He recalled the thoroughness with which she coached him for his escape. She made him do exercises to keep fit. She taught him how to hold a cigarette like a Belgian. She fixed him with a false identity card and with clothes to wear. She even made him carry a brief-case in order that by carrying it he would not swing his arms like an American airman and so give himself away.

During the occupation Madame Brusselmans sheltered under her own roof 176 Allied airmen, all of whom she sent on the road to safety and all of whom successfully escaped and flew again.

It would be an impertinence to praise the courage of a woman like Madame Anne Brusselmans, but at least the B.B.C. can be praised for giving a vast public an opportunity to realise that these great women did exist outside a paragraph in a newspaper. It is so valuable for those millions who look at *This Is Your Life* to see for themselves that women like Mrs. Bloom or Madame Brusselmans are not obvious heroines but people they would not think were different from the other women in a train or a bus.

The third of a trio of courageous women is Mrs. Ellen Field. Her husband and his father were members of the Hong Kong Volunteer Defence Corps and after the surrender of the island were both prisoners in the dreadful Shamshuipo Camp on the mainland. Mrs. Field managed to escape internment by burning her passport and bluffing the Japanese into accepting her as Irish and therefore a neutral. During the years of the Japanese occupation with astonishing energy she with the help of Dr. Selwyn-Clarke, the Chief Medical Officer, who was not interned at first, managed to convey parcels of food to the prisoners and also to help in the escape of some of them. It was a task that required constant courage. She was shot in the leg by a Japanese sentry on one occasion and had to hold her own with some completely intolerable Japanese officers, who were all condemned to various sentences of imprisonment at the war trials and one of whom was hanged. Yet there was one remarkable exception in the shape of a former Lutheran minister in Philadelphia who now had a church of his own in Japan. The Reverend Kinoshi Watanabe had been called up for service as an interpreter. He was a man of

Christian saintliness and is now setting an example in his native land, having returned to his church in spite of losing his wife and children when the bomb obliterated Hiroshima.

Of Sir Selwyn Selwyn-Clarke I wrote at Hong Kong in my diary, *All over the Place*, on 21st March, 1947:

> "Went into see Dr. Selwyn-Clarke who is acting as Honorary Director of Medical Services. He is an outstanding personality. I have rarely been as deeply impressed by the moral force of an individual. He is a barrister as well as a doctor and was sentenced by the Japs to rigorous confinement for many months in prison after severe torture and brutality. He is permanently lame from Jap kicking. His courage and humanity during the ordeal were continuous. Now he is repaying evil with good and tries all the time to help Jap prisoners here. I am told that at Easter he will present each of them with a toothbrush at his own expense."

In that year 1947 Sir Selwyn Selwyn-Clarke was appointed Governor of the Seychelles and there to my own knowledge showed the same outstanding moral courage he had shown in Hong Kong. It is easy for me to understand what an encouragement association with him must have been to Mrs. Field. She has written a full account of those years, in continuous danger with three little girls to look after, in a book called *Twilight in Hong Kong*. Yet if there were only her book from which to gauge her courage we should not have an intimate picture of a woman. In *This Is Your Life* her character revealed itself with perfect clarity and those millions seeing and hearing her on television could understand why she had been able to defy those intolerable Japanese officers.

One last example of moral courage from *This Is Your Life*. This is Major Richard Carr-Gomm, formerly in the Coldstream Guards, who was thirty-five years of age when he was faced with an unexpected public appearance which he would probably have been glad to miss. As a subaltern he had been on active service in Normandy and after the war he had seen service in the Middle East and Cyprus. After fifteen years as a Coldstreamer he could look forward in due course to commanding his battalion. Then one evening in 1955 as Officer of the Guard in the Bank of England he asked Godfrey Winn to dine with him, and to him he announced that he was going to resign his commission because on his visits to Bermondsey where his family had property he had been struck by the number of old people who seemed to be wandering aimlessly and miserably about the streets or huddling in libraries and other public places for warmth. He felt that he could do something to provide them with some kind of companionship and help them in their sad loneliness. He felt that soldiering in peacetime was not good enough. He must do something to help people.

So in September 1955 Major Carr-Gomm turned down a War Office Staff appointment which would have led to promotion and resigned his commission. He went to consult the London County Council Home Help organiser. Miss Marie Monk had already had a letter from him offering his services as a home help, but she had paid no attention to his letter because it had seemed to her that a major in the Brigade of Guards was the last person in the world to become a scrubber of floors or a nurse to old people. Major Carr-Gomm wrote again and finally Miss Monk decided to give him an interview. She was so struck by the sincerity of his desire to become a home helper that she accepted him. And Miss Monk started him off as toughly as she could. She told those millions:

"I well remember his first job because I went with him. We climbed the bare stairs to a shabby landing. We got no reply when we knocked on the door. Eventually we had to break in, and down on the floor lay the man we had called to see. He was an old-age pensioner who had had a stroke. Major Carr-Gomm picked him up and put him on the bed and got hold of a doctor and ambulance. Then he set about cleaning up the room. The place was filthy and I remember I had to show him how to wring out a swab in a bucket to wash the floor. But he was a quick learner and inside a week he could scrub floors as well as anybody."

So Major Carr-Gomm living in one room in Rotherhithe, from half past nine in the morning until late at night devoted himself to scrubbing floors, cleaning windows, making beds and running errands for lonely old people. Then he bought his first house for old people—50 Eugenia Road, Bermondsey.

One of his first two lodgers, Miss Dina Saunders, aged eighty-three, said:

"I'd been living in the same room for fifty-three years, and suddenly I was told I had to get out. I didn't know what to do. I knew nobody who could help. I'd nowhere to go and I was very unhappy. Then the major heard about me and said I could have a front room in his house."

Major Carr-Gomm managed to acquire other houses, and the Abbeyfield Society was formed and registered as a charity. Contributions began to come in, but the problem of lonely old people became continually more urgent. He found one old man who was turned out of his lodging every day from ten to five, wet or fine. He found one old woman ill in bed with practically no food for a fortnight. He found another old woman who had spoken to nobody except an occasional passer-by for ten years.

Major Carr-Gomm's aim is to have a home for old people in every street of the district in which he works. This determination of his to cut himself off from his former life has been rigidly maintained. No doubt he was called a crank; somebody who had left the Coldstream Guards to fuss about lonely old people must be a crank. His mother said a few words which suggest what resolute moral courage Major Carr-Gomm must have:

"I must admit it was a bitter disappointment to us all at first. Indeed, we simply could not understand his action. He had enjoyed so much his life in the Brigade. Of course I admired what he wanted to do, but I just couldn't understand why he had to give up everything to live in one room in a tiny house in Bermondsey with no hot water or even indoor sanitation."

In the end Major Carr-Gomm's singleness of heart silenced criticism.

Some may think it an exaggeration to claim high moral courage for the impulse which led a guards officer to renounce the world he knew because he desired to be useful in the world where poverty and old age and loneliness go hand in hand; the taboos imposed on a man educated at a public school are hardly appreciated by those who have not been subjected to that adamantine mould.

XII

Crumbling under tyranny

IT MAY BE DOUBTED whether we in Britain have yet fully appreciated the immense moral courage that was needed by those Germans who did resist the Nazis. I remember sitting on a cliff above the Atlantic in the early summer of 1933 with a German visitor to the Hebrides and asking how a nation like his could accept the domination of an hysterical revivalist like Hitler.

"If you knew what our position was before Adolf Hitler you would understand that he was necessary." His eyes looked outward across the ocean heaving below in the quiet sunlight. "Yes, he was necessary," he repeated to himself in a murmur.

The assertion made so authoritatively above that stark stretch of ocean, face to face as it were with natural truth, was like a leaden cloud across the face of the sun. I was compelled to believe that Hitler had in fact responded to a primal need of the Teutonic character and that what looked to us on news-reels like an anxious lavatory attendant at a railway terminus was a potential menace to the world; I knew then that this evil caricature of statesmanship must be erased and I never lost an opportunity of declaring this in print.

Some years after this, on a cold dark evening in the late autumn of 1938, I had occasion to visit the German Embassy at the corner of Carlton House Terrace to discuss a newspaper project to send me to Germany and interview all the leaders of the Nazi Party. The great house did not appear even yet to have recovered the life that departed from it on that August day in 1914. It was dim and dingy; the servants were like waiters in a second-rate club. There was not a piece of furniture that did not seem to have outlived its date. The final touch was given to this bizarre decay and prevailing gloom by a floodlit portrait of Adolf Hitler presiding over the entrance hall. It was an execrable picture, the kind of chromolithographic daub uncritical tourists bring back as their souvenir of a honeymoon in the Tyrol. It displayed the Führer in a sort of chamois hunter's pose against a photographer's studio woodland, his cheeks flooded with paint-box roses. That the acknowledged leader of a great nation should suppose himself a worshipful figure thus depicted in the embassy of that great nation revealed to me that the nightmare was already afoot, that a period of civilisation was cracking into ruins, and that a herd of homicidal maniacs had been set loose upon the world. The report in Berlin on my suitability as an emissary of the British Press was unfavourable. I would not be welcomed like Dr. Buchman, Lord Brocket and one or two others who believed that Hitler was a peace-loving idealist.

They are apt to forget in England how closely they have been bound up with the Germans for the past 250 years and are still inclined to underestimate the shock of the break that was made in August 1914. It is true they were beginning to recognise the Germans as serious commercial rivals and to watch with anxiety their growing challenge to Britannia's sea power, but when the British went to war with them in 1914 it was in the spirit of kinsfolk determined to give a lesson in decency to those who had disgraced the family. And the Germans themselves were genuinely hurt and surprised by Britain's action. There was none of the elation with which in days gone by the people of England had welcomed war with France or Spain as natural enemies. There were of course many Scotsmen and Welshmen, and even a few Englishmen, who felt for the Germans the profound antipathy which once upon a time had supported the House of Stuart, but when the First World War came to an end the majority of English people wanted to restore Germany if necessary at the expense of France. It was like a matrimonial reconciliation after a liaison with *la belle France* whose behaviour in demanding material security for herself and thus spoiling the memory of a romantic love-affair was considered unpleasantly cynical and mercenary. France, and France alone, was to blame we felt for not letting Germany settle down to European respectability and a reasonable amount of home comfort.

We can smile, if a little wryly, at the lack of imagination and understanding with which the ordinary man in Britain confronted the catastrophe of the Second World War when it came: but we can thank God for that lack of imagination which prevented his knowing he was beaten in June 1940. It was the same in another June at Hougoumont and Quatre Bras. It did not dawn on the ordinary man until Dunkirk that he was not fighting to prevent recurrent crises which interfered with trade, but for something much more serious, which was for his own survival and for the survival of a system of life that with all its inequalities and inadequacy was more jealous of the rights of the individual than any other.

The first time I ever saw the swastika in action, as it were, was in September 1932. A party of us had gone from Scotland under the auspices of the Polish Foreign Office to exchange those cultural amenities which were a feature of the optimistic but half-hearted attempts to rebuild Europe during the two decades after the First World War.

When our train was passing through the outskirts of Danzig on the way to Warsaw, I saw painted upon one of the palings of a tumbledown fence that separated a row of squalid back-gardens from the railway embankment—the swastika. We had had a brief glimpse from the train of the Free City, but the fleeting impression of picturesque medievalism had vanished in the sordid environs, and what remains much more vividly in my memory is that row of houses topping the slope of the embankment and among the tawdry tattered advertisements upon the fence that small painted swastika, black and poisonous-seeming as a tarantula. At the time I knew too little about the swastika to realise the appropriateness of that setting in which I first beheld it. Yet even then I apprehended something of its vitality, and in that apprehension was caught by a faint malaise about the future. Botanists know that two of the most lethal plants—henbane and deadly nightshade—are found most frequently on rubbish-heaps and that they often spring to life suddenly and unaccountably from the rubble of collapsed buildings. Like henbane or deadly nightshade that swastika on the outskirts of Danzig seemed to have been hatched from decay and collapse. Later I saw the swastika not so much as an evil as a misdirected activity. It seemed a cancer rather than a destructive bacillus, and although it may have begun as an honest effort to achieve regeneration, as my German friend in the Hebrides believed, it was soon clear that even as the cells of the human body in seeking to restore themselves, succeed only in destroying the rest of the body, so too the triumphant swastika would destroy Europe, and lead the body of Western man along a path in which his soul must shrivel.

In the summer of 1933 *The New Statesman* published some anonymous reminiscences of Adolf Hitler during the First World War. As a private in that Bavarian regiment he was already grandiloquent.

> "He was neither popular nor the reverse with his fellows; they just smiled at him, at his vague rambling speeches on everything in the world and out of it... he interested himself particularly in the important question of seeing the officers' washing done or doing it himself. This secured him in the good graces of the colonel, who removed him from the more constant dangers of the trenches and appointed him runner between regimental headquarters and the front line. . . . The regimental records contain not a line concerning an award of the Iron Cross of the First Class to Hitler, though in later years he has taken to wearing it prominently in his self-constructed uniform."

On the evening of 15th November, 1937, the day on which Lord Halifax had gone to Berlin at Goering's invitation to the hunting exhibition, I was sitting after supper in the Savoy Grill with Mr. Winston Churchill and Mr. Robert Boothby. That visit by Lord Halifax was regarded as the first deliberate step along the policy of appeasement, and Mr. Churchill thought that such a policy was the road to ruin. Presently Graf Albrecht von Bernstoff, who had been Counsellor of the German Embassy until the Nazis took over, came into the Grill accompanied by Lady Jowitt.

"Who's that pretty woman with Albrecht?" Mr. Churchill asked.

We told him it was Leslie Jowitt and that he must have met her. He insisted that he never had met her, and the new arrivals were beckoned over to our table.

"Well, Albrecht," said Mr. Churchill, cutting off the end of his cigar as he spoke. "I suppose your countrymen are making a fool of Lord Holyfox to-night?"

"But of course," Albrecht von Bernstoff replied, in the inflection of his voice and the tilt of his shoulders a courteous suggestion that the question was superfluous.

So now Hitler was securing for himself the good graces of Mr. Chamberlain's National Government as once upon a time, twenty years earlier, he had secured the good graces of his colonel. And what a basketful of dirty linen he was going to wash!

Albrecht von Bernstoff was a man of great courage, who never hesitated in Germany and out of it to show that he looked upon the Nazis as ill-bred riff-raff. He urged that National Government of ours to stop Hitler; he might as well have been talking to sleepy peers. In the end the Nazis had their revenge, and they hanged von Bernstoff in April 1945. A memorial to him can be seen in the present German Embassy in Belgrave Square.

At Whitsuntide in 1939 I went to Holland with a German friend of mine to whom the Kaiser's wife, Princess Hermine, had written suggesting he should bring me to Doorn. It appeared that the Kaiser had read *The Windsor Tapestry* and wondered whether I might not be a writer who could present him to the world as he saw himself. The idea was that if he approved of me he would give me access to his papers. My friend Haas-Heye was an artist with many distinguished connections in his own country, but the way it was moving under the direction of what seemed to him a kind of suburbia gone mad had exasperated what even is late as May 1939 we were still able to call a pre-war mind and know what we meant by it, so he had decided to live and work in England, a bold resolution for a man past sixty to take.

On a perfect afternoon in May—Whit Monday to be exact—we drove from Amsterdam to Doorn. The countless little people riding in both directions on bicycles appeared as impersonal as mayflies rising and falling above a stream, as aimless as house-flies round a chandelier. There was hardly any break in the lines of neat little houses on either side of the road. Behind them stretched a seemingly infinite lowland, above the horizon of which the remotest avenues of high trees hung like blue-grey clouds. The farther we drove the more easily I could fancy that Haas-Heye and myself were the only human beings in all that concourse of holiday-makers, for even our chauffeur turned into a kind of mechanical doll whom we directed by prods in the back, being both of us without Dutch.

When at last we reached the village of Doorn we were early for our audience, and we sat outside a café, drinking a liquid that tasted like one of the coffee essences advertised on television. A Dutch policeman resembling the London bobbies one used to laugh at on the earliest American films stood at the cross-roads to rebuke motorists, bicyclists, and hikers who had failed to cross or stop exactly at the right moment and exactly at the right place. The girls' legs were browning rapidly from that fine fortnight of May weather. The young men's faces were tanned and slightly moist. The gilded hands of the clock on the church tower moved slowly on towards the time when we were due at Huize Doorn, and the old church wore the spinster look many an old English church wears nowadays in villages transformed into what seem like picturesque back cloths for polychromatic petrol pumps and swarming cars and bicycles. Here in Holland the bicycles predominated. "There are the people who obey Hitler in Germany," Haas-Heye sighed to himself.

It was a depressing reflection. One could not fancy that these bicyclists were any longer capable of individual thought or action, and yet they lacked the beautiful unanimity and purpose of a flight of birds, so that somehow their swarmlike behaviour seemed a kind of slavery, a conquest of those men and women by their own machines. If I had been told then that thousands of these people would be blown to fragments by bombers in the following May I believe I should have felt as little emotion as to be told of thousands of midges being devoured by dragon-flies. And then a girl was thrown from her machine and struck on the head by the car behind. She lay white and senseless, a jagged cut across her forehead. Instantly one felt a passionate hope that she should not be dead, and a deep relief when she recovered consciousness and was able to limp to a near-by shop. With a lightening of the heart I knew that the individual did still matter.

When it was time for us to leave that whirligig of simple pleasures, we passed from it in a moment as if by some fairy spell into another world when our car drove through a vaulted archway into the domain of Huize Doorn. The sense of magic was enhanced by the necessity to reach the front door at the very first stroke of the hour at which we had been summoned. As soon as the castellated lodge was behind us we might have turned out of Western Avenue into the gardens of the Sleeping Beauty's palace. The air of the afternoon seemed to have been distilled into golden pools of azaleas gleaming against the tall dark pines. The drive took a wide circular sweep to the left to pass a green pond over which rhododendrons leaned, their rosy petals scattered motionless upon the duckweed. The house stood in shade at this hour, which added to the contrast between the white painted windows and the mellow brick. It was such a house as you might see in Norfolk or Suffolk. As we came to the end of the circle of the drive and were ready to turn up along the straight end of it which led to the front door, half-way along what resembled the handle of a great reaping-hook we saw two figures coming towards us.

"The Kaiser himself," my companion murmured and dug our driver sharply in the back to make him stop. "All is well. He has put on a suit of Harris tweed. He wants you to be presented."

That morning Princess Hermine had rung up Haas-Heye at the Amsterdam hotel to ask if I was any relation to Sir Morell Mackenzie, and he had had to admit that Morell Mackenzie was a first cousin of my father's. He had been the throat specialist whom Queen Victoria had sent over to Germany in the hope of keeping the Crown Prince alive long enough to succeed to the throne so that her eldest daughter might become Dowager Empress and Queen instead of Dowager Crown Princess.

Princess Hermine had been disturbed by this information. His Imperial Majesty still felt strongly about Sir Morell Mackenzie's intervention in 1888, although it was now fifty years ago. She said she would welcome us to tea at Doorn, but she could not hold out much hope that His Imperial Majesty would receive us.

The sight of that figure in grey Harris tweed was a relief to Haas-Heye. Even now on the edge of eighty the Kaiser was still meticulous about the appropriate dress for the most trifling occasion.

Conversation was very easy, mostly of trees and flowers because we had brought with us from London all the catalogues we had been able to collect at the Temple Flower Show. The bright eyes of the Kaiser flashed with pleasure to as vivid a blue as a kingfisher's wing as he told his equerry in attendance to gather up the bundle; the effect of suddenly having gone back in time was heightened for me when I noticed that the equerry was wearing a suit cut in the fashion of twenty years before.

Presently the Kaiser told us that the Empress would be expecting us for tea and just before he turned away to continue his walk with the equerry, who was finding some difficulty in carrying the bundle of catalogues, he said pensively:

"Yesterday would have been Chestnut Sunday in Bushey Park. I remember how lovely the avenue was in 1910, when I was in England for the funeral of King Edward."

There was a sudden moisture in those vivid blue eyes, and for me as he spoke the all but thirty years that intervened went rolling away like a handful of stones dislodged by the casual step of a climber up the steep mountain of life.

Towards the end of tea with Princess Hermine in her boudoir something occurred which for the first time brought home to me the power that Hitler wielded. The princess was telling us about some trouble one of her sons had been in with Geobbels over a lady. There had been a challenge to a duel and her son was sent to prison for six months.

"Thank God," she said fervidly, "it was not a concentration camp."

As she spoke one of the servants in a white jacket came in to take away the tea-tray. The princess turned as pale as one of the cups.

"But of course," she said hurriedly, "you know what they are saying for propaganda about the concentration camps is terribly exaggerated. They are not at all bad like that."

And as she spoke she was apprehensively watching the servant whom she obviously believed was one of the Nazi spies planted in the Doorn household. If the Kaiser's wife in Holland could be made to bow before the Nazi terror, what courage must be demanded from those in Germany who refused to bow before it?

Later on that afternoon, the equerry escorted us round the gardens. On a slight mound in the rosarium was a white summer-house immaculately unreal in which upon a curved white bench were disposed two purple velvet cushions with a golden W and and golden H beneath Imperial crowns. It was such a summer-house as once upon a time would not have been out of place in Potsdam, but here it looked beyond the rosarium upon an acre of sandy ground which the Kaiser had presented to the village of Doorn for a children's playground, and beyond through the thin woodland one could see the bicycles endlessly whirring.

Here in this spellbound domain, forbidden to travel more than a few miles away without permission from the Netherlands Government, had lived for nearly twenty years the man whose failure to remould Europe to his heart's desire precipitated the building up of that world of synthetic gentility which was to produce from Central Europe one of its own little human beings to smash it up again. But for the accident of his evil genius Adolf Hitler might have been one of those holiday-makers bicycling about in green corduroy shorts, and finding in such an occupation all that human energy required. Instead, not six months later, he would kick to pieces that gimcrack world whose material comfort had developed so rapidly at the expense of everything else.

The day after our visit to Doorn, Haas-Heye and I lunched at a house in Haarlem which contains perhaps the best private collection of paintings of old masters in Europe. It is an odd experience to sit in a room and, as one sips one's coffee after lunch, to notice on the walls masterpiece after masterpiece with which one has been familiar all one's life. In this room I found myself the centre of conversation among the guests, several of whom were Germans anxious to know what Britain intended to do. The particular masterpieces on the walls of this room were not the lovely interiors of the Dutch School but *quattrocento* paintings from Italy, serene Madonnas against pale blue Umbrian distances, Annunciations and Nativities and Crucifixions, and multicoloured angelic gatherings beneath luminous and placid skies.

Among the guests at lunch was an ex-Minister for one of the minor forms of Nazi energy, a parched pre-occupied man who seemed like a character in an Ibsen play. Then there was an ex-diplomat who had been *en poste* in England before 1914, and who was much more anxious to hear about the Pytchley and the Quorn and hunting with the Galway Blazers in Ireland than to know what England intended to do about the European situation. He appeared as remote from the urgent hour as a joke in *Punch* during the reign of Edward VII. The most voluble of the guests was the wife of one of the great Berlin bankers. At first she was making jokes about the butter in Berlin. Then suddenly feeling that perhaps she was being unbecomingly flippant, she began to wonder how it was possible for anybody to suppose that England would intervene on behalf of a country like Poland.

"I do beg you to believe me when I say that if you attack Danzig we shall fight, and fight to a finish," I said abruptly, with all the passionate emphasis I could impart to a simple statement.

An incredulous silence fell upon the guests gathered in that delightful room. For a moment they were as still as the pictures upon the walls. Then, with that incomprehensible Germanic failure, a failure which what is Teutonic in Anglo-Saxondom shares with them, to grasp the relation between cause and effect, the banker's wife sighed:

"So it is true when they say that England prepares to destroy Germany."

I tried to make it clear to them that Britain would do nothing unless her hand was forced, but it was impossible to convince them of this. Nevertheless, the banker's wife was able to comprehend that something was going wrong with the diplomatic manœuvres, and she complained to me that one of the troubles was our inability to grasp that the men responsible for the direction of Germany's course could not be handled in the traditional gentlemanly English way. It might be possible to do something with Goering because he was on the fringe of gentility and might understand the point of view and the manners of our statesmen, but to all the others their point of view and manners were unintelligible.

"And why," she asked finally, "do you not find an Ambassador who can speak German?"

Suddenly outside on the great lawn two white peacocks shrieked, and the ominous sound seemed to suggest to the banker's wife that she had been talking indiscreetly. She looked furtively and fearfully round over her shoulder for a concealed eavesdropper, and then said to me in tones of a cringing child who has been whipped into submissiveness:

"But our Führer says we must prepare for war because our enemies are plotting to destroy us, and our Führer knows."

That insincere obsequiousness in her voice, like musty olive-oil, gave me a better idea of the terror in which people like her were living in Germany than the most blood-curdling tales from those who had escaped from that terror. She with all her money and with all her influence was as much at the mercy of what Churchill would call "that bloodstained guttersnipe" as a disgraced Sultana. The bowstring might twang, and an indiscreet body be flung into the Bosphorus.

Haas-Heye was depressed by the atmosphere which pervaded that lunch in Haarlem. He longed to be back in England. In the station at Amsterdam we saw a train loaded for Germany, and he shuddered as we passed it. There did emanate from it a kind of menacing black squalor.

At Harwich next morning Haas-Heye inhaled the English air.

" Even Holland is too near," he murmured with a sigh, his eyes clouded.

Naturally, with a crassness worthy of the Germans themselves, the suet-brained guardians of our security interned him when war was declared.

In August, ten days before that declaration, I went over to Holland again, crossing this time by Gravesend to Rotterdam. The country was still a-whirr with bicycles, many of their riders loaded with great bunches of heather from the few stretches of land that were not cultivated. The Kaiser had gout and I was unable to see him, but I sat with the Princess Hermine and her daughter on the balcony of her boudoir, and the sense of impending catastrophe was hardly bearable. Her two sons had already been called up, and her thoughts were far away beyond the trees, in Germany. We were like two people trying to talk to one another across the roar of an ever widening cataract. The westerly sun behind the house drew from the scarlet salvias and orange cannas, growing in great beds among the lawns and wreathing the woodland with an edge of hot colour, an added heat and depth of hue. They seemed the very flames of war kindling. As we drove away through the arch of the castellated lodge a company of Dutch soldiers in pale sage-green uniform were marching in to billet themselves in the orangery.

The situation was growing worse hourly. I look back at that last motor-drive across Holland as to a phantasmagoria of bicycles and cars in the last whirling dance of death of a chromium-plated Cellophane-wrapped world which had substituted make-believe for faith, a phantasmagoria lighted by menacing oranges. We stopped at Hilversum to admire what was said to be the most beautiful broadcasting station in Europe. It seemed to sum up in its design the illusory streamlined progress of two decades of human history.

Then on again with the swarming bicyclists to The Hague where we stopped the car for a moment to take a glimpse at the Palace of Peace. A group of seedy postcard-mongers ceased to lounge disconsolately and hurried across the great courtyard in the hope of selling a souvenir of peace to the last tourists they might expect perhaps for years.

What seemed a truer expression of peace was the Queen's house in one of the squares, the front door of which opened directly on the sidewalk like the house of any burgher. The trees in the square opposite were hung with orange globes for festival illumination. I had hoped to get one more look at the glorious Rembrandts in the Mauritshuis, but a placard was being hung on the door on which was scrawled in ink " closed until further notice " and the first wagon-load of sandbags had just pulled up before it. I gazed across the bottle-green water of the Vyver to an old sundial the colour of verdigris, high up on the wall of a house on the other side, and wondered when the moving shadow of the gnomon would again record hours of peace.

In Rotterdam we drove through the very portion of the city which was to be obliterated nine months hence. The boat for Gravesend was almost empty. The sea was glassy all the way across, and southward to port Mars hung like an orange in the sky. I have never seen the planet of war so large and so ruddy nor the reflection of him streak the water with such long metallic gleams.

We reached Gravesend very early on the Sunday morning a week before war was declared. The official examining passports had lost his holiday look. The few passengers wore an anxious haggard air. They passed along the platform like the first pale leaves that fall at summer's end. Outside Victoria Station the garish posters of the Sunday papers were already in shreds; they seemed as fatuous as trodden confetti, with their catchpenny scare lines.

The porter who took our bags to be inspected for I.R.A. bombs before putting them in the left-luggage office told me he thought Hitler was the greatest man in the world and that it was a pity we hadn't got his equal in England.

"What I mean to say is, look what he's done for his own people! Well, he comes from the people himself, and he knows what they want."

With the impression still fresh upon the mind of the terror that what had once been as seemingly insignificant a man as this porter with cloudy brooding eyes was capable of rousing in the wife of an ex-Emperor and the wife of a rich banker, it was reassuring to remind oneself that Oliver Cromwell had probably cured the English for ever of indulging in the experiment of a dictatorship as a way of putting right a time that was out of joint.

We in Britain were never called upon before or during the Second World War to display moral courage to the extent that it was demanded from the individual on the Continent. Let it be granted at once that the willingness of the nation to follow the inspiring lead of Winston Churchill was in his own words the nation's finest hour, but it was much nearer to physical than to moral courage. The old saying about the British not knowing when they are beaten is a literal truth.

That inability to grasp a self-evident fact is baffling to an enemy. The Italians misled by Mussolini thought they would be on the winning side and from the moment they received the lesson administered by the Fleet Air Arm at Taranto followed a month later by the even sharper lesson administered by Wavell in Northern Africa, the Italians knew that they were beaten and with that knowledge became less and less inclined to prolong what they felt was a struggle for nothing.

The French in June 1940 knew that they were beaten and in that knowledge abandoned all pride and bowed to Hitler. Moreover, the French, before the war began at all, knew that they could be beaten, and even in those dark days of June 1940 it never occurred to the British nation as a whole that it could be beaten; if a nation lacks the imagination to realise that it could be beaten, it is obvious that it will also lack the imagination to know when it is beaten. It was from the nations which either knew that they were beaten or that they could be beaten that the examples of moral courage came. Who that heard General de Gaulle's broadcast, spurring his countrymen who disdained to surrender to fight on with him, can forget that voice of France? From that moment until he marched from the Arc de Triomphe to the Te Deum sung in Notre Dame by a liberated Paris his moral courage never flinched through just over four years. During that time he had to maintain his leadership of the Free French against the prejudice of Franklin Roosevelt, against British complaints of his lack of humour, and against at least one jealous French general who thought he should be recognised as head of the French Government. And now when after years of retirement he has come back to lead the French people his enduring moral courage is as firm as ever.

And what moral courage was called for from Dr. Benes to sustain his political life after his country was fed to the Nazi wolves in the hope of keeping them occupied long enough for Great Britain and France to reach safety first. Then there was John Metaxas of Greece roused from bed in the small hours of a night at October's end and called upon to reply to an ultimatum handed to him by the Italian Minister in Greece. It took a great draught of moral courage to give an immediate " No " with the certainty of his country's being invaded within a few hours of his giving it. That reply of Metaxas has made " No " an almost sacred word in the Hellas of to-day. OXI.

Then there were the Serbians who threw out the Yugoslav Government and drove the Prince-Regent Paul out of the country in March 1941 rather than surrender their land to a Hitler, and this decision was taken in the almost certain knowledge that it would be the end of Yugoslavia until the Nazis were conquered.

These were all glorious feats of moral courage but those who performed them were at least assured of an opportunity to fortify their resolution with feats of physical courage.

That opportunity was denied to the Germans living in Germany who believed that if the Nazis were not destroyed the

Germany of religion, science, philosophy and music would be destroyed. God knows that physical courage of the highest order was exacted from those Germans who opposed the Nazis because it involved the certainty of execution with the axe or slow strangling with the rope or the protracted death agony of the concentration camp. But that kind of physical courage requires much greater moral courage behind it than the physical courage required to fight the enemy on the battlefield or in the mountains or the maquis. When an implied criticism of the established order uttered in a neutral country can make the Kaiser's wife turn pale or an indiscreet remark of a banker's wife let slip in a neutral drawing-room can make her burst into grovelling flattery of a Hitler for fear of reprisals when she is back home, the strain upon decent opinion in Germany during the Nazi domination hurts one to contemplate.

Figures from the past like Sir Walter Raleigh, Sir Thomas More, Charles James Fox, Abraham Lincoln, Eleutherios Venizelos, and many another about whose moral courage I had supposed I should be expatiating have been ignored in order to remind readers here and in America what men and women in Germany did to redeem their country's good name.

XIII

A handful of German heroes

THERE WAS ONE GREAT DIFFERENCE between the German Resistance Movement and the other Resistance Movements in Europe. The latter were fighting against an invader: the invaders in Germany were Germans. The time for an active German Resistance to have had any possibility of success was before the war started when the German General Staff believed that Hitler's foreign policy was imperilling the future of the country by bringing about war between Great Britain and France and what was then an unprepared Germany. A date had actually been fixed for certain generals to take action on 14th September, 1938, but such action was called off after Munich. The German people were longing for an assurance of peace and would almost certainly have welcomed Hitler's downfall if his downfall had made peace secure. Then at Munich Hitler triumphed and the German people hailed him as a magician who would take back what had been taken from them by the Treaty of Versailles without having to fight. After the outbreak of war the success of German arms everywhere for two years would have made any attempt to eliminate Hitler from power seem unpatriotic. When war starts, reason departs. To criticise the conduct of a war is defeatism, and in the hysteria of war defeatism soon becomes high treason. One serious attempt to blow up Hitler in a plane was made in 1943, but the Devil was still looking after his own, and the business miscarried without anybody's being aware of the attempt. No obvious attempt was made again until it was apparent to all in Germany that the war was lost.

It may be doubted whether, even if the No Surrender terms

agreed upon between the American President and the British Prime Minister had not been published, the German Resistance would have tried seriously to obliterate Hitler earlier. The mood of the Germans can be recaptured from an entry in the diary for 1943 of Ulrich von Hassell, the German Ambassador in Rome for six years before the war:

"The longer the war lasts the less I think of the Generals. They have undoubted technical ability and physical courage, but little moral courage, absolutely no broad world vision, no inner spiritual independence or that strength of resistance which rests on a genuine cultural basis. For this reason Hitler was able to make them subservient and bind them hand and foot . . . all those on whom we set our hopes are failing, the more miserably so since they agree with all they have been told and permit themselves to indulge in the most anti-Nazi talk, but are unable to summon up enough courage to act."

Ernst von Weizsacker, who was Secretary of State in the German Foreign Office until 1943 and associated with von Stauffenberg in the attempt to erase Hitler on 20th July, 1944, wrote of the German people in his memoirs:

"Germans are by nature not at all adapted to play the part of revolutionaries. They have an inborn respect for the authority of the State. Riots and civil wars have often occurred in other countries, but they have almost never occurred in German history. Anyone who attempts to interfere with the existing authorities has to reckon with strong opposition, however right he may be from the objective point of view."

Finally to illustrate the background against which the courageous few had to display their courage, the words of the Chief Prosecutor for the United States at the Nuremberg trials may be quoted:

"Under the clutch of the most intricate web of espionage and intrigue that any modern state has endured, persecution and torture of a kind that had not been visited upon the world in many centuries, the elements of the German population which were both decent and courageous were annihilated. Those which were decent and weak were intimidated. Open resistance, which had never been more than feeble and irresolute, disappeared. But resistance, I am happy to say, always remained, although it was manifest in only such events as the abortive effort to assassinate Hitler."

When Hitler became Chancellor in 1933 Sophie Scholl was twelve years old: her brother Hans was fifteen. They were two of the five children of the burgomaster of a small town in Württemberg. At first the future seemed wonderful. Hans became an enthusiastic member of the Hitler Youth organisation until gradually it was borne in on him that its influence was an evil influence and he cut himself off from it. As the years went on he became more and more convinced that the Nazis, already corrupting the soul of Germany, would end by destroying it altogether unless a spirit of resistance to such corruption could be roused among the people. In due course Hans Scholl entered Munich University to study medicine and he was there when war came. He was called up for service with the Medical Corps and served as a medical orderly during the invasion of France. Later he was attached to a student company in Munich and was able to continue his studies, although he had to spend a good deal of his time in barracks.

Sophie Scholl, after being called up for a year first with the Labour Service and then with the Auxiliary Military Service, was at last able to enter Munich University to study biology and philosophy on the eve of her twenty-first birthday in 1942. Her imagination was stirred by mysterious leaflets in hectograph which were slipped into people's letter-boxes in Munich. They came from some association which called itself the White Rose and at the end of the leaflet was a request to type it out with as many carbons as possible and pass it on. Those leaflets were frank. The first one began:

"Nothing is less worthy of a civilised country than passively to allow itself to be 'governed' by an irresponsible gang of bosses who have surrendered to their lower instincts.... Goethe speaks of the Germans as a tragic people, like the Jews and the Greeks, but to-day the German people seems to be a shallow, will-less mob of yes-men, who have no marrow in their bones, no faith in their souls, and are willing to let themselves be driven to destruction."

Another leaflet said:

"Hitler himself writes in an earlier edition of 'his' book (the worst-written book I have ever read, imposed as a bible on a 'nation of poets and thinkers'): 'you cannot believe how much you have to deceive a nation in order to govern it.'"

And again:

"Since the conquest of Poland three hundred thousand Jews have been murdered in the most bestial fashion. This is the most frightful crime ever committed against human dignity, a crime without parallel in all history. . . . Perhaps someone will say that the Jews deserved their fate—such a statement would be a piece of monstrous arrogance, but suppose someone made it—what would he say to the fact that all the youths and girls of the Polish nobility have been destroyed (though pray God, some have escaped)? How, you ask was this done? All males of noble family between the ages of fifteen and twenty were carried away to forced labour in concentration camps in Germany; all girls between the same ages were sent to the S.S. brothels in Norway. . . . Why does the German people show such apathy towards all these frightful and inhuman crimes? Hardly anyone seems to trouble about them. They are accepted as facts and put aside, and the German people falls again into its dull obtuse sleep, giving those Nazi criminals the courage and the opportunity to continue their havoc—and they take it."

Sophie Scholl had suspected that her brother Hans was in league with other students to circulate these leaflets, but before she could be perfectly sure Hans and the other medical students were sent off to the Russian front that summer.

One day Sophie was visited by one of the sisters in charge of a hospital for mentally defective children who told her that from time to time the S.S. were bringing black lorries to the hospital and taking away some of these children to be gassed. Sophie was determined that she must fight against such horrors. In the late autumn of 1942 Hans came back from Russia with memories of Nazi cruelty, and he and the others set to work again on circulating leaflets. Sophie was now an active member of "The White Rose." The emotion roused by the terrible news about Stalingrad made these young people hope that they would fire the German people to a revolution.

One night Hans and a couple of other students painted DOWN WITH HITLER seventy times along a main street of Munich and above the entrance to the university FREEDOM. However, the main business was hectographing leaflets in the cellar where they worked. They were encouraged by news that students were starting on the same lines in Berlin, in Freiburg and in Hamburg. But the Gestapo was also getting busy. On the morning of 18th February, 1943, Hans and Sophie arrived at the university with a suitcase full of leaflets a few minutes before the lecture-rooms opened. They scattered their leaflets along the corridors and emptied some from the first floor into the entrance hall. The head-porter had seen what they were doing and ordered all the doors in the university to be locked at once. Then he notified the Gestapo who arrived and arrested Hans and Sophie; soon afterwards they arrested Christopher Probst, a friend of Hans. Four days later the young people were tried in the People's Court and sentenced to death by the infamous Freisler; a few hours afterwards they were beheaded. Sophie was executed first and astonished the warders and the executioner by her serenity; Hans before he laid his head upon the block cried in a voice that rang through the prison, "Long live freedom!"

Kurt Huber, one of the professors at Munich University, probably drafted most of the leaflets which these courageous young students distributed. He was arrested some days after Hans and Sophie Scholl, together with two more students, and they were all beheaded five months later.

In his final speech to the court Huber pleaded for the two students arraigned with him, Willi Graf and Alexander Schorell:

> "I beg and entreat you to judge these young defendants opposite in a truly constructive manner; to seek and to hear not lip-service to power, but the clear voice of conscience

and so to consider the motives which prompted the deed. These motives were in fact the most selfless and the most idealistic that one can imagine. They were striving for absolute justice, integrity and truthfulness in public life."

Those young students were sustained by their faith but there was not a word of this in the leaflets and Catholics have to remember what a blow to German Catholics that Concordat made with Hitler in 1934 had been and may be forgiven for wondering if the Vatican is always inspired by political prescience and spiritual courage. And that is equally true of the Lutheran Church. Priests and pastors who gave their lives rather than yield to the damnable Nazi doctrine were unsupported officially by their Churches and could therefore be treated as rebels against the State. So those who died were martyrs for moral courage not for religious faith, and without doubt that has been a great loss to religion.

Carl von Ossietsky was a Catholic, and a journalist of great repute who died as a prisoner of the Gestapo.

In his journalistic youth in Hamburg he had denounced the influence of the Army in politics, and when at the age of thirty he came back to Germany after four years of fighting as a private soldier on the Western Front he came back determined to fight with his pen against any political forces that might bring about another war.

With this object in view he went to Berlin as a secretary of the German Peace Society and was a contributor to various Liberal newspapers and periodicals, finally in 1927 becoming editor of the *Weltbühne* in which he wrote brilliantly against the forces of reaction and with particular fierceness against the National Socialists whose rise he regarded as a menace to the future. He was equally critical of Moscow.

In 1931 Ossietsky was sentenced after a trial held in secret to eighteen months' imprisonment for betraying military secrets. This " betrayal " was his publication of the fact that air armaments were being secretly produced in Russia with the co-operation of the Soviet Government. Ossietsky refused to avoid prison by going abroad; he felt it was his editorial duty to go to prison. Seven months later he was released under the Christmas amnesty of the Chancellor von Schleicher.

When Hitler became Chancellor his friends urged Ossietsky to leave Germany. He refused to go until he had published his final warning against what he believed to be the disastrous choice of Hitler to lead the nation. On the night this article was printed the Reichstag was set on fire, and early in the morning he was arrested. While he was in prison Ossietsky was awarded the Nobel Peace Prize in 1935. This was such a great annoyance to the Nazis that Hermann Goering had him brought to his office, where he was told that if he would decline the prize on the grounds of his unworthiness he would be released. Ossietsky flatly refused and was then sent to a municipal hospital under strict arrest. From here somehow he managed to telegraph to the Nobel Prize Committee that he was grateful for the unexpected honour.

Ossietsky was now sent to a concentration camp where he was badly knocked about. When he collapsed from a heart attack during hard labour, he used to be allowed a few days' rest after which he would be visited by some important Nazi official and invited to sign a petition for his release on the ground that he had changed his opinions. This Ossietsky always refused to do until at last the Nazis decided to have him slowly put to death by "special treatment" and in May 1938 Ossietsky ceased to embarrass them.

Ossietsky's ability to hold out against the temptation to recant unquestionably owed much to what must have been an immense reserve of physical courage, but the demand upon that physical courage was the result of Ossietsky's moral courage, and he was not even allowed to live long enough to have the melancholy gratification of seeing come true all his most pessimistic prophecies of what would happen to Germany under Nazi domination.

Example after example of the kind of moral courage displayed by men like Ossietsky might be recorded, and if there are few examples of such reckless defiance as was shown by those young students of Munich University that is because the omnipotence of the Nazi means of repression made reckless defiance an utterly useless gesture. The lives of many and the liberty of thousands more paid for what was the heinous offence of having the courage of their opinions. It became increasingly obvious that the only way to challenge the Nazi savages was to destroy the evil medicine man who swayed them.

The question is often asked whether political assassination is justifiable on moral grounds. It is difficult to grasp why political assassination should be disapproved of by those who still maintain that society is morally justified in the infliction of capital punishment. The only people entitled to disapprove of political assassination, when the creature to be assassinated is abhorred for his sins against God and his crimes against man, are those who believe that it is wrong to take life in any circumstances. In the case of Hitler one might suppose that even the most devout Buddhist would hesitate to subscribe to his creed.

It is remarkable that during those dreadful years of Hitler's domination none of the millions he put to death was accused of a conspiracy against his life. There were one or two abortive attempts within the Army to rid Germany of Hitler but these attempts went wrong because the hell-hound was on the Devil's lead; none of them was frustrated by the vigilance of Hitler's human guardians.

The moral courage and resolution to which were added physical courage and resolution did not appear until Claus Schenck Graf von Stauffenberg, a young colonel in his thirty-sixth year, was inspired to action.

Stauffenberg was a Swabian aristocrat and when he was training to be an officer his superior officers and his own contemporaries looked forward to a military career for him as brilliant as that of Gneisenau, one of his ancestors.

When war came in 1939 Stauffenberg was a lieutenant in a Panzer division and fought in Poland and in France. Then he was called from active service in the field to a job at Headquarters where his talent for organisation, which may have been an inheritance from the great Gneisenau, was valuable. Stauffenberg did not relish being taken away from the fighting troops, but no doubt it was during his time at Headquarters that he began to realise what a menace Hitler was to the future of the German Army. At the beginning of 1943 Stauffenberg was in the field again, fighting in North Africa where not long afterwards he was very severely wounded in the face, the hands, and the knee by fire from a low-flying plane. He lay for days in a military hospital in Carthage, wondering whether he would be completely blind when he came out. In the end he kept the sight of one eye, but lost his right hand and half the fingers of his left.

When he returned to Germany after his convalescence Stauffenberg was appointed Chief of Staff to General Olbricht in charge of the Army Ordnance Department. By now he was convinced that the only hope for the future of the German Army and indeed for Germany itself was to kill Hitler. He set to work to build up a military conspiracy without any interference by General Olbricht and indeed with his implied approval.

Stauffenberg was now in touch with what was known as the Kreisau Circle, a group of idealists planning out a future for a Germany emerging from the wreck of the war. The outstanding figure in this group was Helmuth James Graf von Moltke, a great-great-nephew of the Field-Marshal, with an English mother. Moltke could not bring himself to approve of assassination as a way out, but some of the members of the Kreisau Circle believed it was the only thing to do. He was arrested in January 1944 because he had warned a man who was wanted by the Gestapo, and he was in prison when Stauffenberg so nearly succeeded in obliterating Hitler a few months later. Moltke was tried in January 1945 in the People's Court with Roland Freisler as the presiding Judge. Moltke had known some of those who had been involved in the conspiracy. That was enough. Moltke was condemned to death because as a Christian gentleman he made no secret of the repulsion with which the Nazi creed filled him.

Shortly before he was executed Moltke wrote these words to his sons:

"All my life, even when I was at school, I have fought against narrow-mindedness and violence, against presumption, intolerance and that absolute and pitiless regimentation which is part of the German character and which has found expression in the National Socialist state. I have also dedicated myself to overcome this spirit with all the harm it brings in its train: excessive nationalism, racial persecution, unbelief and materialism."

Ten days after Moltke's execution on 23rd January, 1945, the vile Freisler who had condemned so many to death was killed in a daylight raid on Berlin by the United States Air Force. The People's Court was sitting when the warning sounded, but Freisler did not immediately adjourn the proceedings. On his way to the shelter what had been a foul moral mess of humanity was struck by one of the first bombs that dropped and became a physical mess. That Hitler, Himmler and Freisler escaped being tried for their crimes is one of the great regrets of history.

Stauffenberg did not lightly make up his mind to assassinate Hitler, and let it be remembered that he took upon himself the sole responsibility of carrying out the deed. To Jakob Kaiser, a former leader of the Catholic Trade Unions, he said:

"We have put ourselves to the test before God and before our conscience; it must be done, for this man is evil incarnate."

With the arrests increasing month by month and with the Allied landing in Europe known to be imminent it was vital that Hitler should be exterminated as soon as possible. Stauffenberg was now Chief of Staff to General Fromm commanding the Army of Reserve, and on the morning of 20th July, 1944, he flew to Hitler's Headquarters in East Prussia to report on the creation of new front-line divisions for the Army of Reserve. The conference in what was called the Wolf's Lair was held in a wooden house instead of as usual in Hitler's concrete bunker. This was unfortunate. Had the bomb exploded in the bunker it must have killed everybody in it.

Stauffenberg was taken in by Keitel to be presented to Hitler and make his report. In a brief-case he carried besides his papers a time-bomb weighing over five pounds set to explode a few minutes later. In the conference room there were about a couple of dozen people standing round a large and very heavy table covered with papers. Neither Goering, Ribbentrop nor Himmler were present. Hitler was poring over the maps with Keitel and Jodl. Stauffenberg placed under the table his brief-case in which the bomb was already alive. Then, with the excuse of making a telephone call to Berlin, Stauffenberg left the conference room. A couple of minutes later the walls and the roof were shattered by an explosion.

Stauffenberg drove off to the airport, feeling sure that all had gone according to plan. Alas, Hitler was not killed because when the bomb exploded he had been leaning over the table which had protected him. One of his trouser-legs was blown off but his head was not, and the Chief Signals Officer who was in the conspiracy lost his nerve and failed to put the communications centre out of order.

When Stauffenberg got back to the airfield outside Berlin he notified the conspirators gathered in General Olbricht's office at the Headquarters of the General Staff in the Bendlerstrasse that Hitler was dead, and here he joined them as soon as his car reached Berlin. An announcement was sent out to all Commanders-in-Chief at home and in the various theatres of operations in the occupied countries that some of the Nazi leaders who had survived Hitler's death were trying to seize power and that General Beck and Field-Marshal von Witzleben who had taken over the command of the Army had issued orders to all senior Party leaders, S.S. and police officers to be placed under arrest. At the same time troops were to be brought in from barracks outside Berlin to secure the Gestapo Headquarters and the radio station, and to disarm the S.S. Owing to the failure to disrupt the communications at Hitler's Headquarters Keitel was able to announce that Hitler was not dead and to countermand all the orders from Berlin.

In the evening officers placed under arrest in the Bendlerstrasse earlier that afternoon broke out and disarmed the conspirators. Stauffenberg and Olbricht were shot at once by orders of General Fromm, the commander of the Army of Reserve who, having been involved in the conspiracy himself, thought it wise to get rid of Stauffenberg, his Chief of Staff, and Olbricht before they could talk. General Beck took his own life. Other officers would have been shot if Kaltenbrunner who was Himmler's second-in-command had not arrived in time to stop further action. Himmler himself arrived later in the evening and in Goebbels's house that night the examinations of those involved or suspected of being involved in the plot to kill Hitler began.

The Nazis took advantage of the situation not merely to put to death all those, military or civilian, who were suspected of being involved in the plot but also to put to death or send to concentration camps anybody who had even shown any signs of opposition to their damnable creed. The names of 4980 put to death are definitely known, but many more thousands were sent to concentration camps where many of them perished slowly.

The first trial of conspirators was held on 8th August and ended in the death by slow hanging of Field-Marshal Witzleben, General Höppner, and six other officers. The executions were filmed and on the same evening Hitler gloated over their death agonies in the Reich Chancellery. It was a pity that Hitler managed to kill himself less than a year later. He should have been carted round the five continents of the world in a cage and exhibited like a captive animal until he expired of mortification.

Stauffenberg's physical courage in carrying that live bomb into the conference room at the Wolf's Lair—a man with one eye only and only half a hand—must not be allowed to outshine the moral courage that such an action demanded. It should be remembered that it would not have necessarily followed from the death of Hitler that the object for which he dared so much would have been achieved. It was, indeed, to put it crudely, a gamble. He knew that if he failed his own end was certain, but he also knew that even if he succeeded his own end was uncertain. His conscience was clear. He could affirm that, in trying to rescue his countrymen from the moral degradation in which, except for the comparatively very few, they were sunk because they had passively accepted the monstrous crimes begotten by the Nazi creed, he had himself passed through a change of heart. At the beginning of the war he had been exhilarated by victory in Poland and in France. Disillusionment had slowly crept over him when he was working on the Staff at Headquarters, but it was not until he lay in that Carthage hospital threatened with blindness and left with only half a hand that he realised what he owed to himself and to his country, a debt which he would pay with his life and which he believed that one day his country would honour. As the command to fire was given to the shooting party, his voice rang out, "Long live the eternal Germany." On 20th July, 1955, the Bendlerstrasse where stood the German War Office, in the courtyard of which he was shot by the light of a car lamp, was re-named the Stauffenbergstrasse. Indeed, Claus von Stauffenberg was a heroic figure in the grand style; he even looked the part, tall, handsome and young. Of him we might echo the words of Shakespeare, and say, "This was the noblest German of them all."

Those who have written about the attempt to rid the world of Hitler have failed within my reading experience to pay the tributes to Stauffenberg that his memory deserves. There has seemed an inclination to explain Stauffenberg's act as merely an expression of the Army's resentment and anxiety for its future. In fact, although some of those associated with him less directly may have been actuated mainly by such motives, Stauffenberg himself was looking beyond the future of the Army to the future of his country. He spent time before the moment came for action in drawing up a political confession of faith by which what Hitler in broadcasting to Germany about his survival called a "tiny clique of traitors and saboteurs" dedicated themselves under oath to the "forces of truth, justice, and right long since tried and proven and just re-awakened." The value of that attempt in spite of its failure was to reveal for the first time to the world outside that the tales of Germans who were resisting the Nazis were indeed true. We had come to think of them as all completely hypnotised by that foul and evil mesmerist. We had heard nothing of that small band of Munich students who had circulated those leaflets written by Kurt Huber. We had heard nothing of the Kreisau Circle and the courageous quietism of

Helmuth von Moltke. And certainly we had not heard of Admiral Wilhelm Canaris.

Wilhelm Canaris who was born in 1887 was a young lieutenant in the light cruiser *Dresden* when war came in 1914. He was at the battle of Coronel when the only British ship to survive was the light cruiser *Glasgow* saved by her speed. Later at the battle of the Falkland Islands the *Dresden* got away thanks to her speed and ironically was discovered in Chilean territorial waters three months later by the *Glasgow*. In the certainty of being sunk by the superior fire of the British cruiser the captain of the *Dresden* scuttled his ship, and he and his crew were interned.

Canaris effected a remarkable escape from South America thanks to his knowledge of Spanish, and at last with a Chilean passport in the name of Reed Rosas found himself on board a Dutch Lloyd liner bound for Rotterdam. The liner was stopped at the entrance of the English Channel and ordered to put in to Plymouth. Canaris was unsuspected by the sleuths of Passport Control and was allowed to go on to Holland, whence he reached Germany. In 1916 the German Admiralty sent him to Spain which he reached successfully, with his Chilean passport. After a year of secret service activity in Spain Canaris who had done valuable work on behalf of U-boats decided he should like to serve in a U-boat himself and applied to be recalled home. Still travelling on that Chilean passport, he reached Italy where he was arrested at Domodossola and kept in prison for some time. Finally he was released, but he was not allowed to continue his journey to Switzerland and was put on board a Spanish freighter in Genoa harbour, bound for Cartagena by way of Marseilles.

Canaris did not like the notion of being detained by the French counter-espionage authorities, with the record they would have of his activities in Spain as Reed Rosas. So he decided to throw himself on the mercy of the Spanish captain of the freighter to whom he admitted that he was not Reed Rosas but a German naval officer and therefore certain to be shot as a spy if he fell into the hands of the French. The Spaniard's chivalry was stirred and he took his ship right on to Cartagena without putting in at Marseilles.

Canaris was still anxious to return to Germany for active service and finally he managed to get on board a German submarine based on Pola, whence he reached Berlin. In the spring of 1918 he was given command of a U-boat based on Cattaro, which he brought back to Kiel just after the Kaiser abdicated and went to Holland.

For the next sixteen years Canaris served at the German Admiralty and with the diminutive navy that was left to Germany until in 1934 he was put in charge of the Abwehr, the centre of Military Intelligence. Here with persistent courage he worked hard to thwart Nazi excesses. It is not true that he ever transgressed in loyalty when operations according to the accepted rules of war were being carried out. He did what he could to shield all those in the "opposition" and in particular the courageous Major-General Hans Oster who became his Number Two.

Throughout the war Oster never allowed the General Staff to plead ignorance of what the Nazis were doing. The mass extermination of Jews, the shooting of hostages, the putting to death of incurables, the gassing of defective children, every vile act was brought to the notice of the Army by Oster so that they should know what kind of set of criminals they were serving. On their consciences he placed the responsibility of allowing the Nazis to violate every kind of civilised behaviour. He lost no opportunity of warning those in danger of the Gestapo and always tried to help those who had been arrested. Yet he would not use his influence to save his own son who was defending a hopeless position at Stalingrad because "suffering and distress must be shared by all."

In February 1944 the Abwehr was taken over by Himmler's Secret Intelligence. Canaris was given a job of no importance by now as Chief of the Department for Economic Warfare. Immediately after Stauffenberg's attempt on 20th July Canaris and Oster were both arrested and taken to the dreaded Gestapo Headquarters in the Prinz Albrechtstrasse. Canaris received only a third of the normal ration for prisoners in the cellars who were being interrogated. He had to sleep on a wooden bunk, his hands were tightly handcuffed all the time, a very bright electric light was so fixed as to shine in his eyes all night, and it was forbidden to turn the body or the head. All the cells were unheated. The interrogations went on endlessly. By Christmas Canaris was in a starved state and compelled to do menial tasks like scrubbing the corridor. In February 1945 some of the prisoners, among them Canaris and Oster, were moved to the concentration camp of Flossenbürg on the frontier of Bavaria with Bohemia. Here in addition to the handcuffs his legs were shackled. And the endless interrogations went on without breaking the admiral's spirit.

The next cell to Canaris was occupied by Colonel Lunding who had been head of Danish Military Intelligence until by Hitler's orders he was dismissed and interned in Germany. The door of Lunding's cell had a thin crack across it through which it was possible to see what went on in the corridor. During the ten months of his incarceration at Flossenbürg the Danish colonel was able to count over eight hundred executions because a window in the corridor opposite the door of his cell looked out on the way to the place of execution. During his daily exercise in the camp courtyard Lunding saw six rings fastened to the wall under a projecting ledge from which those condemned to be hanged were strangled and close by a square of lead plating on the wall in front of which those condemned to be shot had to kneel to receive the bullets in the napes of their necks.

Lunding found out from the warder, whose goodwill he had gained with presents out of comforts sent to him from home, the name of the prisoner in the next cell to himself. He had never met Canaris on his visits to Copenhagen, but he was aware of how much he had done to check the outrages of the S.S. and the Gestapo. Then he recognised the admiral at exercise when for half an hour every day the handcuffs and shackles were taken off. Lunding was struck by his bearing and by the neatness of his personal appearance. He seemed an unbroken man.

Presently after several failures Canaris and Lunding found a method of communicating with each other by taps, and it was apparent to Lunding that until now, in spite of daily interrogations by officials within the camp and by emissaries sent down to Flossenbürg from Berlin, Canaris had baffled all the efforts of his enemies to extract from him any of the secrets which they knew were his. Towards the latter end of March Kaltenbrunner[1] himself tried. Lunding through the crack in his door could see Himmler's huge Number Two threatening Canaris like an ogre or monstrous grizzly bear and the small slender admiral answering his threats with live gestures of defiance. The Danish colonel felt that the German admiral was far from being "finished off" yet.

At the beginning of April physical torture was added to mental torture. At last on 8th April what was called an S.S. Summary Court was held at which Canaris, Oster and several others had to endure the protracted mockery of a trial. Round about 1 a.m. of the 9th Canaris returned to his cell after hours of interrogation. He tapped upon the wall that this was probably the last interrogation. He added that he had been badly knocked about and that the bridge of his nose was broken.

Then he tapped out his last message to the world:

> "I die for my country and with a clear conscience. You, as an officer, will realise that I was only doing my duty to my country when I endeavoured to oppose Hitler and to hinder the senseless crimes by which he has dragged down Germany to ruin. I know that all I did was in vain, for Germany will be completely defeated. I knew that she would be, as far back as 1942."

To this was added a last message to his wife, and about 3 a.m. the tapping was finished.

About six in the morning when it was still dark outside, Lunding heard the Admiral being called out of his cell and the noise of the handcuffs and shackles being struck off. There were other prisoners in the corridor. Then came the command:

"Strip!"

Through the crack in his door Lunding could see the naked white bodies.

[1] It is a relief to know that Kaltenbrunner was executed after his trial at Nuremberg.

" March! "

The morning was still enough for Lunding to have heard any shots from his cell. There was no sound. That meant slow strangling by the ropes attached to those iron rings.

The words above were written exactly sixteen years to a day after Admiral Wilhelm Canaris and General Hans Oster died for their country, on the eve of the trial of Adolf Eichmann in Jerusalem.

In the old story Almighty God was willing to spare Sodom if ten just men could be found in the city. We may wonder what epithet the vulgarisers of the New Testament will find to substitute for " just " when the Old Testament is being vulgarised. Try they never so hard they will not find a better epithet than just, and there were enough just men in Germany for the Divine mercy to spare their country and restore it to the comity of civilised nations.

XIV

Conclusions

WE MAY ASSERT without any possibility of contradiction that the Nazi crime against the individual was the most heinous yet committed by any tyranny whether that tyranny was exercised by a dictatorship, a triumvirate, an oligarchy, a democracy or a mob. Nevertheless, although such a strain was put on the moral courage of Germans even to dare to criticise in conversation the Nazi behaviour, it is wise to remember that the abolition of that tyranny has not set humanity free from any possible resurgence of it. It is equally wise to remember that, although the individual will certainly cease to exist under doctrinaire Communism in course of time, the individual is by no means sure of preservation should what is called the free world be able to maintain itself economically against Communism. The tyranny of mass opinion could be as destructive of true freedom in the country which believes itself to be the shrine of liberty as the official worship of regimentation in Moscow and Peking. Fortunately for the prospect of the future in the West the United States have repeatedly produced men of unassailable moral courage at times when moral courage has been most needed, and most of all when those United States still seemed fundamentally disunited after the Civil War.

President Kennedy's book *Profiles in Courage* brought together some inspiring examples of moral courage in American political life and that book is a refreshment after the hot air of so many political speeches of to-day, all the less excusable because nearly all of them are written and read by the " orator." Some words in the speech of Lucius Quintus Cincinnatus Lamar of Mississippi spoken in 1878 in the Senate define moral courage in politics. He was refusing to accept the directive of the Mississippi Legislature that its two Senators should vote for the Bland Silver Bill which he thought could lead to disastrous inflation:

> "Upon the youth of my state whom it has been my privilege to assist in education I have always endeavoured to impress the belief that truth was better than falsehood, honesty better than policy, courage better than cowardice. To-day my lessons confront me. To-day I must be true or false, honest or cunning, faithful or unfaithful to my people. Even in this hour of their legislative displeasure and disapprobation, I cannot vote as their resolutions direct.
>
> "My reasons for my vote shall be given to my people. Then it will be for them to determine if adherence to my honest convictions has disqualified me from representing them; whether a difference of opinion upon a difficult and complicated subject to which I have given patient, long-continued conscientious study, to which I have brought entire honesty and singleness of purpose, and upon which I have spent whatever ability God has given me, is now to separate us; . . . but be their present decision what it may, I know that the time is not far distant when they will recognise my action to-day as wise and just; and armed with honest convictions of my duty, I shall calmly await the results, believing in the utterance of a great American that 'truth is omnipotent, and public justice certain.'"

Senator Lamar's belief may have sounded over-optimistic at the time, but it was justified. Although he was declared by general opinion to be politically dead, he toured the whole State and by force of sincerity armed with eloquence he regained the confidence of his constituents.

> "I prize the confidence of the people of Mississippi, but I never made popularity the standard of my action. I profoundly respect public opinion, but I believe that there is in conscious rectitude of purpose a sustaining power which will support a man of ordinary firmness under any circumstances whatever.

"The liberty of this country and its great interests will never be secure if its public men become mere menials to do the biddings of their constituents instead of being representatives in the true sense of the word, looking to the lasting prosperity and future interests of the whole country."

At the time of the Suez crisis Mr. Nigel Nicolson, the Conservative member for Bournemouth, one of those South of England constituencies which are the guardians of conventional and commonplace opinion, upset his constituents by voting with his conscience instead of with the Government, the result of which was that he was not adopted as the Conservative candidate at the next General Election. He was penalised for a display of moral courage in expressing his belief that the Government's policy and action over Suez had been wrong. The penalty for such independent behaviour was exclusion from Parliament as a recognised cog in the Conservative machine, although of course he would have been at liberty to offer himself for re-election without the official blessing of his party. In Nazi Germany or in Stalinist Russia the penalty for displaying independence would no doubt have been much more unpleasant, and to-day in Communist Russia, in Spain, and even in Portugal, it is impossible to oppose the ruling régime without unpleasant consequences.

Nevertheless, it will not do to be too complacent about the freedom of speech and the liberty of the Press we enjoy in Great Britain; the transformation of party politics into party machines is one way of imposing on the electors a form of totalitarianism, a very mild form of totalitarianism no doubt, but still a menace to the political health of the country. This increasingly cynical attitude of the public about the moral integrity and mental honesty of politicians is a distressing feature of present-day opinion. The general grief when Aneurin Bevan died was profound, for he was a politician whose moral integrity and mental honesty were never found wanting. There were plenty of times when popular opinion was against him because he refused to bow to it, but that refusal was remembered to his renown not to his discredit.

Yet most ambitious young politicians of to-day are disinclined to consider a posthumous fame any compensation for a career ruined because they refused to give up to party what was meant for mankind. In the competitive stress of our times the party man out of step with his party cannot hope to reach the heights of what is no longer an art but an ever more jealously hidebound profession. The party machine is naturally intolerant of those who throw spanners into the works. The moral courage of a politician only too often appears to the rest of the party pack or the party herd as the behaviour of a lone wolf or a rogue elephant. And let us be fair. It is not always easy to distinguish between a gesture of moral courage and a display of self-opinionated conceit. Only time can decide, and not always time, which of the two the gesture was. What the individual owes to society and what the individual owes to himself is a problem of assay which has never been resolved to the satisfaction of everybody. It was the basis of the struggle for the soul of Western man between Catholicism and Protestantism, but the moral courage inspired by a religious faith even to bear martyrdom is outside the scope of the present examination of a few aspects and examples of moral courage.

I ask myself at this point when I was first made aware of the imperative claim of moral courage if one was to be able to respect oneself and not allow what one believed to be truth and justice to surrender to expediency. I think it was in the last summer of the nineteenth century. The occasion was a family gathering in the house of a French uncle at Charnay in the Lyonnais. Among the guests was a Captain Degoutte of the Zouaves, with whom, after one of those interminable and superb repasts in which the French indulge at these reunions, I found myself walking in my uncle's orchard. He was a slim serious-looking man with pince-nez.

During the re-trial of Dreyfus at Rennes the year before I had been exasperated by the self-righteousness of the British Press and the opportunity they took of getting back on the French for the Fashoda incident and their anti-British attitude in the Boer War.

I decided to make it clear to this French officer in his mid-thirties that I was too much a man of the world at the ripe age of seventeen to follow the blind leadership of the British Press.

" *Vous savez, M. le capitaine,*" I said. " *Moi, je suis anti-Dreyfusard.*"

Instead of the congratulations I had hopefully expected to receive Captain Degoutte looked at me through his pince-nez like a schoolmaster.

" *Alors, vous êtes idiot, vous êtes imbécile.*"

And then he went on to denounce those who were dragging the honour of the French Army into the dust.

" And now I, because I was one of those who would not accept lies and injustice, have ruined my military future. Next week I am ordered to Cochin-Chine, and that means the end of my career."

As he spoke Captain Degoutte looked eastward a hundred miles across the great vale of the Saône to where the Alps bounded the wide horizon, their snowy tips rose-pink in the setting sun. I can see now the expression of despair in his eyes behind those pince-nez, and I recall my own shamed realisation of how intolerable my silly adolescent remark must have seemed to him. I gulped an apology which must have struck him as sincere because he took the trouble to explain to me, walking up and down in my uncle's orchard, why the Dreyfus case was a blot on the French Army, and what it had cost those officers who had stood out against the great majority. And that was my first practical lesson in moral courage.

This story has a happy ending because service in Indo-China was not the end of Captain Degoutte's military career.

Before 1914 he had seen active service in Tunis, Madagascar, China, Algeria and Morocco and had spent his leisure hours in studying law and languages, making himself proficient in Madagascan, Chinese, and German, had passed through the École de Guerre and had commanded a battalion. He started the First World War as Chief of Staff of the IV Army Corps, and before the war ended he commanded the VI Army. After the armistice he commanded the Army of the Rhine until he was recalled to France in 1924 where he became a member of the Superior Council for War, devoting the rest of his life to Alpine defence in which he was much interested. Probably as a boy in Charnay he had been stirred by that view of the Alps across the wide vale of the Saône. On reaching the age limit he was retained on the active list and in 1928 he was given France's supreme military honour—the Médaille Militaire. He died in 1938, still on the active list at the age of seventy-two.

An ambitious captain of Zouaves had everything to lose in those years at the end of the nineteenth century by speaking out for truth and justice, and Captain Degoutte's willingness to sacrifice what promised to be a brilliant career has always remained with me as an outstanding example of moral courage. Virtue has all too often to be its own reward; in the case of General Degoutte it was richly and rightly rewarded.

One more story of moral courage which exceedingly impressed me in my youth, although at the time I was told it such an example seemed to set an impossible standard of achievement for myself.

I quote from a memoir of Mother Isabel Mary of the Community of St. Mary the Virgin, Wantage, where it speaks of her early life as a young American actress of nineteen who was playing with Henry Irving as his leading lady at the Lyceum Theatre under the management of her father.

> " The prestige of the American impressario's success had considerably enhanced the dignity of English acting, and the position she and her sister occupied in contemporary social life had no kind of resemblance to that usually occupied by young actresses at that date. They knew practically all the famous people of the time—statesmen, barristers, musicians, painters, poets, not to mention all the leading actors, dancers and singers. . . . She and her mother were once at a large luncheon party where all the rest of the guests were famous or fashionable people of the great world, and one of the leading politicians of the period told a story in French about a fancy-dress ball in Paris at which a man had appeared dressed as Jesus Christ. Isabel, who was by far the youngest

person at the table, rose from her place, and left the house. Not even the most flippant of human beings could deny great courage to the girl of nineteen capable of such an action."

The leading politician was Sir Charles Dilke who wrote to congratulate that young American actress on her strength of mind. He did not use the phrase " moral courage," and reflecting on that I ask myself whether the various instances cited in these pages might not have been better cited as examples of strength of mind. Further reflection rejected this. It would be possible to have strength of mind without the moral courage to defend it. No fortress is stronger than he who commands it. However deep may be one's own religious feelings an affront to them will often be passed over in silence to avoid embarrassing the rest of the company.

Yet what does the embarrassment of others matter if a conviction of truth and justice demands the courage of the individual to express his conviction by words or actions?

The decent impulse to make things comfortable all round must not be allowed to degenerate into the sacrifice of principles to comfort. Whether in politics, in bureaucratic and managerial administration, or in trade unions the moral courage of the individual will be called upon with ever sharper urgency to maintain itself and preserve its integrity under the relentless pressure of mankind's material progress.

These words had just been penned when over the radio came the news of the first cosmonaut's encirclement of the earth in space. Another momentous date has been inscribed upon the age-long calendar of life upon this earth, a date that may one day be considered to mark a turning-point in the history of man.

The feat is being hailed in the Soviet Union as a triumph of collective effort over individualistic capitalism. But what would all that collective effort have achieved without the courage of an individual?

A leader by George Murray in the *Daily Mail* of 13th April, 1961, commented upon that individual in moving words:

" Let us first think of the man who has been out there, that warm, throbbing amalgam of blood, bones and tissue; a human creature like the rest of us, with a heart, a brain—a soul.

"The first since the dawn of time to escape from the trammels of this earth-bound life—and live. The first to have 'left the warm precincts of the cheerful day'—and return. The first to soar out towards the stars.

"We think with awe of this man in the void, spinning through endless space. Lasting fame has come to him. The name of Gagarin will rank with that of Columbus and all the scientists and explorers who have ventured into dark, unknown realms.

"New lustre is added to the fame of his country, Soviet Russia, which has pioneered the journeys into space. First 'a lump of iron.' Then a dog. Now—a man."

Russia has asked for her achievement to be recognised by general disarmament. Dare we hope that any nation, including Russia, will have the moral courage to respond? Yuri Gagarin had the physical courage to hazard his life for a dream. Dare we hope that any individual statesman will have the moral courage to hazard his future for another dream?

Even as that question is asked he who asks it realises that he has begged the question by assuming that moral courage can be granted only to those whose beliefs accord with his own. Yet those who differ from him are entitled to claim as much moral courage for those who adhere without flinching to what they believe is the right course of action or the valuable expression of opinion. Superficially it will always seem less courageous to support a majority than a minority, but it demanded greater courage from Aneurin Bevan to oppose unilateral disarmament in a majority than to advocate it in a minority.

Perhaps the surest test of an individual's moral courage is his refusal to do or say anything to damage his own self-respect. "The fortitude of Monmouth," wrote Macaulay, "was not that highest sort of fortitude which is derived from reflection and self-respect."

Reflection as Macaulay used the word presumably means a

decision taken in the mind about what is the truth and justice of political or private behaviour and, that decision having been taken, to have the courage to proclaim it or if the need arises to act upon it. A failure of such courage could be a lack of self-respect which amounts to the betrayal of a man's soul. To Christians confident of a future life, martyrdom was an imperative manifestation of the individual's courage. Martyrdom is less attractive all over the world to-day.

The trial of Adolf Eichmann has been a revelation of cold-blooded atrocities against human beings on a scale not yet recorded in history. Eichmann's explanation of his behaviour, and indeed his implied excuse for it, was that he lacked the civic courage, or as we should say in English the moral courage, to disobey the orders of his superiors. The dreadful obliteration of six million Jews is so monstrous a crime that a figure as conspicuous as Eichmann was in the commission of that crime condemned by all for his part in it and his plea that he was compelled to obey orders by military discipline appears as a pitiably lame excuse.

But under what stress of disagreement with the orders of his superiors is a soldier justified in disobeying them? William Douglas Home was sentenced to a year's imprisonment because he disobeyed an order in protest against the needless bombing of some thousands of French civilians. He was cited earlier as an example of moral courage in full awareness by the present writer that it was the citation of a minority opinion. Military discipline may demand obedience if it is to be preserved, but let us remember that in the event of nuclear warfare young men all over the world will be called upon to commit hideous crimes against their fellow-men without any likelihood of being tried for such crimes by those who survive them. Should one of them have the moral courage to refuse to obliterate some hundreds of thousands of human beings, he will find that the State does not allow the individual to obey his conscience if such obedience be held to imperil the safety of the State.

When Eichmann admitted his lack of civic courage in carrying out the orders of Hitler, Himmler, and the rest of the Nazis, it was clear that he did not believe any blame was attached to him for such a lack. The prosecution argued that in his zest for extermination he had gone beyond his orders. If that be true the explanation of such zeal is the approval of which it was received by his superiors. It is not an individual who has been tried in Israel but a whole nation. The long hideous story that was related week by week seemed preoccupied with the crimes of one man for which millions of Germans were in fact responsible, Germans with an abundance of physical courage and not a vestige of moral courage, and therefore all of them as guilty as Eichmann save only those comparatively few whose courage was indomitable.

Let the last note on moral courage be given to Lord Russell who can look back through a life of ninety years, in which he has achieved the peak of intellectual eminence, to a constancy of moral courage rarely equalled. He has never feared the unpopularity that comes from expressing his own opinions out of favour with the mood of the time, even to the extent of going to prison for them during the First World War. Now he is the outstanding leader of those prepared at whatever discomfort for themselves to demonstrate against the threat of nuclear warfare. Lord Russell is not a Christian. He does not believe in immortality. He is the perfect example of human fortitude sustained by reflection and self-respect.

Index

Index

Index

Index

Index

Index

Index